Worship & Praise

Full Music Edition

Augsburg Fortress
Minneapolis

Worship & Praise

Full Music Edition

Also available:
Worship & Praise Songbook (3-850) ISBN 0-8066-3850-8
Worship & Praise compact disc (3-852) ISBN 0-8066-3852-4

The paper used in this publication meets the minimum requirements of American National Standard for Information Sciences—Permanence of Paper for Printed Materials, ANSI Z329.48-1984.
Printed in the USA.

Manufactured in the U.S.A.   ISBN 0-8066-3851-6   3-851

09 08 07 06 05 04 03 02 01 00 99   2 3 4 5 6 7 8 9 10 11 12 13 14 15 16 17 18 19 20

Contents

Welcome...

to *Worship & Praise*, a collection of carefully selected songs of the Christian faith, suitable for use in worship and at other times. Here are songs of adoration and praise, prayer and lament, thanksgiving and trust, justice and joy. Here are brief choruses and refrains, songs that tell a story, songs that use warm and personal faith language, well-loved Bible verses set to music, classic texts of Christian worship set to new rhythms and melodies. Here are songs for many times and seasons of the church's year and the Christian's life.

Many congregations are supplementing their repertoire of congregational song with worship songs such as these, blending the richness of the church's tradition with the freshness of more recent expressions in words and music. Since no single volume could contain the many songs that have emerged in the last generation, one goal of this collection is to present a sampling of the most widely used and the most broadly useful songs for congregations at worship in the first years of the 21st century. Talented song writers have added a limited number of new materials as well. Contemporary music and worship leaders, pastors, and theologians have graciously assisted worship staff members of the publisher and of the Division for Congregational Ministries of the Evangelical Lutheran Church in America in selecting and carefully reviewing the words and music of these songs.

Worship & Praise Songbook contains core materials for worshiping assemblies: the words and a single melody line for each song. Basic chord symbols are also provided. A few songs often sung in harmony are included as four-part arrangements. The songs are ordered alphabetically by their common titles for ease in locating them. Indexes of topics, themes, and scripture references identify songs suitable for particular seasons and occasions. Copyright information appears at the end of each song, with more details in an appendix, to simplify obtaining permission for reproducing in any form the words and/or music of a song.

Worship & Praise Full Music Edition is an essential companion to the Songbook. Keyboard players, guitarists, percussionists, and other ensemble musicians will find the full musical arrangement of each song in this volume, including keyboard score and complete chord symbols. Drum kit patterns are contained in an appendix, along with a musical key index. Pastors, musicians, and worship planners will find the section "Using *Worship & Praise*" and the expanded indexes to be helpful tools for using these songs within basic patterns of worship. A recording of selected songs from *Worship & Praise* is available separately as a tool for those who learn and lead this music.

In the astounding diversity of worship, God's people on earth participate even now in the vision of Revelation 5: in the assembly of "...a great multitude that no one could count from every nation, from all tribes and peoples and languages, standing before the throne and before the Lamb, with palm branches in their hands." May these songs in musical languages of our day add to the breadth of the church's timeless song.

A song of unity

1

As a moth-er hen gath-ers her chicks, as an ea - gle
lifts up her young, you have called to your ta - ble all
peo-ple as one; God, we thank you for your pres-ence here.
As we share in the bread and the wine, come to us, ho - ly
Je - sus, in love. Let the gift of your sac-ri-fice

o - pen our eyes; we are one in your bo-dy and blood.

Text and music: David M. Jahn
Text and music © 1999 Augsburg Fortress

A story for all people

2

1 As peo - ple wait in dark - ness, in fear of end - less
2 We come in - to your pres - ence, in hope and joy re -
3 A time of prep - a - ra - tion: the guest is draw - ing
4 You call us to re - pen - tance, to turn and start a -
5 Re - newed by this en - coun - ter, we'll go out and pro -

night, send forth your word of com - fort, a mes - sage of great
stored. With ea - ger hearts we lis - ten, and gath - er 'round your
near, as moun - tain plac - es crum - ble and straight-ened paths ap -
gain. You send your Ho - ly Spir - it to drown the pow'r of
claim. We'll tell of your sal - va - tion, and mag - ni - fy your

light. The world stands proud be - fore you, con - flict - ed, hun - gry,
word. We watch and wait your com - ing and pray for great - er
pear. Pre - pare a hum - ble wel - come in ev - 'ry heart and
sin. We won - der in your mer - cy, your sing - ing fes - tal
name. The ser - vant words of Mar - y will swell the faith - ful

poor. Come, scat - ter pride and fool - ish - ness, and
trust, to know that while we wait for you, Em -
home, and cel - e - brate the prom - ise of our
voice; and in your meal of bread and wine we
soul, and you will bring your chil - dren home that

mend all souls with Sav - ior love once more.
man - u - el, you watch and wait with us.
God who is, and was, and is to come.
join the in - vi - ta - tion to re - joice!
day when all cre - a - tion will be whole.

Refrain

A sto - ry for all peo - ple, old
sto - ry new to - day. A song of love and
heal - ing, a light to show the
way.

Text: Dori Erwin Collins
Music: Dori Erwin Collins; arr. Daniel Kallman
Text and music © 1999 Augsburg Fortress

All hail King Jesus

All hail King Je - sus! All hail Em - man - u - el,

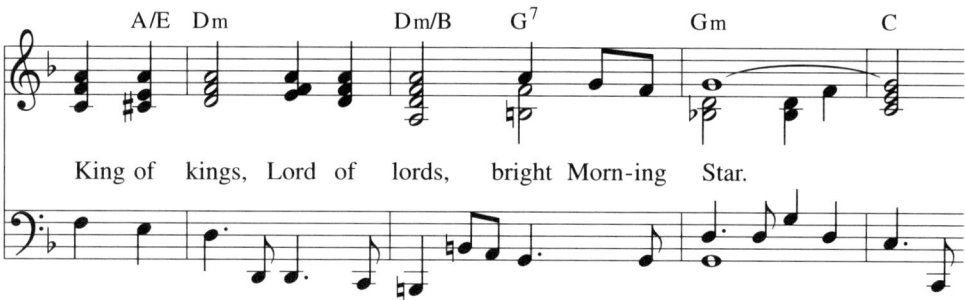

King of kings, Lord of lords, bright Morn-ing Star.

And through - out e - ter - ni - ty, I'll sing your prais - es;

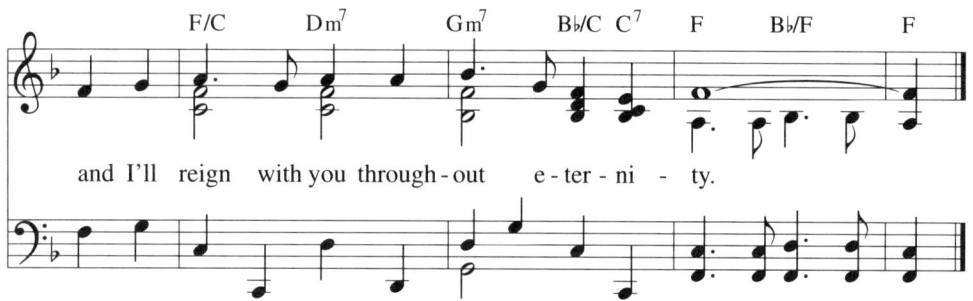

and I'll reign with you through-out e - ter - ni - ty.

Text and music: Dave Moody
Text and music © 1981 Dayspring Music, admin. Word Music, Inc.

All is ready now

4

Chords (system 1): D — B⁹sus — Bm

1 Qui - et - ly into the sta - ble where the
2 'Cross the thresh - old of cre - a - tion, Je - sus
3 Now en - throned as king of heav - en, blaz - ing

Chords: Em — Asus — A⁷ — G

Sav - ior sleep - ing lies, we can go, for all are
comes to dwell with us, as he was in the be -
glo - ry like the sun: in his hands are pow'r and

Chords: D/F♯ — E⁹sus — E⁷ — Asus — A⁷

wel - come: shep - herd, an - gel, poor, and wise. What we
gin - ning, ev - er - more God's gift of love. Now he
jus - tice, on his lips are peace and love. As our

Chords: D — D/F♯ — A/G — G — Bm

have we bring and of - fer, earth - ly gifts for Child di -
calls us to the ta - ble, gift of love to bleed and
gifts are turned to ash - es, fall - ing down in awe we

Chords: E — Em — D/F♯

vine, giv - ing that which we were giv - en, fruits of
die; man - ger here be - comes an al - tar, sta - ble
bow, emp - ty - hand - ed, we a - dore him. "Come, for

Chords: G⁶ — A⁷sus | 1. D — B⁹sus Bm — Em — A⁷sus

har - vest, bread and wine.
Lamb is sac - ri -
all is read - y

Chords: D | 2. D — B⁹sus — Bm — Em

ficed.

Chords: F♯m — G⁶ — A⁷sus — Dsus D | 3. Dm⁷/F — E⁷sus — Em⁷ — D²

now."

Text and music: Jay Beech
Text and music © 1999 Jay Beech

5 All that we have

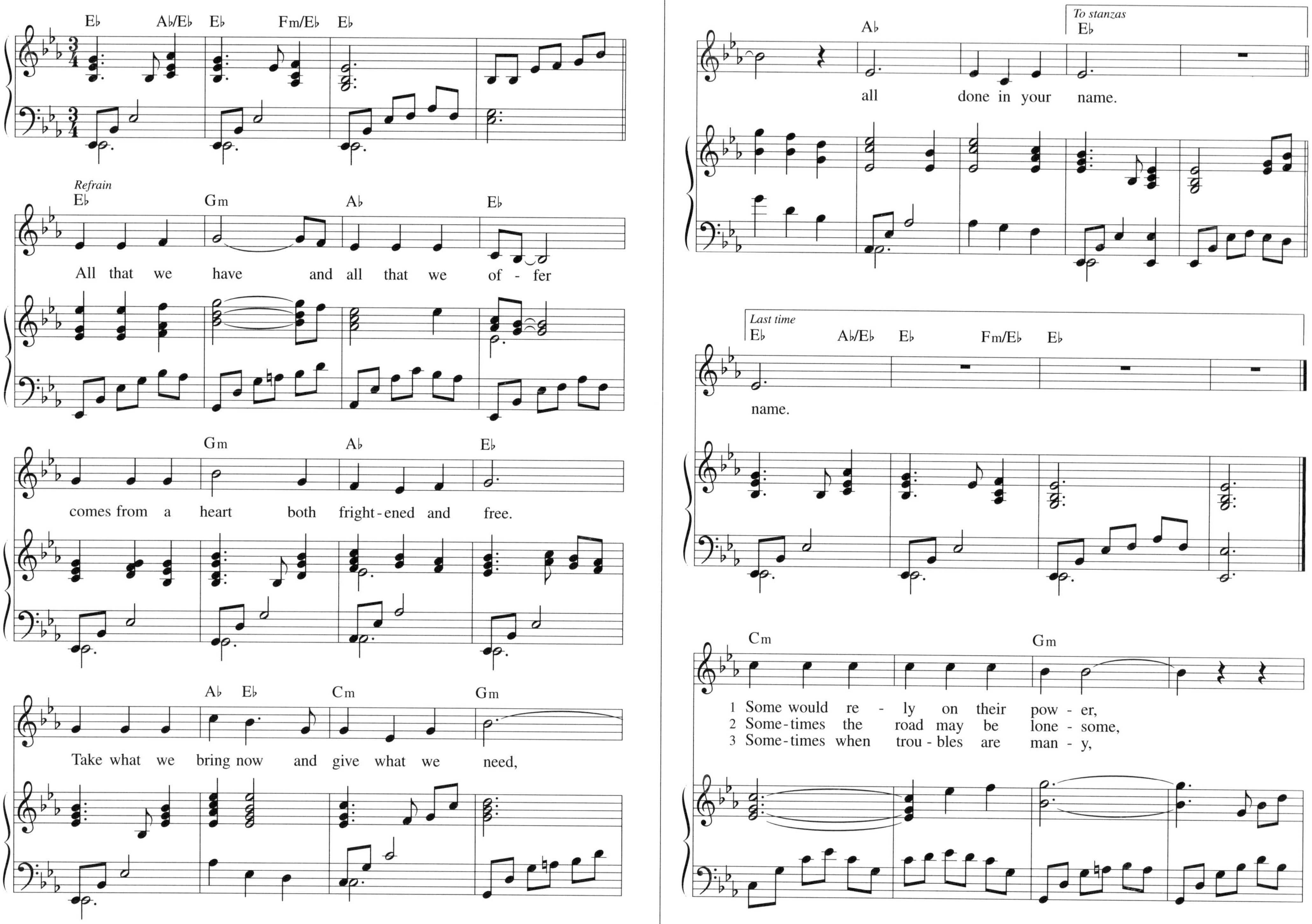
E♭ A♭/E♭ E♭ Fm/E♭ E♭
Refrain
E♭ Gm A♭ E♭
All that we have and all that we of - fer
Gm A♭ E♭
comes from a heart both fright-ened and free.
A♭ E♭ Cm Gm
Take what we bring now and give what we need,
A♭
To stanzas
E♭
all done in your name.
Last time
E♭ A♭/E♭ E♭ Fm/E♭ E♭
name.
Cm Gm
1 Some would re - ly on their pow - er,
2 Some-times the road may be lone - some,
3 Some-times when trou - bles are man - y,

oth - ers put trust in their gold.
of - ten we may lose our way.   Take
life can seem emp - ty, it's true.   But

Some have on - ly their Sav - ior,   whose
cour - age and al - ways re - mem - ber
look at the life of the Mas - ter,   who

faith - ful - ness nev - er grows old.
love is - n't just for a day.
lov - ing - ly suf - fered for you.

Text: Gary Ault
Music: Gary Ault; arr. Gary Daigle
Text and music © 1969, 1979 Damean Music, admin. GIA Publications

1 Al - le - lu - ia, al - le - lu - ia, al - le - lu - ia, al - le - lu - ia;
2 He's my Sav - ior, al - le - lu - ia, he's my Sav - ior, al - le - lu - ia;
3 He is wor - thy, al - le - lu - ia, he is wor - thy, al - le - lu - ia;
4 I will praise him, al - le - lu - ia, I will praise him, al - le - lu - ia;

al - le - lu - ia, al - le - lu - ia, al - le - lu - ia, al - le - lu - ia.
he's my Sav - ior, al - le - lu - ia, he's my Sav - ior, al - le - lu - ia.
he is wor - thy, al - le - lu - ia, he is wor - thy, al - le - lu - ia.
I will praise him, al - le - lu - ia, I will praise him, al - le - lu - ia.

Text and music: Jerry Sinclair
Text and music © 1972 Manna Music, Inc.

Alleluia. Lord, to whom shall we go?

F/A B♭2 Csus Dm7 Gm7

C7sus C7 F B♭/F F B♭/F F

F C/E Gm7 C C/B♭

Al-le-lu - ia. Lord, to whom shall we go?

F/A B♭ C Dm

You have the words of e-ter - nal life. Al-le -

F/A B♭2 Csus Dm

lu - ia. Al-le -

Gm7 C7sus C7 [1] F/A B♭ C F

lu - ia, al - le - lu - ia. Al-le -

[2] F B♭/F F B♭/F F

ia.

Text: John 6:68, adapt. *Lutheran Book of Worship*
Music: Robin Cain; arr. Phil Kadidlo
Text © 1978 *Lutheran Book of Worship*; music © 1999 Augsburg Fortress

Amazing love

C Dm7

1 My Lord,   what love is this   that
2 And so   they watched him die,   de-
3 And now   this love of Christ   shall

Gsus G Csus C G C

pays   so dear - ly,   that I,   the
spised,   re - ject - ed;   but, oh,   the
flow   like riv - ers;   come, wash   your

As the deer

Dm7 · F/G · G · C

guilt - y one, may go free?
blood he shed flowed for me.
guilt a - way, live a - gain.

Refrain

Gm7 · C · Eb

A - maz-ing love, oh, what sac - ri - fice, the Son of God giv'n for

G · Gm7 · C

me; my debt he pays and my death he dies, that

Gm7 · C · Gm7 · C

I might live, that I might live.

D · A/C# · Bm · Bm/A · G · Asus · A · D

As the deer pants for the wa-ter, so my soul longs af - ter you.

A/C# · Bm · D/A · D/F# · Em7 · A7sus · A7 · D

You a - lone are my heart's de-sire and I long to wor - ship you.

Bm · Bm/A · G · D/F# · G · Bm/F# · Em · F#sus · F#

You a - lone are my strength, my shield, to you a - lone may my spir-it yield;

D · A/C# · Bm · D/A · D/F# · Em7 · A7sus · A7 · D

you a - lone are my heart's de - sire, and I long to wor - ship you.

As the grains of wheat

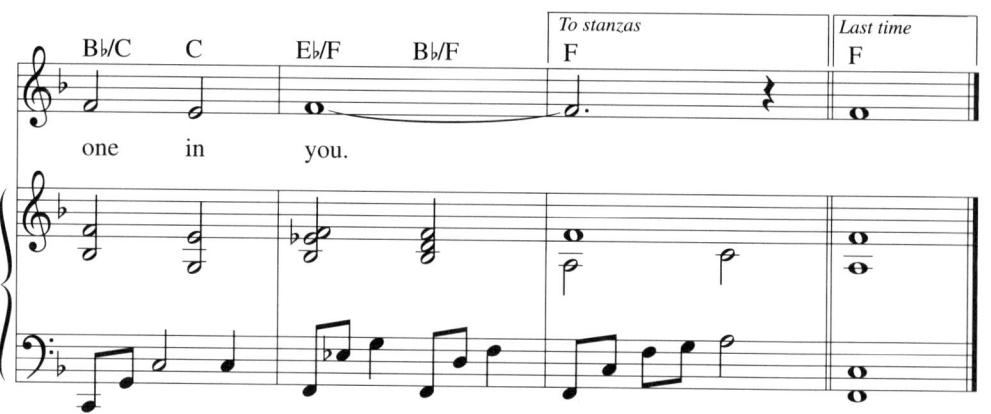

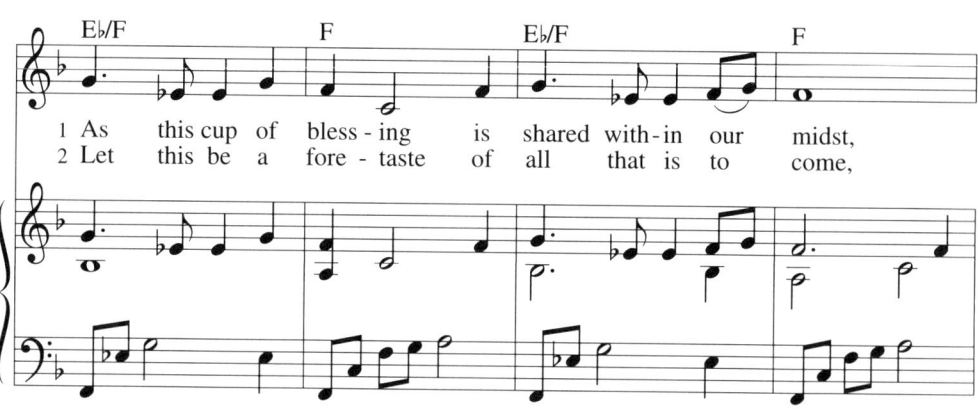

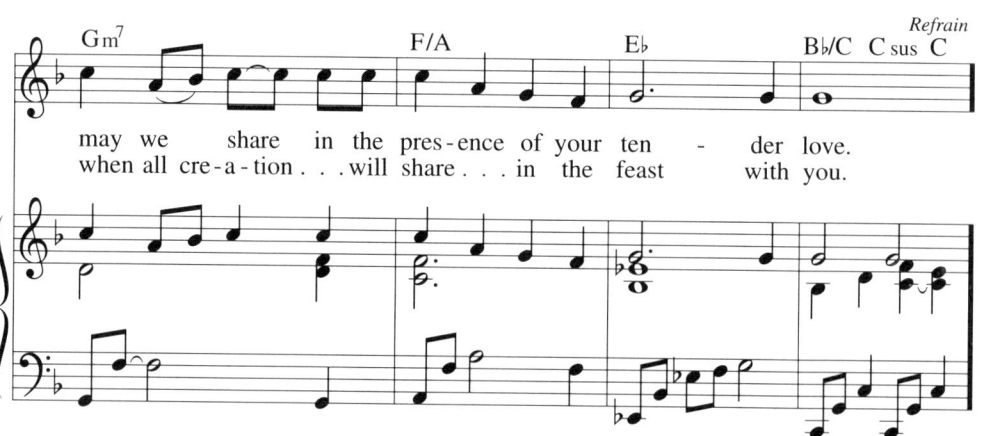

Refrain

As the grains of wheat once scat - tered on the hill were gath - ered in - to one, were gath - ered in - to one to be - come our bread; so may all your peo-ple from the ends of the earth be gath - ered in - to one in you.

1 As this cup of bless - ing is shared with - in our midst,
2 Let this be a fore - taste of all that is to come,

may we share in the pres - ence of your ten - der love.
when all cre - a - tion . . . will share . . . in the feast with you.

Text: Didache, 2nd cent., refrain; Marty Haugen, stanzas
Music: David Haas
Text and music © 1999 GIA Publications

At the foot of the cross

At the foot of the cross, I can hard-ly take it in, that the King of all cre-a-tion was dy-ing for my sin; and the pain and ag-o-ny, and the thorns that pierced your head, and the hard-ness of my sin-ful heart that left you there for dead. And,

oh, what mer-cy I have found at the cross of Cal-va-ry; I will nev-er know your lone-li-ness, all on ac-count of me. And I will bow my knee be-fore your throne, 'cause your love has set me free; and I will give my life to you, dear Lord, and praise your maj-es-ty, and praise your maj-es-ty.

Text and music: Derek Bond
Text and music © 1992 Sovereign Music UK

At the name of Je - sus,

at the name of Je - sus.

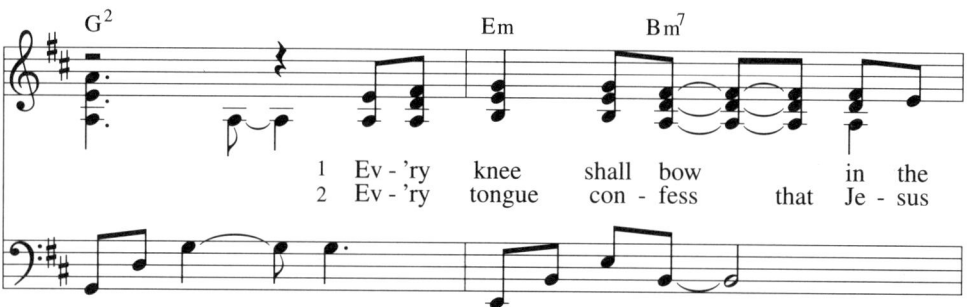

1 Ev - 'ry knee shall bow in the
2 Ev - 'ry tongue con - fess that Je - sus

Text: Philippians 2:10-11, adapt. Richard Webb
Music: Richard Webb
Text and music © 1998 Richard Webb, admin. Faith Inkubators

Awesome God

Our God is an awe-some God, he reigns from

heav-en a-bove with wis - dom, pow'r, and love— our

God is an awe-some God! Our God! Our God is an awe-some

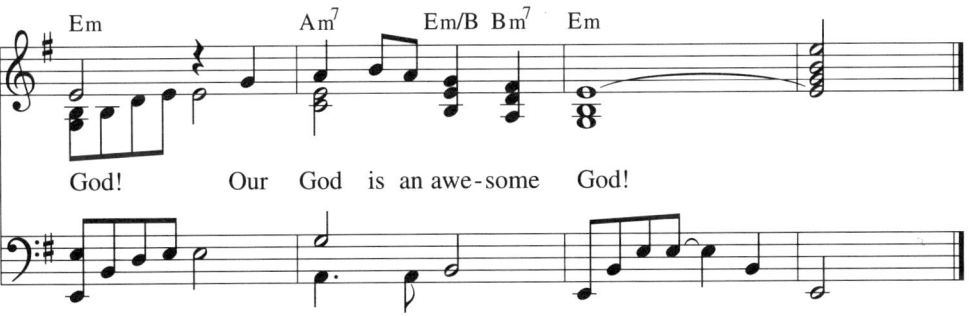

God! Our God is an awe-some God!

Text and music: Rich Mullins
Text and music © 1988 BMG Songs, Inc.

Baptized and set free

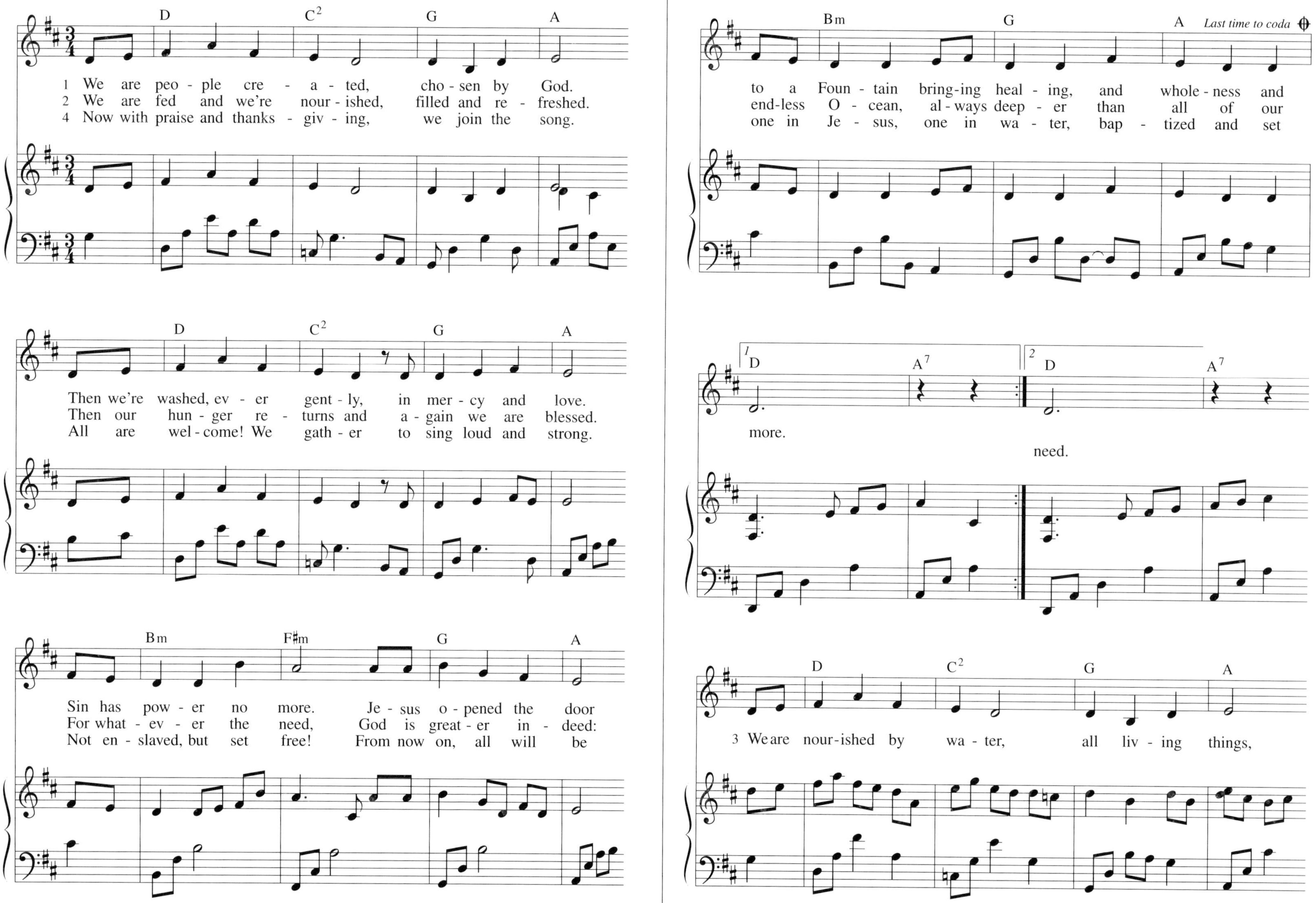
D C2 G A
1 We are peo - ple cre - a - ted, cho - sen by God.
2 We are fed and we're nour - ished, filled and re - freshed.
4 Now with praise and thanks - giv - ing, we join the song.
D C2 G A
Then we're washed, ev - er gent - ly, in mer - cy and love.
Then our hun - ger re - turns and a - gain we are blessed.
All are wel - come! We gath - er to sing loud and strong.
Bm F♯m G A
Sin has pow - er no more. Je - sus o - pened the door
For what - ev - er the need, God is great - er in - deed:
Not en - slaved, but set free! From now on, all will be
Bm G A Last time to coda
to a Foun - tain bring - ing heal - ing, and whole - ness and
end - less O - cean, al - ways deep - er than all of our
one in Je - sus, one in wa - ter, bap - tized and set
1 D A7 2 D A7
more.
need.
D C2 G A
3 We are nour - ished by wa - ter, all liv - ing things,

and by life that the Spir - it a - bun - dant - ly brings.

home. free!

As we jour - ney toward home, may your pres - ence be known:

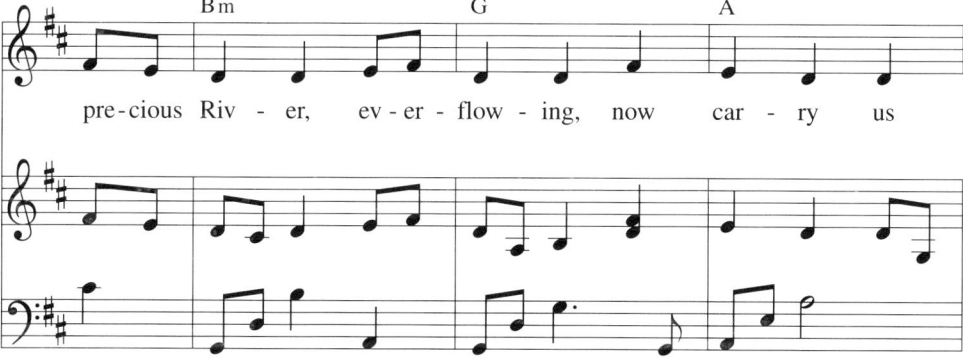

pre - cious Riv - er, ev - er - flow - ing, now car - ry us

Text and music: Cathy Skogen-Soldner
Text and music © 1999 Augsburg Fortress

Be bold, be strong

Text and Music: Morris Chapman
Text and music © 1984 by Word Music, Inc.

Be my home

Be my Sav - ior; be my heart's de - light.

Be my vi - sion;

be my guid - ing light. Storms may press a - gainst me, threat - en to pre - vail.

Be my ref - uge; be my shel - ter from the storm.

Be my love that keeps me warm; be my Sav - ior, be my light; be my home.

Text and music: Handt Hanson and Paul Murakami
Text and music © 1996 Prince of Peace Publishing, Changing Church, Inc.

Beauty for brokenness

1 Beau - ty for bro - ken - ness, hope for de - spair:
2 Shel - ter for fra - gile lives, cures for their ills,
3 Ref - uge from cru - el wars, ha - vens from fear,
4 Rest for the rav - aged earth, o - ceans and streams,
5 Light - en our dark - ness, breathe on this flame,

Lord, in the suf - fer - ing this is our prayer.
work for the crafts - men, trade for their skills;
cit - ies for sanc - tu - a - ry, free - doms to share;
plun - dered and poi - soned, our fu - ture, our dreams,
un - til your jus - tice burns bright - ly a - gain;

Bread for the chil - dren, jus - tice, joy, peace;
land for the dis - pos - sessed, rights for the weak,
peace to the kill - ing fields, scorched earth to green,
Lord, end our mad - ness, care - less - ness, greed;
un - til the na - tions learn of your ways,

sun - rise to sun - set your king - dom in - crease.
voic - es to plead the cause of those who can't speak.
Christ for the bit - ter - ness, his cross for the pain.
make us con - tent with the things that we need.
seek your sal - va - tion, and bring you their praise.

Refrain

God of the poor, friend of the weak, give us com - pas -

- sion, we pray; melt our cold hearts, let tears fall like

rain. Come, change our love from a spark

to a flame.

To stanzas   *Last time*

Text and music: Graham Kendrick
Text and music © 1975 Make Way Music, admin. Integrity Music, Inc.

Bind us together

Bless his holy name

Blessed be the Lord God of Israel

Bless the Lord, O my soul: and all that is with-

in me, bless his ho - ly name. *Fine*

He has done great things, he has done great things,

he has done great things: bless his ho - ly name! *D.C. al fine*

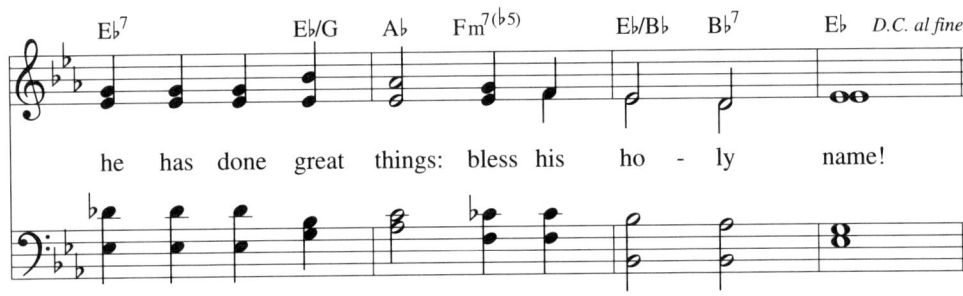

Bless'd be the Lord God of Is - ra - el! Ho - ly is your

name: you have come to save your

peo - ple from death and from the grave.

Text and music: Andraé Crouch
Text and music © 1973 Bud John Songs, Inc., admin. EMI Christian Music Publishing

1 You have spo-ken through the proph - ets
2 Lit - tle child, . . you . . shall be called

from age up-on age:
the proph-et of the Lord;

the prom-ise giv-en to our
the way of God . . you . .

an - ces - tors
will pre - pare,

for - ev - er true will re -
bring-ing sal - va - tion through the

main.
Word.

De-liv-'ring us from our en - em - ies,
With ten-der mer - cy . . . from our God,

our God is al - ways near;
the day-spring from on high

in ho - li - ness and
brings us the light to

righ - teous - ness we wor - ship with - out fear.
guide our feet and drive a - way the night.

Text: Luke 1:68-79, adapt.
Music: Ralph C. Sappington
Text and music © 1999 Augsburg Fortress

Blessing, honor, and glory

Bless - ing, hon - or, glo - ry to the

Seat-ed up-on the throne, he is the Lamb of God!

Lamb. Ho - ly, righ - teous,

God! Bless-ing, hon - or,

wor - thy is the Lamb. Death could not hold him down,

glo - ry to the Lamb. Ho - ly, righ - teous,

for he is ris - en!

wor - thy is the Lamb of God.

Text and music: Geoff Bullock and David Reidy
Text and music © 1990 Word Music, Inc., and Maranatha! Music, admin. Word Music, Inc.

Bring forth the kingdom

Leader
D   G/D   D   D/F#   All G   D/F#   A   D

1 You are salt for the earth, O peo-ple: salt for the king-dom of God!
2 You are a light on the hill, O peo-ple: light for the cit-y of God!
3 You are a seed of the word, O peo-ple: bring forth the king-dom of God!
4 We are a blest and a pil-grim peo-ple: bound for the king-dom of God!

G   D/F#   Em/G   A   D   G   D/F#   A   D

bring forth the cit-y of God!

Leader
G   D/F#   G   A   D   All G   D/F#   A   D

Share the fla-vor of life, O peo-ple: life in the king-dom of God!
Shine so ho-ly and bright, O peo-ple: shine for the king-dom of God!
Seeds of mer-cy and seeds of jus-tice, grow in the king-dom of God!
Love our jour-ney and love our home-land: love is the king-dom of God!

Refrain
G   D/F#   Em   A   D   G   D/F#

Bring forth the king-dom of mer-cy, bring forth the

Em   A   D   G   D/F#   G   A   D

king-dom of peace; bring forth the king-dom of jus-tice,

Text and music: Marty Haugen
Text and music © 1986 GIA Publications

Broken for me

Refrain

E — AM⁷ F♯m⁷ B⁷sus B⁷

Bro-ken for me, bro-ken for you;

Last time to coda ⊕

E AM⁷ F♯m⁷ B⁷

the bod-y of Je - sus bro-ken for you.

E AM⁷ F♯m⁷

1 He of - fered his bod - y, he poured out his
2 Come to my ta - ble and with me
3 This is my bod - y giv - en for
4 This is my blood . . . . . I shed for

Bsus B E AM⁷

soul; Je - sus was bro - ken
dine; eat of my bread . . . .
you; eat it, re - mem - b'ring
you; for your for - give - ness,

F♯m⁷ B⁷sus B⁷ *Refrain*

that we might be whole.
and drink of my wine.
I died for you.
mak - ing you new.

⊕ *Coda*

F♯m⁷ A/B E

bro - ken for you.

Text: Janet Lunt
Music: Janet Lunt; arr. Mimi Farra
Text and music © 1978 Sovereign Music UK

Broken in love

This is my bod - y, bro - ken in love; take it and eat and re - mem - ber me.

This is my blood, poured out in love; take it and drink and re - mem - ber me. For

love is will - ing ev - 'ry day to die in or - der to live, and

love is pa - tient for a way to share the gifts that I give.

Text: Handt Hanson
Music: Handt Hanson; arr. Henry Wiens
Text and music © 1991 Prince of Peace Publishing, Changing Church, Inc.

By grace we have been saved

1 By grace we have been saved through faith and not by keep-ing law.
2 For all have sinned and fall - en short. God's plan, not one o - beyed.
3 God gave to earth a per - fect love through Je - sus on the cross.
4 We know the wage of sin is death; thank God, we shall re - vive.
5 Set free, we now have peace with God. Sal - va - tion is se - cured.

God's saints be - lieved by what they heard and not by what they saw.
Christ has for all ful - filled the law. Be - lieve, con - fess, be saved.
While we were foes, Christ died for us. We gained by God's own loss.
For just as Je - sus rose a - gain, we too are made a - live.
How beau - ti - ful the feet of those who share this gos - pel word.

Refrain

Oh, how I love Je - sus! Oh, how I love Je - sus!

Oh, how I love Je - sus, be - cause he first loved me!

Text: Rusty Edwards, stanzas; Frederick Whitfield, refrain
Music: North American traditional, arr. Rusty Edwards
Text © 1997 Selah Publishing Co.; arr. © 1999 Augsburg Fortress

Canticle of the turning

1 My soul cries out with a joy - ful shout that the
2 Though I am small, my God, my all, you
3 From the halls of power to the for - tress tower, not a
4 Though the na - tions rage from age to age, we re -

God of my heart is great, and my spir - it sings of the
work great things in me, and your mer - cy will last from the
stone will be left on stone. Let the king be - ware for your
mem - ber who holds us fast: God's mer - cy must de -

won - drous things that you bring to the ones who wait. You
depths of the past to the end of the age to be. Your
jus - tice tears ev - 'ry ty - rant from his throne. The
liv - er us from the con - quer - or's crush - ing grasp. This

fixed your sight on your ser - vant's plight, and my weak - ness you did not
ver - y name puts the proud to shame, and to those who would for you
hun - gry poor shall weep no more, for the food they can nev - er
sav - ing word that our fore - bears heard is the prom - ise which holds us

spurn, so from east to west shall my name be blest. Could the
yearn, you will show your might, put the strong to flight, for the
earn; there are ta - bles spread, ev - 'ry mouth be fed, for the
bound, 'til the spear and rod can be crushed by God, who is

world be a - bout to turn?
world is a - bout to turn.
world is a - bout to turn.   My   heart shall sing of the
turn - ing the world a - round.

day you bring. Let the fires of your jus - tice burn.   Wipe a -

way all tears, for the dawn draws near, and the world is a - bout to turn.

Cares chorus

I   cast   all my cares up - on you;   I

lay   all of my bur - dens down at your feet.   And

an - y - time that I don't know   what   to   do,   I will

cast   all my cares   up - on   you.

Text: Rory Cooney, based on Luke 1:46-55
Music: Irish traditional, adapt. Rory Cooney
Text and music © 1990 GIA Publications

Text and music: Kelly Willard
Text and tune © 1978 Maranatha Praise, Inc., admin. The Copyright Company

Change my heart, O God

Text and music: Eddie Espinosa
Text and music © 1982 Mercy/Vineyard Publishing

Come and see

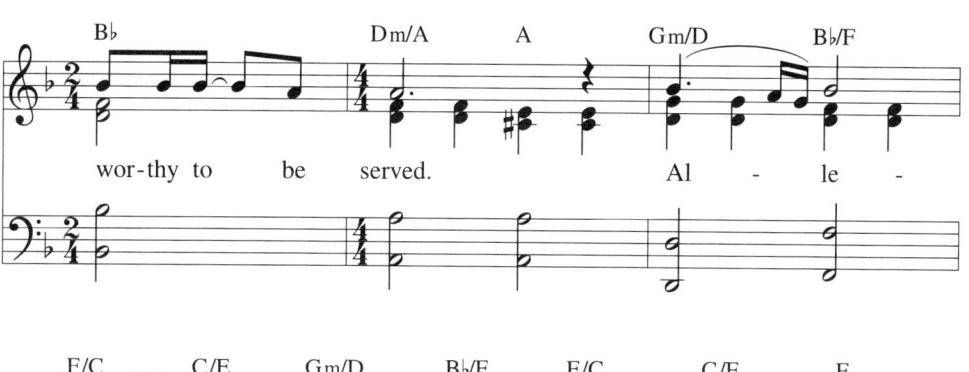

1 Come and see the glo-ry of the Lord. Come, be-hold the
2 Come and give thanks un-to the Lord. Come, be-hold the

Lamb. Come and see the mer-cy of the King,
Lamb. Come and sing the prais-es of the King,

bow-ing down be-fore him.
bow-ing down be-fore him. For he is

Lord a-bove the heav-ens, Lord in all the earth, Lord of all the an-gels,

wor-thy to be served. Al - le -
lu - ia. Al - le - lu - ia, Lord.

Text and music: Lenny LeBlanc
Text and tune © 1989 Doulos Publishing, admin. The Copyright Company

Come and taste

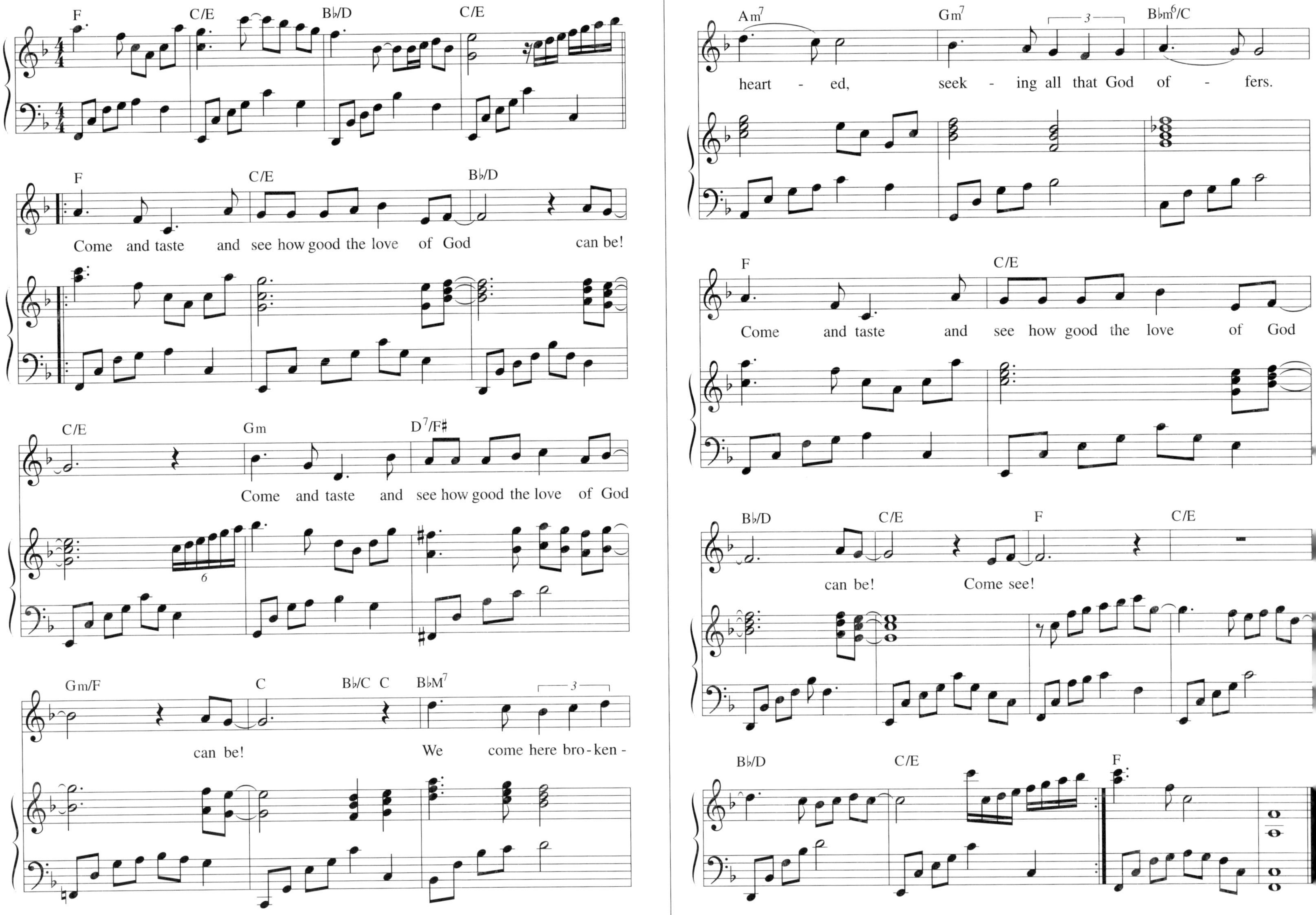
F C/E B♭/D C/E
F C/E B♭/D
Come and taste and see how good the love of God can be!
C/E Gm D7/F♯
Come and taste and see how good the love of God
Gm/F C B♭/C C B♭M7
can be! We come here bro-ken -
Am7 Gm7 B♭m6/C
heart - ed, seek - ing all that God of - fers.
F C/E
Come and taste and see how good the love of God
B♭/D C/E F C/E
can be! Come see!
B♭/D C/E F

Text: Handt Hanson and Paul Murakami
Music: Handt Hanson and Paul Murakami; arr. Henry Wiens

Come, let us worship and bow down

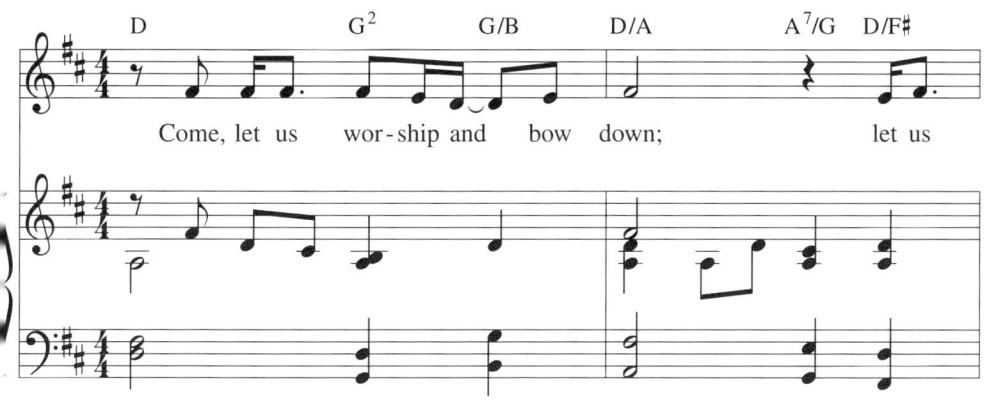

Come, let us wor-ship and bow down; let us

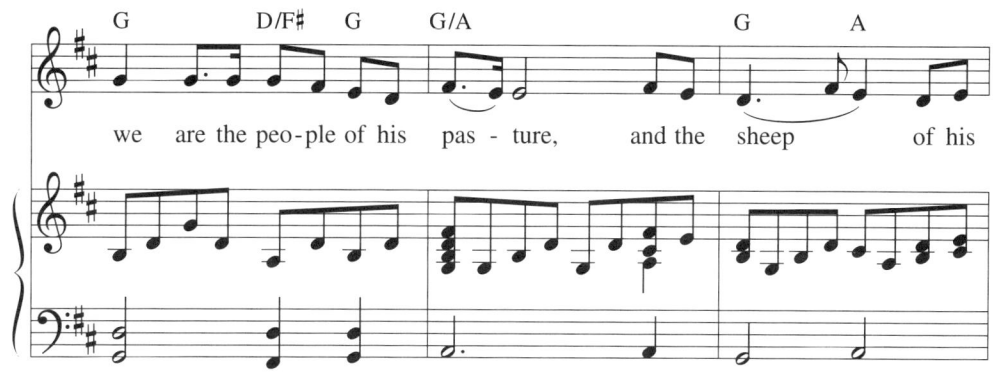

we are the peo-ple of his pas - ture, and the sheep of his

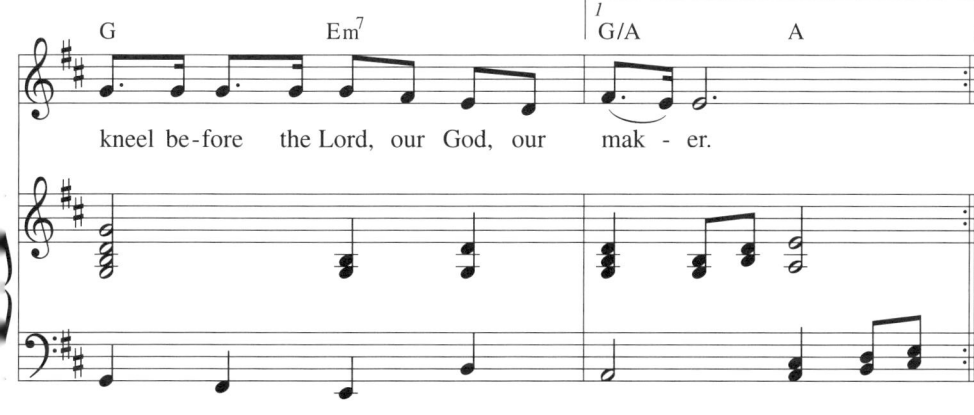

kneel be-fore the Lord, our God, our mak - er.

hand, and the sheep of his hand.

mak - er. For he is our God, and

Text: Psalm 95:6-7
Music: Dave Doherty
Music © 1980 Maranatha Praise, Inc., admin. The Copyright Company

Come to the mountain

Refrain

Eb

1 Je - sus took Pet - er, James, and John
2 "This is my Son!" said a voice from the cloud.
3 We will be changed like Je - sus our Lord,

Ab · Eb · Eb/Bb · Eb

Come to the moun - tain to see the light.

Eb/Bb · Bb

up to the moun - tain to be a - lone.
"Lis - ten to him . . . . . and do what he says!"
and live with him . . . . . in heav - en a - bove.

Ab · Eb · F7 · Bb

Come to the moun - tain to hear God's word.

Eb · G7 · Cm

While they were watch - ing Je - sus was changed;
Soon as it came . . . . . that vis - ion was gone,
But while we live on this earth - ly home,

Ab · Eb · G7 · Cm

Go to the val - ley, it is your home.

Ab · Eb/Bb · Ab · Eb

and they saw Mo - ses face to face.
and they saw Je - sus stand - ing a - lone.
our work as ser - vants nev - er is done.

Ab · Eb/Bb · Ab/Bb Bb7 · Eb

Go to the val - ley to serve the Lord.

Text: Scott Tunseth
Music: Kathy Donlan Tunseth
Text and music © 1996 Scott Tunseth and Kathy Donlan Tunseth

Come to the table

F | Bb/F | C/E Dsus⁴₂ Dm⁷/C | Bb | C⁷sus | F | Gm⁷ Bb/C

Come to the ta-ble of mer-cy, pre-pared with the wine and the bread.

F | Bb/F | Dsus⁴₂ Dm⁷/C | Bb | C⁷sus | Fsus F

All who are hun-gry and thirst-y, come and your souls will be fed.

Am | BbM⁷ | C⁷/Bb Am Dm⁷ Gm⁷ | Dm/F | C/E Bb/D C

Come at the Lord's in-vi-ta-tion; re-ceive from his nail-scarred hand.

F | Bb/F | C/E Dsus⁴₂ Dm⁷/C | Bb | C⁷sus | Fsus F

Eat of the bread of sal-va-tion; drink of the blood of the Lamb.

Text: Claire Cloninger
Music: Martin J. Nystrom
Text and music © 1991 Integrity's Hosanna Music and Word Music

Create in me a clean heart

G | D C | G C/D G

Cre-ate in me a clean heart, O God, and re-new a right

D | Dsus D | G | C/D | ¹G | ²G⁷

spir-it with-in me. Cre-

C | G/C D | G | Gsus G

Cast me not a-way from your pres-ence, O Lord, and

C | G/C D | G | G⁷

take not your Ho-ly Spir-it from me. Re-

C | G/C D | G | D/F♯ Em

store un-to me the joy of your sal-va-tion,

C | D | Dsus D | G

and re-new a right spir-it with-in me.

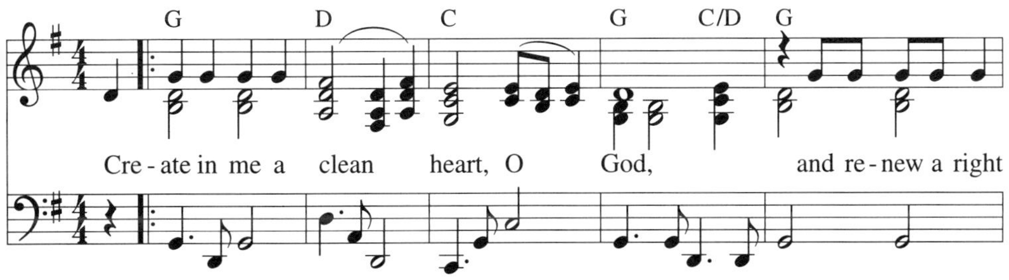

Text: Psalm 51:10-12
Music: anonymous
Arr. © 1986 Maranatha! Music, admin. The Copyright Company

Create in me a clean heart

Emmanuel

Text and music: Mary Rice Hopkins
Text and music © 1989 Big Steps 4 U, admin. Music Services/Maranatha! Music, admin. The Copyright Company

Text and music: Bob McGee
Text and music © 1976 C. A. Music

37 Father, I adore you

1 Fa - ther,
2 Je - sus, I a - dore you, lay my life be -
3 Spir - it,

fore you; how I love you.

*may be sung in canon

Text and music: Terry Coelho
Text and music © 1972 Maranatha! Music, admin. The Copyright Company

38 For by grace

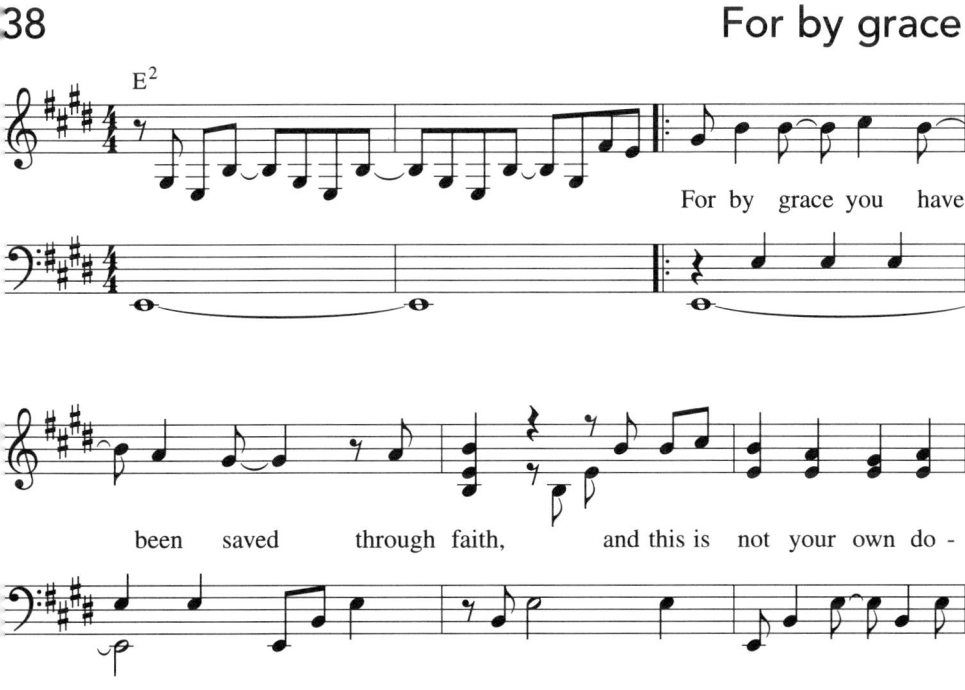

For by grace you have

been saved through faith, and this is not your own do -

ing; it is the gift of God.

Sal - va - tion, sal -

va - tion, sal -

va - tion, sal - va - tion:

it is the gift of God.

Text: Ephesians 2:8
Music: Thomas Ian Nicholas
Music © 1998 Thomas Ian Nicholas, admin. Faith Inkubators

For God so loved

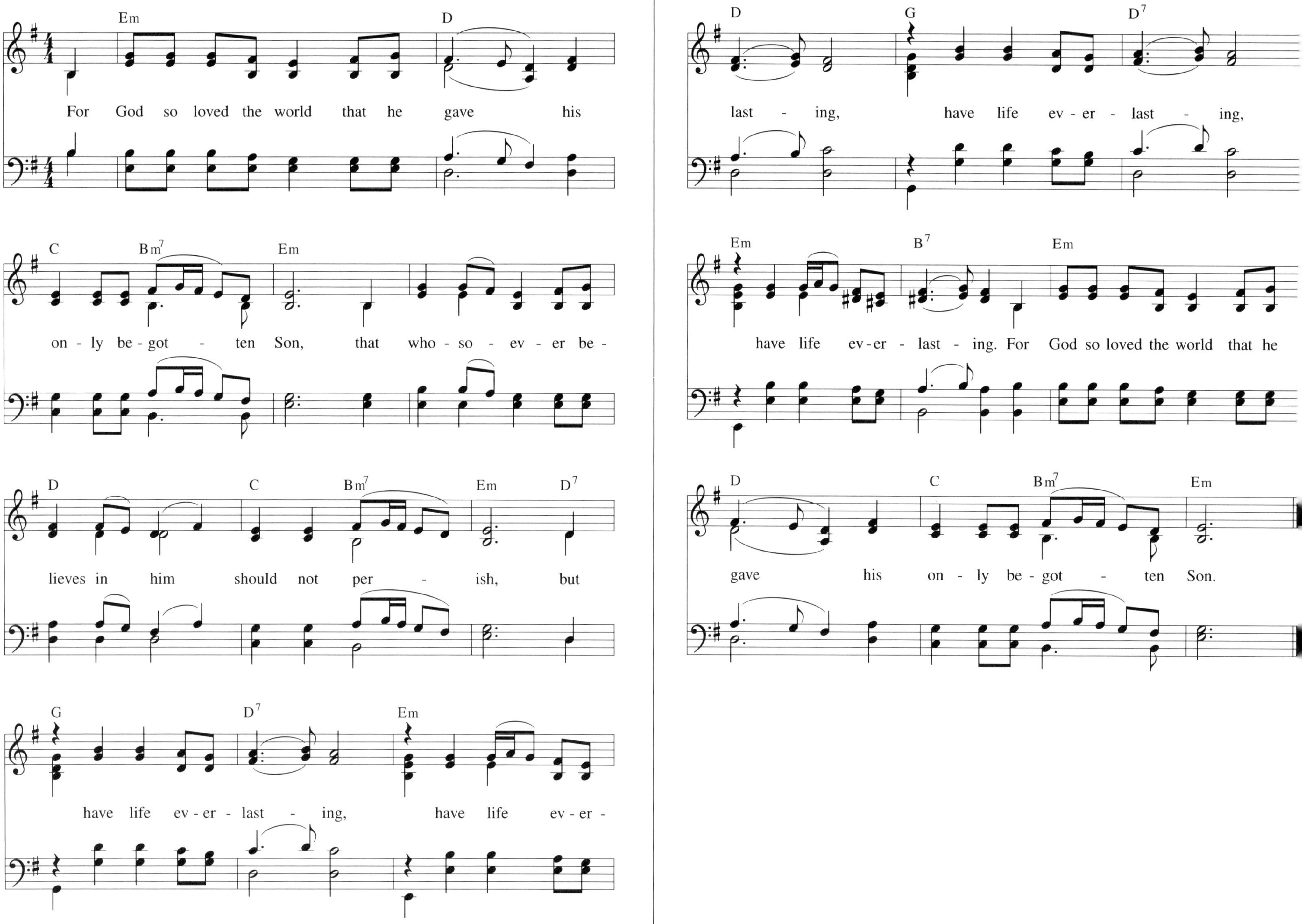

For God so loved the world that he gave his
on - ly be - got - ten Son, that who - so - ev - er be-
lieves in him should not per - ish, but
have life ev - er - last - ing, have life ev - er -
last - ing, have life ev - er - last - ing,
have life ev - er - last - ing. For God so loved the world that he
gave his on - ly be - got - ten Son.

Text: John 3:16, adapt. Stuart Dauermann
Music: Stuart Dauermann

From where the sun rises

1 From where the sun ris - es, e - ven to the
2 We're lift - ing our fac - es, look - ing at the

place it goes down, we're giv - ing you praise,
one we all love: we're giv - ing you praise,

giv - ing you praise.
giv - ing you praise. From sun - kissed
All col - ors and

is - lands, and e - ven where the cold wind blows,
rac - es, join - ing with the an - gels a - bove,

we're giv - ing you praise,
we're giv - ing you praise,

Fine

giv - ing you praise.
giv - ing you praise.

E - ven in the night when the sun goes down, we're giv - ing you praise;

pass - ing it a - long as the world goes 'round, we're

D.C. al fine

giv - ing you praise.

Text and music: Graham Kendrick
Text and music © 1996 Make Way Music, admin. Integrity Music, Inc.

Give thanks

Text and music: Henry Smith
Text and music © 1978 Integrity's Hosanna! Music

Glorify thy name

1 Fa - ther,
2 Je - sus, we love you, we wor-ship and a - dore you,
3 Spir - it,

glo - ri - fy thy name in all the earth;

glo - ri - fy thy name, glo - ri - fy thy name,

glo - ri - fy thy name in all the earth.

Text and music: Donna Adkins
Text and music © 1976 Maranatha! Music, admin. The Copyright Company

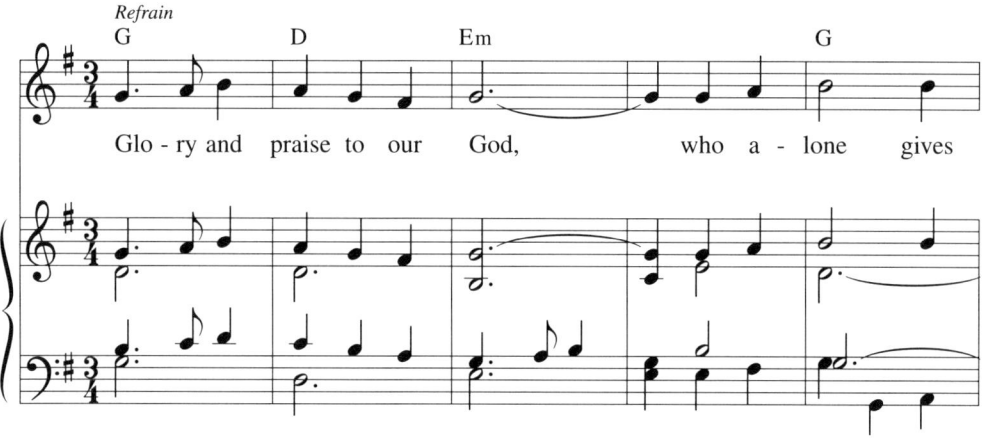

43 Glory and praise to our God

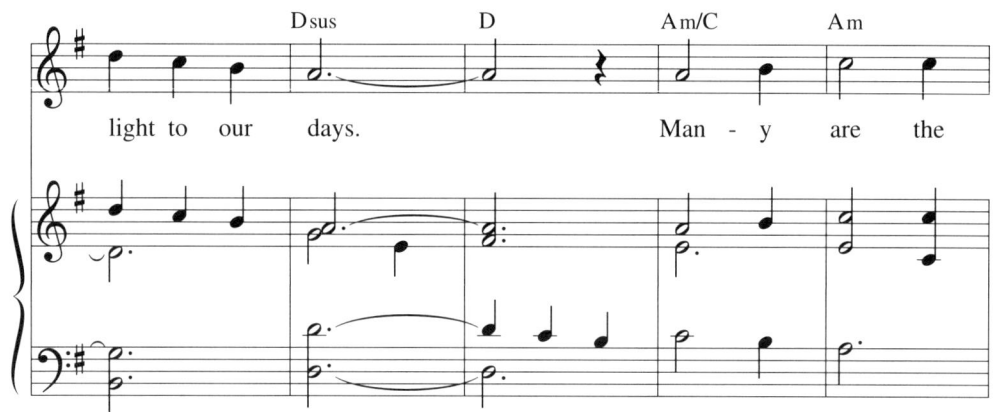

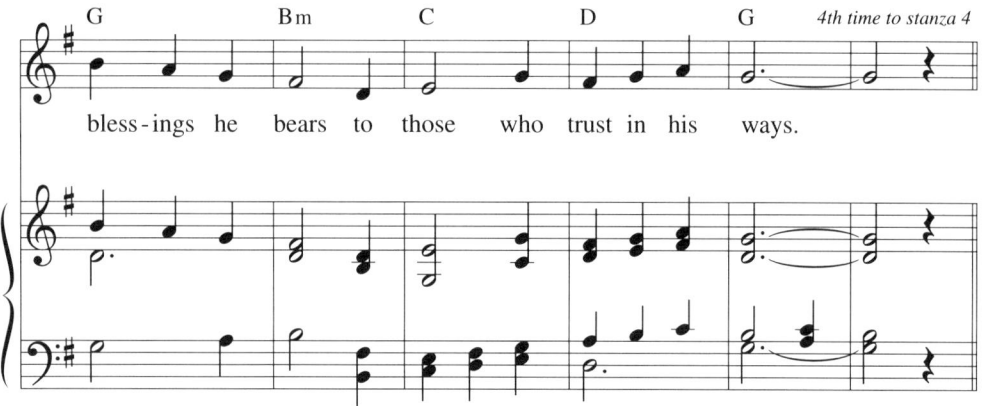

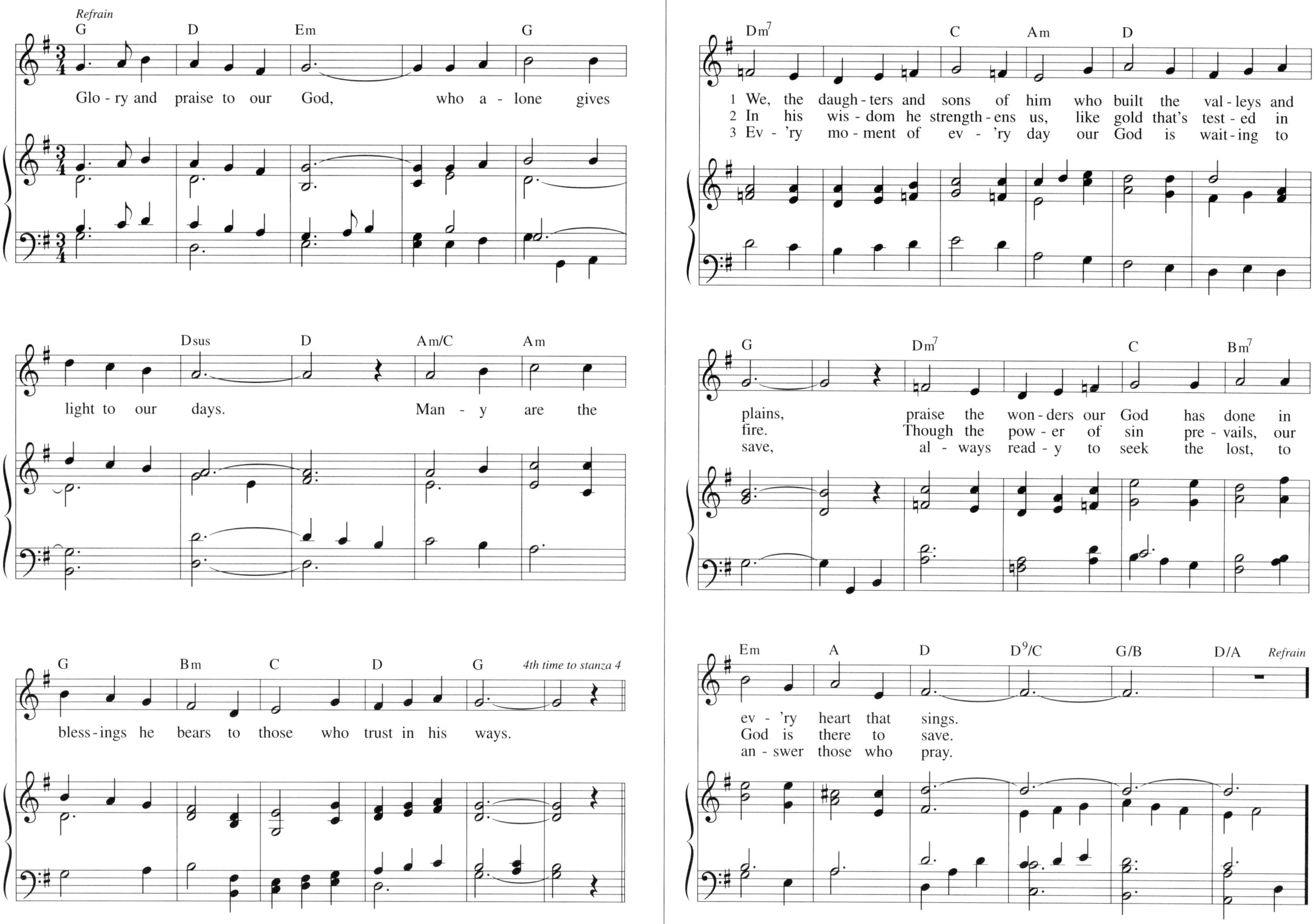
Refrain
Glory and praise to our God, who alone gives light to our days. Many are the blessings he bears to those who trust in his ways.
4th time to stanza 4
1 We, the daughters and sons of him who built the valleys and plains, praise the wonders our God has done in every heart that sings.
2 In his wisdom he strengthens us, like gold that's tested in fire. Though the power of sin prevails, our God is there to save.
3 Every moment of every day our God is waiting to save, always ready to seek the lost, to answer those who pray.
Refrain

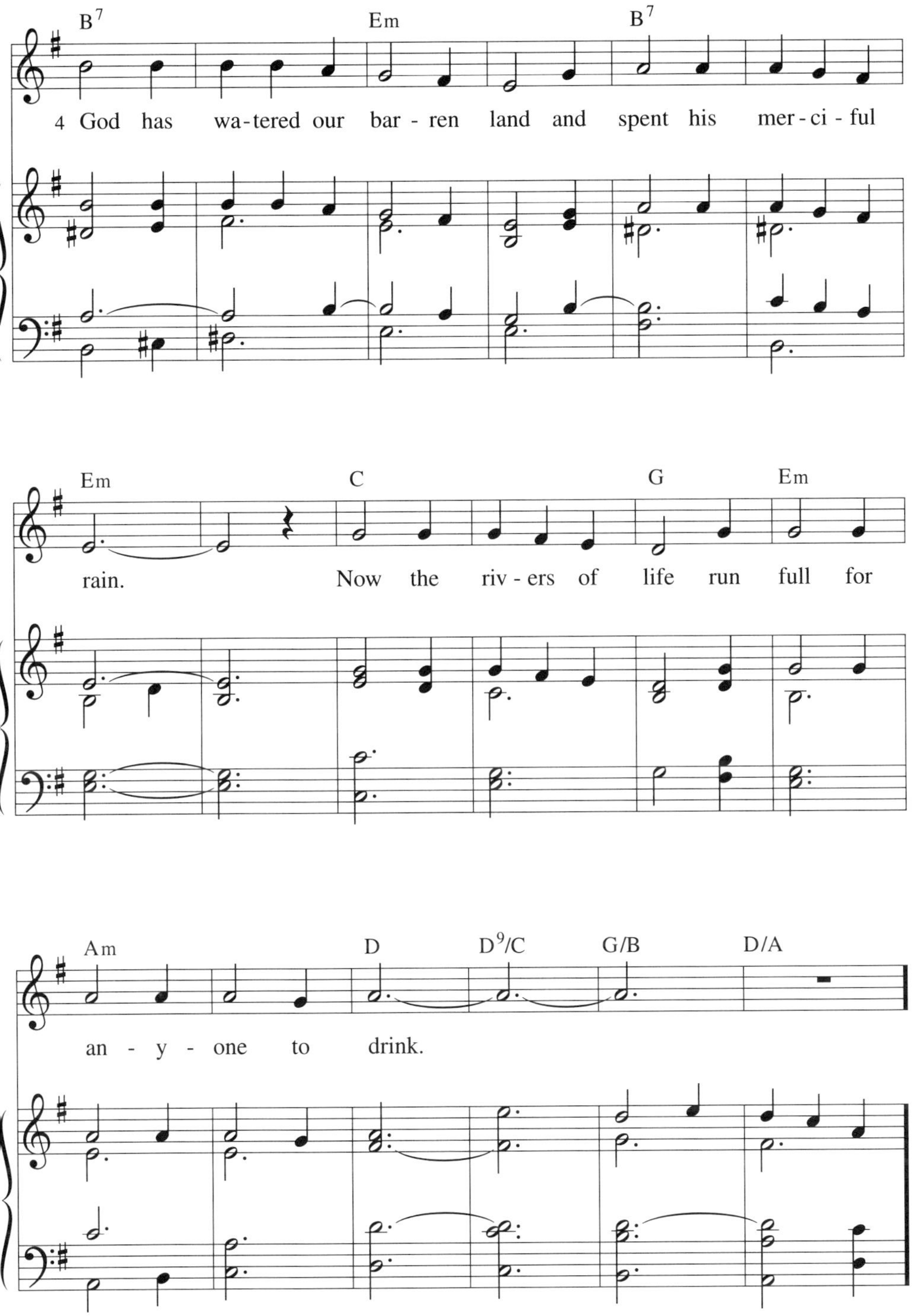

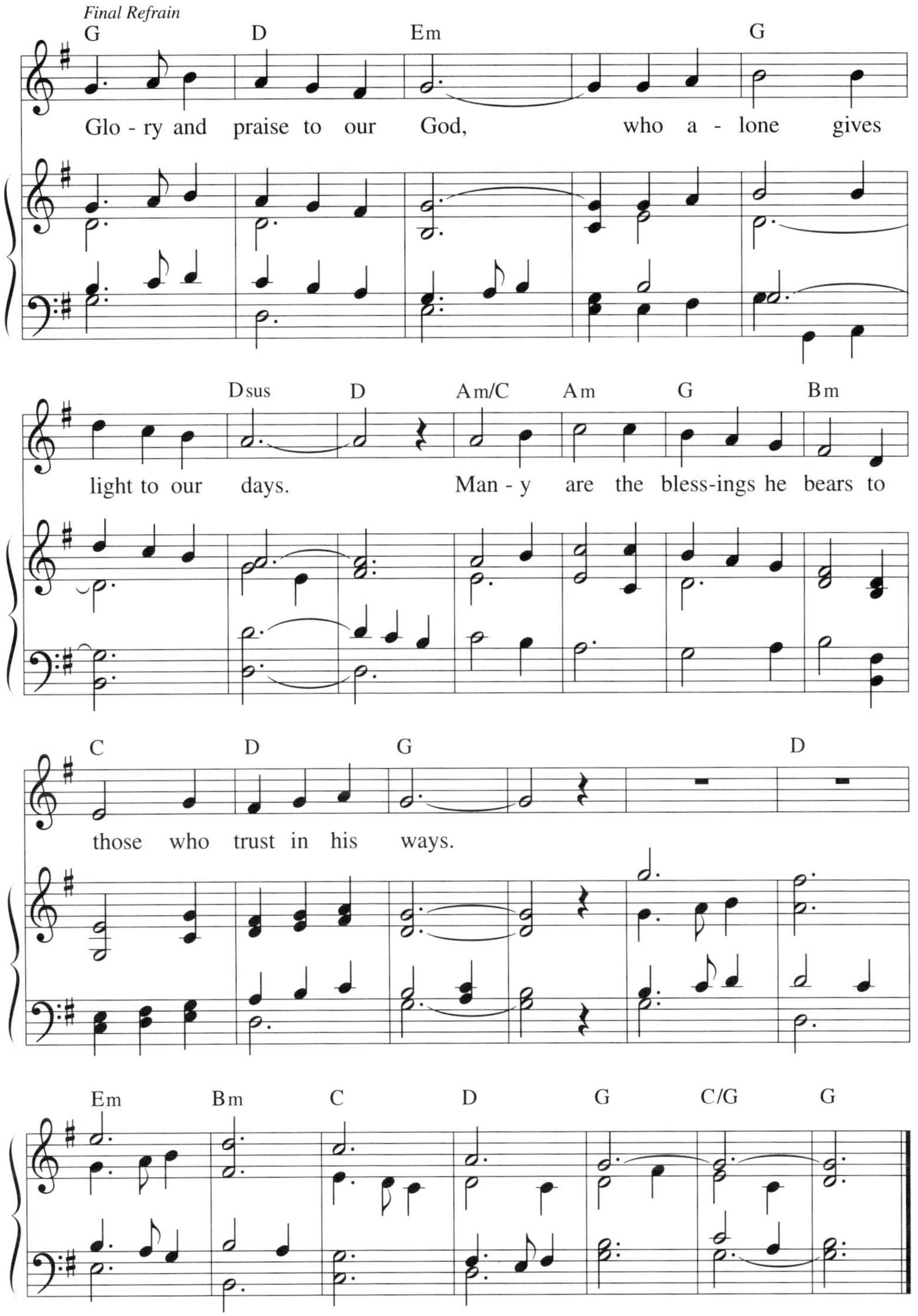

4 God has wa-tered our bar-ren land and spent his mer-ci-ful rain. Now the riv-ers of life run full for an-y-one to drink.

Final Refrain

Glo-ry and praise to our God, who a-lone gives light to our days. Man-y are the bless-ings he bears to those who trust in his ways.

Text and music: Daniel Schutte
Text and music © 1976 Daniel Schutte and New Dawn Music

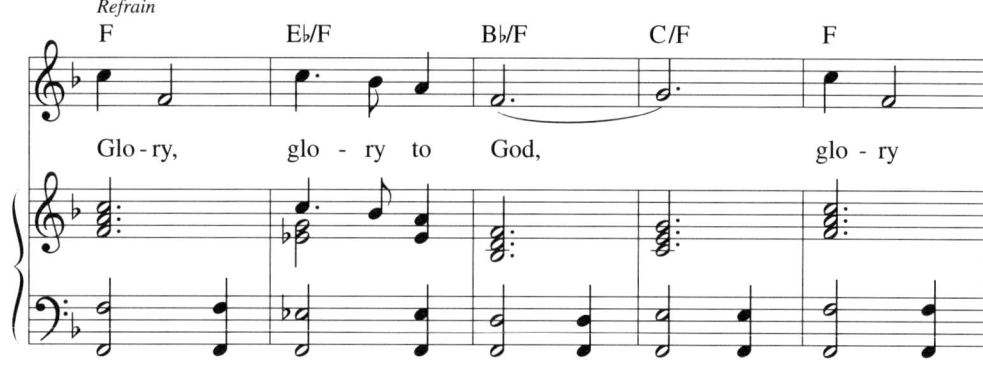
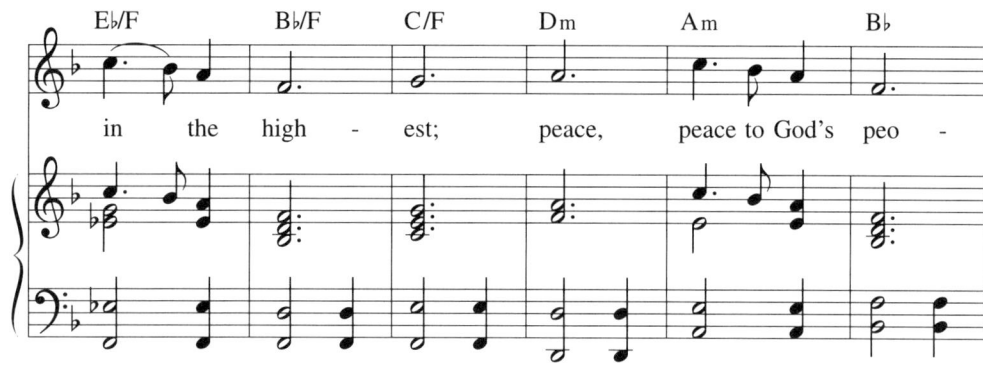

Fa - ther, Lord God, Lamb of God,

you take a - way the sin of the world: have mer -

cy on us; you are seat - ed at the right hand

of the Fa - ther: re - ceive our prayer.

3 For you a - lone are the Ho - ly One, you a - lone are the

Lord, you a - lone are the Most High, Je - sus

Christ, with the Ho - ly Spir-it, in the glo-ry of

God the Fa - ther. A - men

Refrain

Text: "Gloria," tr. English Language Liturgical Consultation
Music: David Haas
Music © 1999 GIA Publications

Glory to God

We praise you for your glory

Dm   C   B♭   C   Dm   C

1 Glo-ry to God in the high-est,   peace to his peo-ple on earth;
2 Je-sus, our Lord .. and Sav - ior,   rul-ing in glo-ry a-bove,

Dm   C   B♭   C   Dm   C²/D

al-might-y God,   the Fa - ther, the heav-en-ly   king.
O Lamb of God,   so wor - thy, for-give us our   sin.

B♭   C   Dm   C   B♭   C

al-might-y God,   the Fa - ther, the heav-en-ly
au-thor of life and cre-a - tor of in-fi-nite

Refrain

Dm   C/E   F   C/E   C⁷   Dm   B♭M⁷

We wor - ship you,   we give thanks to you,   we

Dm   C²/D   Dm   C²/D   Am⁷   Dm   C

king.
love:

Glo-ry to God in the high-
We call on you now . . . for mer-

F/A   C   B♭   F   C/E   C⁷

praise you for   your glo - ry.   We wor - ship you,   we give

B♭   C   Dm   C   B♭   C

- est,   peace to his peo - ple on earth;
- cy,   we pray for your heal - ing with-in;

Dm   B♭M⁷   F/A   F   Gm   F/C   C⁷   F

thanks to you,   we praise you for   your glo - ry.

Text: "Gloria," adapt. Rick Founds and Bill Batstone
Music: Rick Founds and Bill Batstone

You alone are the Holy

You alone are the Holy;
you alone are the Lord;
you alone are the Most High, the Most High God:
Jesus, our Lord and Messiah,
Spirit of power and love,
one with the Father in glory forever. Amen

This stanza completes the traditional "Glory to God" hymn text begun on the previous page.

Text: "Gloria," adapt. *Worship & Praise*
Text © 1999 Augsburg Fortress

46 Go in peace and serve the Lord

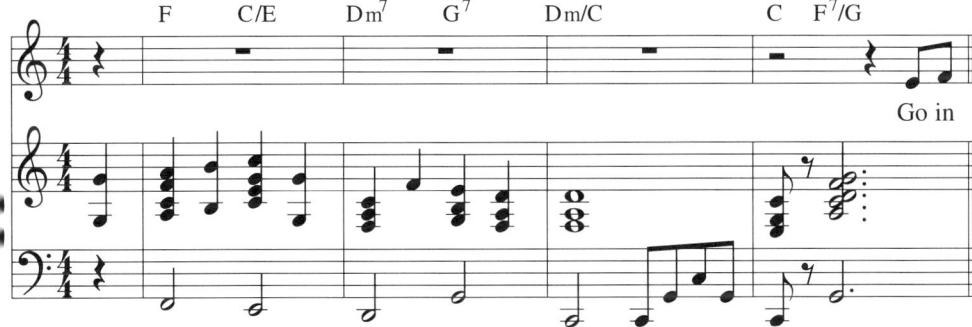

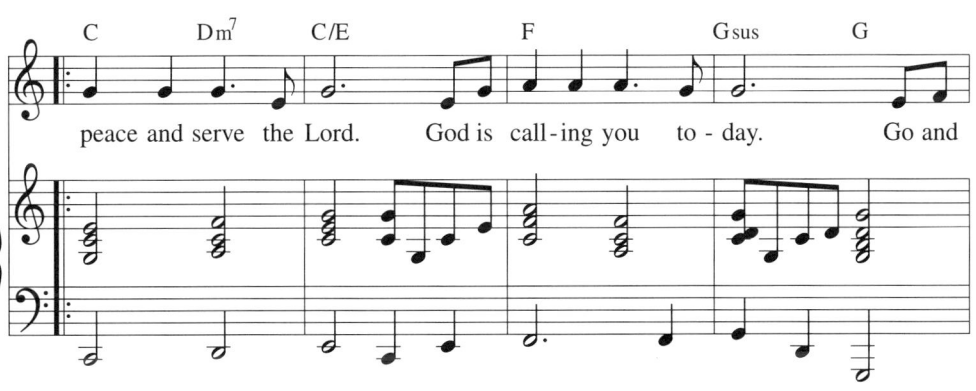

Text: Handt Hanson
Music: Handt Hanson; arr. Henry Wiens
Text and music © 1996 Prince of Peace Publishing, Changing Church, Inc.

Go, make disciples

salt of the earth. Go, be the light for the world.

Go, make dis - ci - ples, bap - tiz - ing them,

teach - ing them. Go, make dis - ci - ples, for

Go, be a cit - y on a hill, so all can see that you're

I am with you till the end of time. Go, be the

serv - ing me. Go, make dis - ci - ples.

Text: Handt Hanson
Music: Handt Hanson; arr. Henry Wiens
Text and music © 1996 Prince of Peace Publishing, Changing Church, Inc.

Go out with joy

Text and Music: Leila Huerta and Joe Huerta
Text and music © 1984 Maranatha Praise, Inc., admin. The Copyright Company

Go ye therefore

Go ye there-fore and make dis-ci-ples of all na-tions, of all na-tions.

Go ye there-fore and make dis-ci-ples of all na-tions, of all na-tions,

bap-tiz-ing them in the name of the Fa-ther and the Son and the Ho-ly Spir-it.

Go ye there-fore and make dis-ci-ples of all na-tions, of all na-tions. Go!

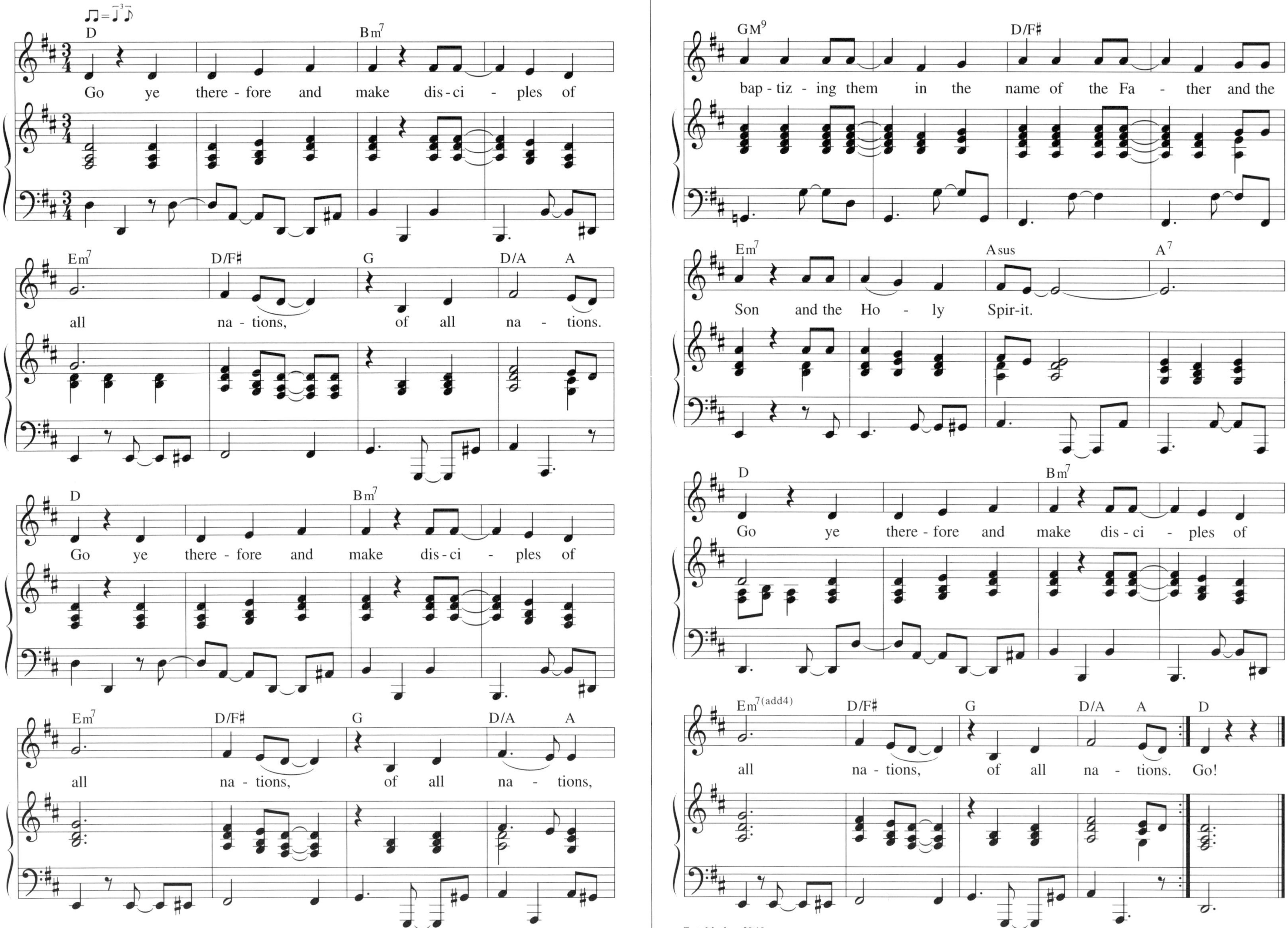

Text: Matthew 28:19
Music: Robin Cain; arr. Richard Webb
Tune © 1997 Robin Cain
Arr. © 1997 Richard Webb

God be with you

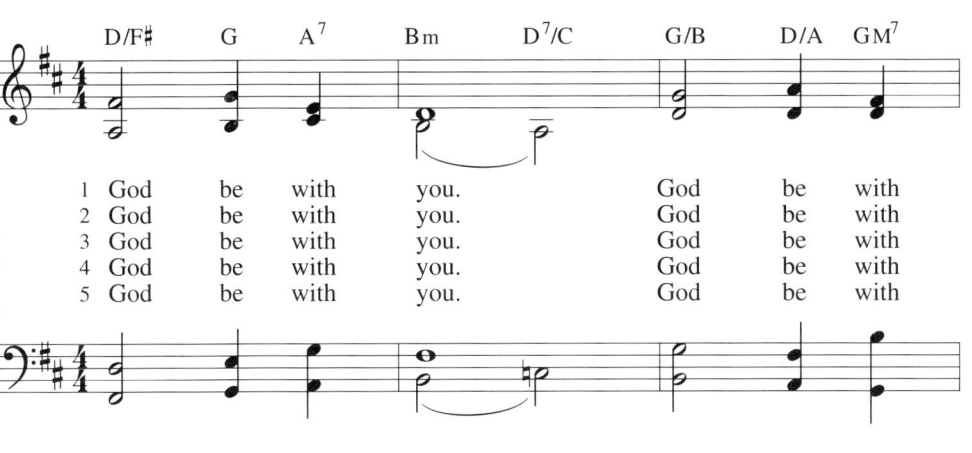

1 God be with you. God be with
2 God be with you. God be with
3 God be with you. God be with
4 God be with you. God be with
5 God be with you. God be with

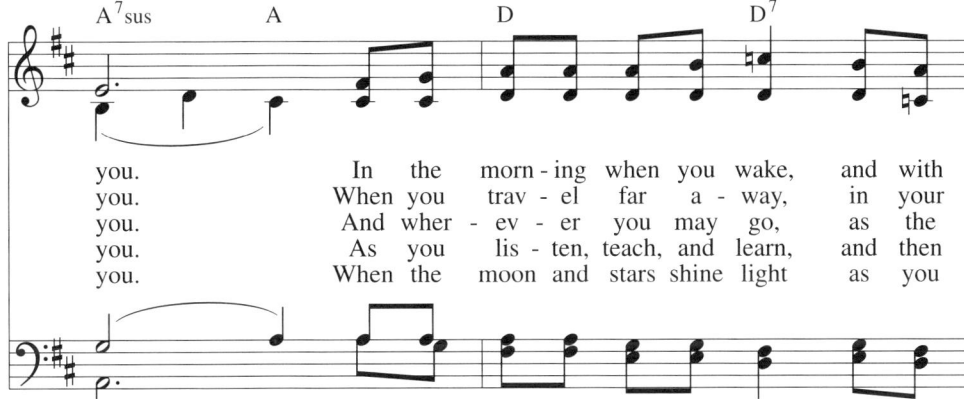

you. In the morn-ing when you wake, and with
you. When you trav-el far a-way, in your
you. And wher-ev-er you may go, as the
you. As you lis-ten, teach, and learn, and then
you. When the moon and stars shine light as you

ev-'ry breath you take, God be with you.
dai-ly work and play, God be with you.
spir-it winds will blow, God be with you.
safe-ly home re-turn, God be with you.
slum-ber through the night, God be with you.

Text and music: Rusty Edwards
Text and music © 1997 Selah Publishing Co.

God has done marvelous things

1 Earth and all stars!
2 Hail, wind, and rain!
3 Trum - pet and pipes!
4 En - gines and steel!

Loud rush - ing plan - ets!
Loud blow - ing snow - storm!
Loud clash - ing cym - bals!
Loud pound - ing ham - mers!

Oh, vic - to - ry!
Flow - ers and trees!
Harp, lute, and lyre!
Lime - stone and beams!

Loud shout - ing ar - my!
Loud rust - ling dry leaves!
Loud hum - ming cel - los!
Loud build - ing work - ers!

Sing to the Lord a new song!

Refrain

God has done mar - vel - ous things. I too, I

too sing prais - es with a new song!

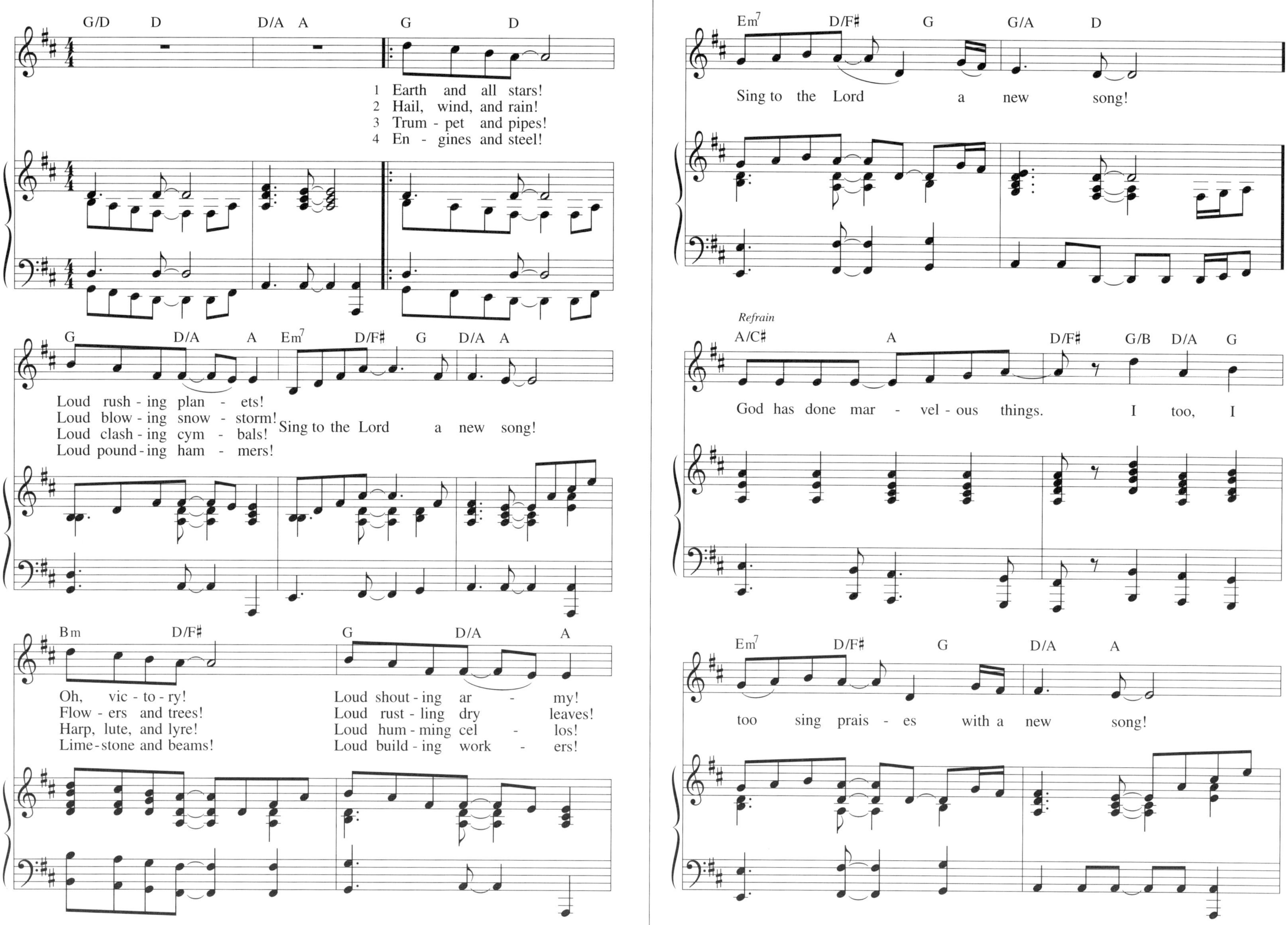

God has done mar - vel - ous things. I too, I too sing prais - es with a new song!

I too sing prais - es with a new song!

To stanzas

new song!

Last time

5 Classrooms and labs!
  Loud boiling test-tubes!
  Sing to the Lord a new song!
  Athlete and band!
  Loud cheering people!
  Sing to the Lord a new song!
  Refrain

6 Knowledge and truth!
  Loud sounding wisdom!
  Sing to the Lord a new song!
  Daughter and son!
  Loud praying members!
  Sing to the Lord a new song!
  Refrain

Text: Herbert Brokering
Music: David Haas
Text © 1968 Augsburg Publishing House; music © 1997 Augsburg Fortress

Good soil

Lord, let my heart be good soil, o-pen to the seed of your

word. Lord, let my heart be good soil, where

love can grow and peace is un-der-stood. When my heart is hard,

break the stone a-way. When my heart is cold, warm it with the day.

When my heart is lost, lead me on your way. Lord, let my heart,

Lord, let my heart, Lord, let my heart be good soil.

Text: Handt Hanson
Music: Handt Hanson; arr. Henry Wiens

Music: Handt Hanson; arr. Henry Wiens

Music © 1991 Prince of Peace Publishing, Changing Church, Inc.

Great is the Lord

Great is the Lord, he is ho-ly and just, by his pow-er we trust in his

love. Great is the Lord, he is faith-ful and true, by his

mer-cy he proves he is love. Great is the Lord, and

wor-thy of glo-ry. Great is the Lord, and wor-thy of praise.

Great is the Lord, now lift up your voice, now lift up your voice:

Great is the Lord!

Great is the Lord!

Text and music: Michael W. Smith and Deborah D. Smith
Text and music © 1982 Meadowgreen Music, admin. EMI Christian Music Publishing

54 He has made me glad

I will en-ter his gates with thanks-giv-ing in my heart,

I will en-ter his courts with praise.

I will say this is the day that the Lord has made;

I will re-joice for he has made me glad.

He has made me glad, he has made me glad,

I will re-joice for he has made me glad.

He has made me glad, he has made me glad,

I will re-joice for he has made me glad.

Text: Psalm 100:4 and 118:24, adapt. Leona von Brethorst
Music: Leona von Brethorst

He is ex-alt-ed, the King is ex-alt-ed on high; I will praise him.

He is ex-alt-ed, for-ev-er ex-alt-ed, and I will praise his

name. Je - sus is Lord, for-ev-er his truth shall

reign; hea - ven and earth re-joice in his ho - ly

name. He is ex-alt-ed, the King is ex-alt-ed on high.

He who be-gan a good work in you,

he who be-gan a good work in you

will be faith - ful to com-plete it,

will be faith - ful to com-plete it. He who start-

- ed the work will be faith - ful to com-plete it in you.

Text and music: Twila Paris

Text and music © 1985 Straightway Music, admin. EMI Christian Music Publishing

Text and music: Jon Mohr

Text and music © 1987 Jonathan Mark Music, admin. Gaither Music; and Birdwing Music, admin. EMI Christian Music Publishing

57 Hear the angels

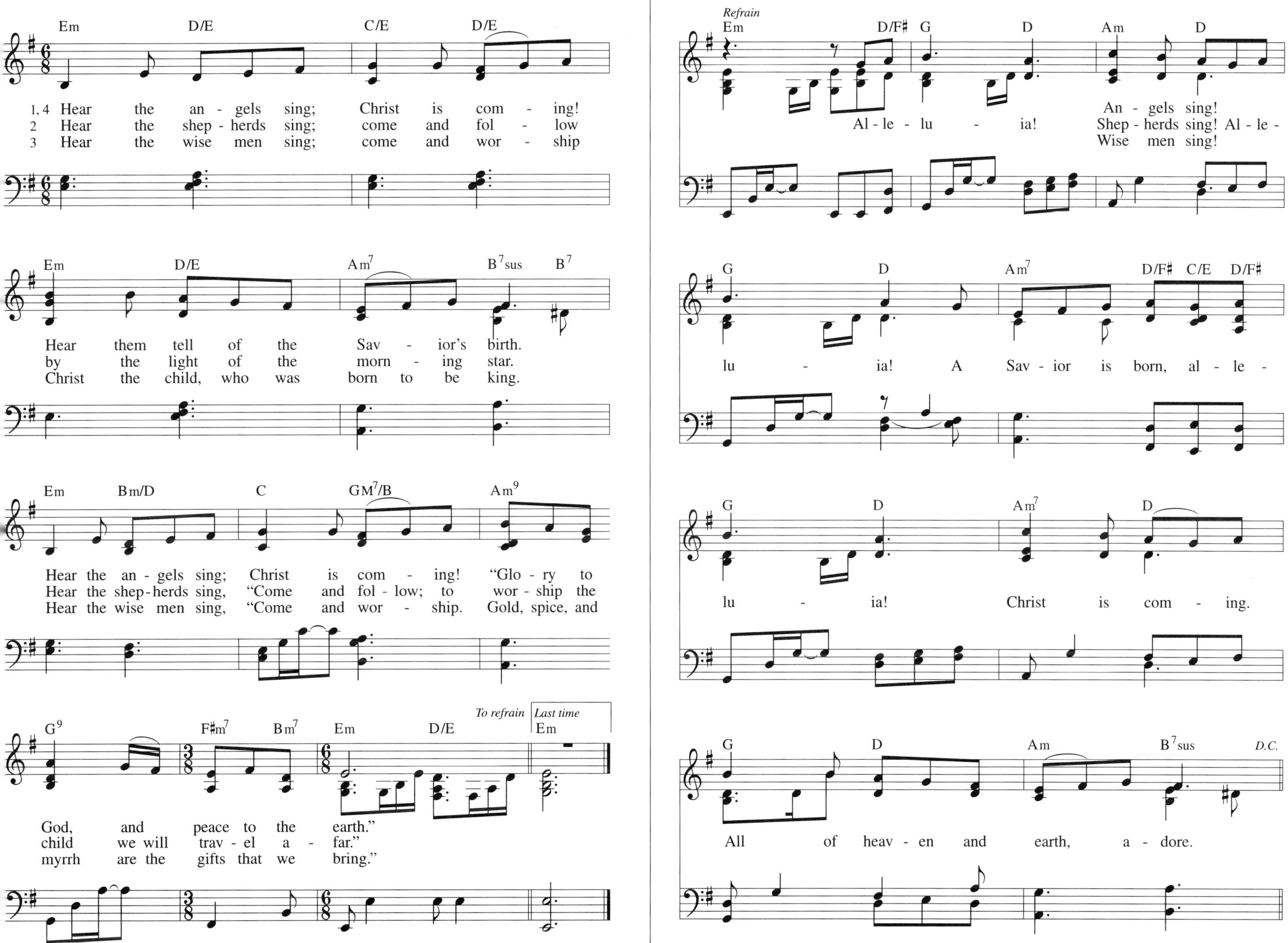

1,4 Hear the an - gels sing; Christ is com - ing!
2 Hear the shep - herds sing; come and fol - low
3 Hear the wise men sing; come and wor - ship

Hear them tell of the Sav - ior's birth.
by the light of the morn - ing star.
Christ the child, who was born to be king.

Hear the an - gels sing; Christ is com - ing! "Glo - ry to
Hear the shep-herds sing, "Come and fol - low; to wor - ship the
Hear the wise men sing, "Come and wor - ship. Gold, spice, and

God, and peace to the earth."
child we will trav - el a - far."
myrrh are the gifts that we bring."

Refrain

An - gels sing!
Shep - herds sing! Al - le -
Wise men sing!

Al - le - lu - ia!

lu - ia! A Sav - ior is born, al - le -

lu - ia! Christ is com - ing.

All of heav - en and earth, a - dore.

Text: Robin Cain
Music: Robin Cain and Phil Kadidlo
Text and music © 1999 Robin Cain and Phil Kadidlo

Here is bread

1 Here is bread,   here is wine,   Christ is with us,
2 Here is grace,   here is peace,   Christ is with us,
3 Here we are,   joined in one,   Christ is with us,

he is with us.   Break the bread,   taste the wine,
he is with us.   Know his grace,   find his peace,
he is with us.   We'll pro-claim   till he comes

Christ is with us   here.
feast on Je - sus
Je - sus cru - ci -   fied.

Refrain

In this bread   there is heal - ing,   in this cup   is

life for - ev - er.   In this mo - ment,   by the Spir - it,

Christ is with   us   here.

Text and music: Graham Kendrick
Text and music © 1993 Make Way Music, admin. Integrity Music, Inc.

Holy ground

We are stand-ing on ho-ly ground,

and I know that there are an-gels all a-round.

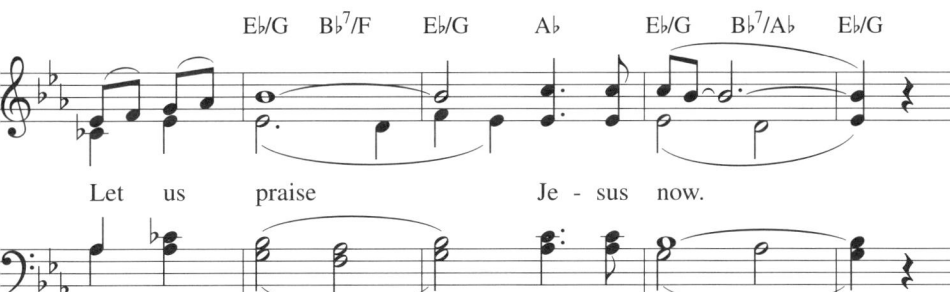

Let us praise Je-sus now.

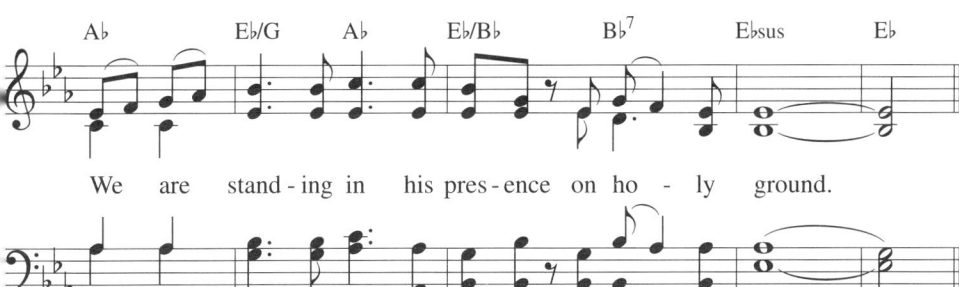

We are stand-ing in his pres-ence on ho-ly ground.

Text and music: Geron Davis

Holy, holy

1 Ho-ly, ho-ly, ho-ly, ho-ly, ho-ly, ho-ly,
2 Gra-cious Fa-ther, gra-cious Fa-ther, we're so blest to be your
3 Pre-cious Je-sus, pre-cious Je-sus, we're so glad that you've re-
4 Ho-ly Spir-it, Ho-ly Spir-it, come and fill our hearts a-
5 Hal-le-lu-jah, hal-le-lu-jah, hal-le-lu-jah, . . .

Lord God Al-might-y; and we lift our hearts be-fore you as a
chil-dren, gra-cious Fa-ther; and we lift our heads be-fore you as a
deemed us, pre-cious Je-sus; and we lift our hands be-fore you as a
new, . . . Ho-ly Spir-it; and we lift our voice be-fore you as a
. . . . . . hal-le-lu-jah; and we lift our hearts be-fore you as a

to-ken of our love, ho-ly, ho-ly, ho-ly, ho-ly.
to-ken of our love, gra-cious Fa-ther, gra-cious Fa-ther.
to-ken of our love, pre-cious Je-sus, pre-cious Je-sus.
to-ken of our love, Ho-ly Spir-it, Ho-ly Spir-it.
to-ken of our love, hal-le-lu-jah, hal-le-lu-jah.

Text and music: Jimmy Owens

Holy, holy, holy/*Santo, santo, santo*

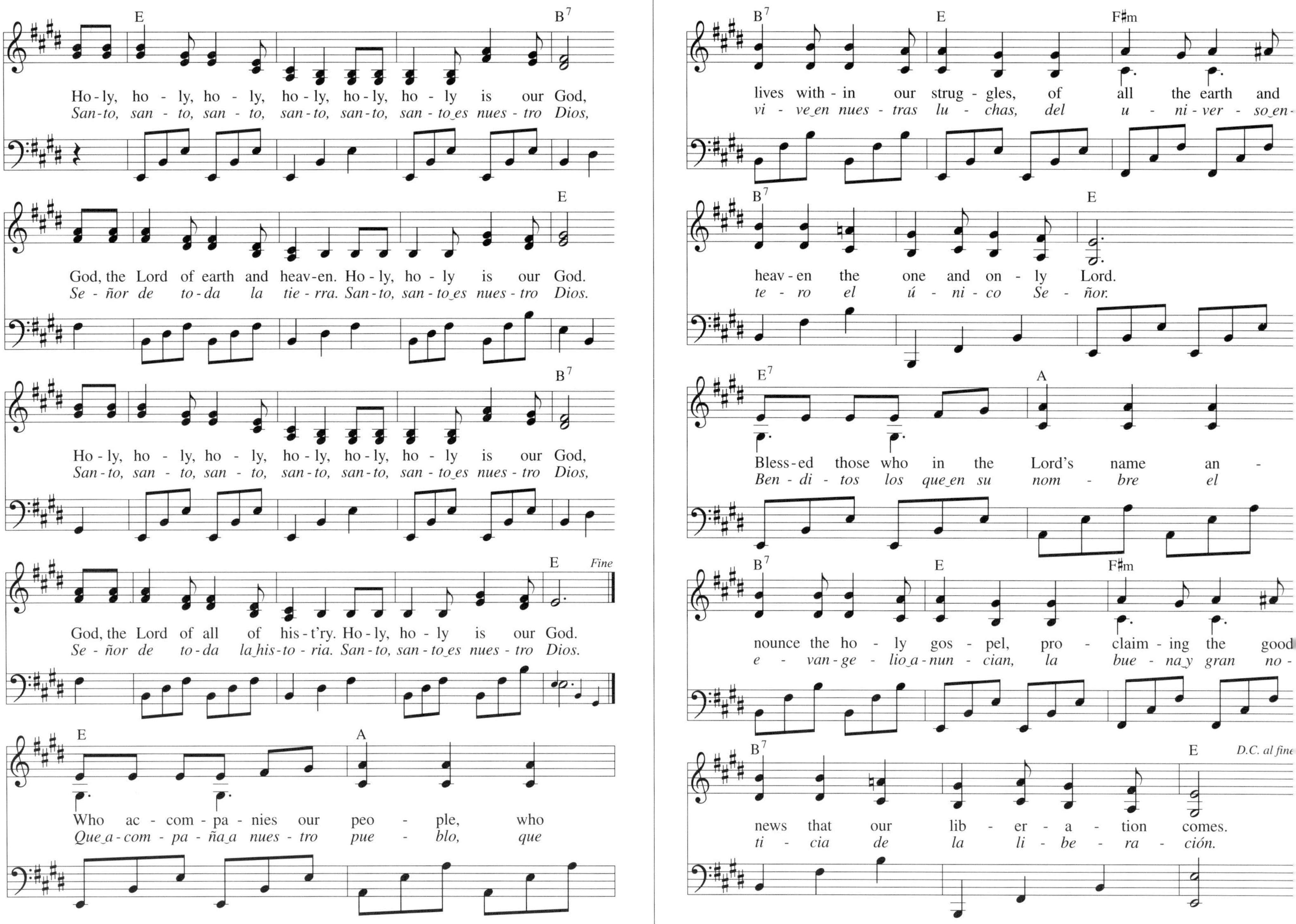
E B7
Ho-ly, ho-ly, ho-ly, ho-ly, ho-ly, ho-ly is our God,
San-to, san-to, san-to, san-to, san-to, san-to es nues-tro Dios,
E
God, the Lord of earth and heav-en. Ho-ly, ho-ly is our God.
Se-ñor de to-da la tie-rra. San-to, san-to es nues-tro Dios.
B7
Ho-ly, ho-ly, ho-ly, ho-ly, ho-ly, ho-ly is our God,
San-to, san-to, san-to, san-to, san-to, san-to es nues-tro Dios,
E Fine
God, the Lord of all of his-t'ry. Ho-ly, ho-ly is our God.
Se-ñor de to-da la his-to-ria. San-to, san-to es nues-tro Dios.
E A
Who ac-com-pa-nies our peo-ple, who
Que a-com-pa-ña a nues-tro pue-blo, que
B7 E F♯m
lives with-in our strug-gles, of all the earth and
vi-ve en nues-tras lu-chas, del u-ni-ver-so en-
B7 E
heav-en the one and on-ly Lord.
te-ro el ú-ni-co Se-ñor.
E7 A
Bless-ed those who in the Lord's name an-
Ben-di-tos los que en su nom-bre el
B7 E F♯m
nounce the ho-ly gos-pel, pro-claim-ing the good
e-van-ge-lio a-nun-cian, la bue-na y gran no-
B7 E D.C. al fine
news that our lib-er-a-tion comes.
ti-cia de la li-be-ra-ción.

Text: Guillermo Cuéllar; tr. Linda McCrae
Music: Guillermo Cuéllar, arr. Diana Kodner

Holy, holy, holy/*Santo, santo, santo*

Ho-ly, ho-ly, ho-ly, my heart, my heart a-dores you! My
San - to, san - to, san - to, mi cor - a - zon te_a - do - ra! Mi

heart is glad to say the words: you are ho-ly, Lord.
cor - a - zon te sa - be de - cir: san - to_e - res Se - ñor.

Text: anonymous
Music: anonymous; arr. Pablo Sosa
Arr. © 1990 Iona Community, admin. GIA Publications

Holy, holy, holy Lord

Ho-ly, ho-ly, ho-ly Lord, God of pow'r and might,

heav-en and earth are full of your glo-ry, full of your glo-ry; ho-

san - na, ho - san - na, ho - san - na in the

high-est; ho - san - na, ho - san - na, ho -

san - na in the high - est.

Bless-ed is he who comes in the name of the Lord. Ho-

Text: "Sanctus," tr. English Language Liturgical Consultation
Music: Jay Beech
Music © 1995 Augsburg Fortress

Holy, holy, holy Lord

Holy, ho - ly, ho - ly

Lord, God of pow - er and

might, heav - en and

earth are full of your glo - ry. Ho -

san - na in the high - est.

Bless - ed is he who comes in the

name of the Lord. Ho - san - na

in the high - est.

Text: "Sanctus," tr. English Language Liturgical Consultation
Music: Richard Webb and Daniel Vazquez
Music © 1999 Augsburg Fortress

How can I be free from sin?

Text and music: Graham Kendrick and Steve Thompson
Text and music © 1991 Make Way Music, admin. Integrity Music, Inc.

How majestic is your name

O Lord, our Lord, how ma-jes-tic is your name in all the earth!

O Lord, our Lord, how ma-jes-tic is your name in all the earth!

O Lord, we praise your name. O

Lord, we mag-ni-fy your name, Prince of

Peace, might-y God, O Lord God Al-might - y.

I love you, Lord

I love you, Lord, and I lift my voice to

wor - ship you; O my soul, re - joice. Take

joy, my King, in what you hear; may it be a

sweet, sweet sound in your ear.

I was glad

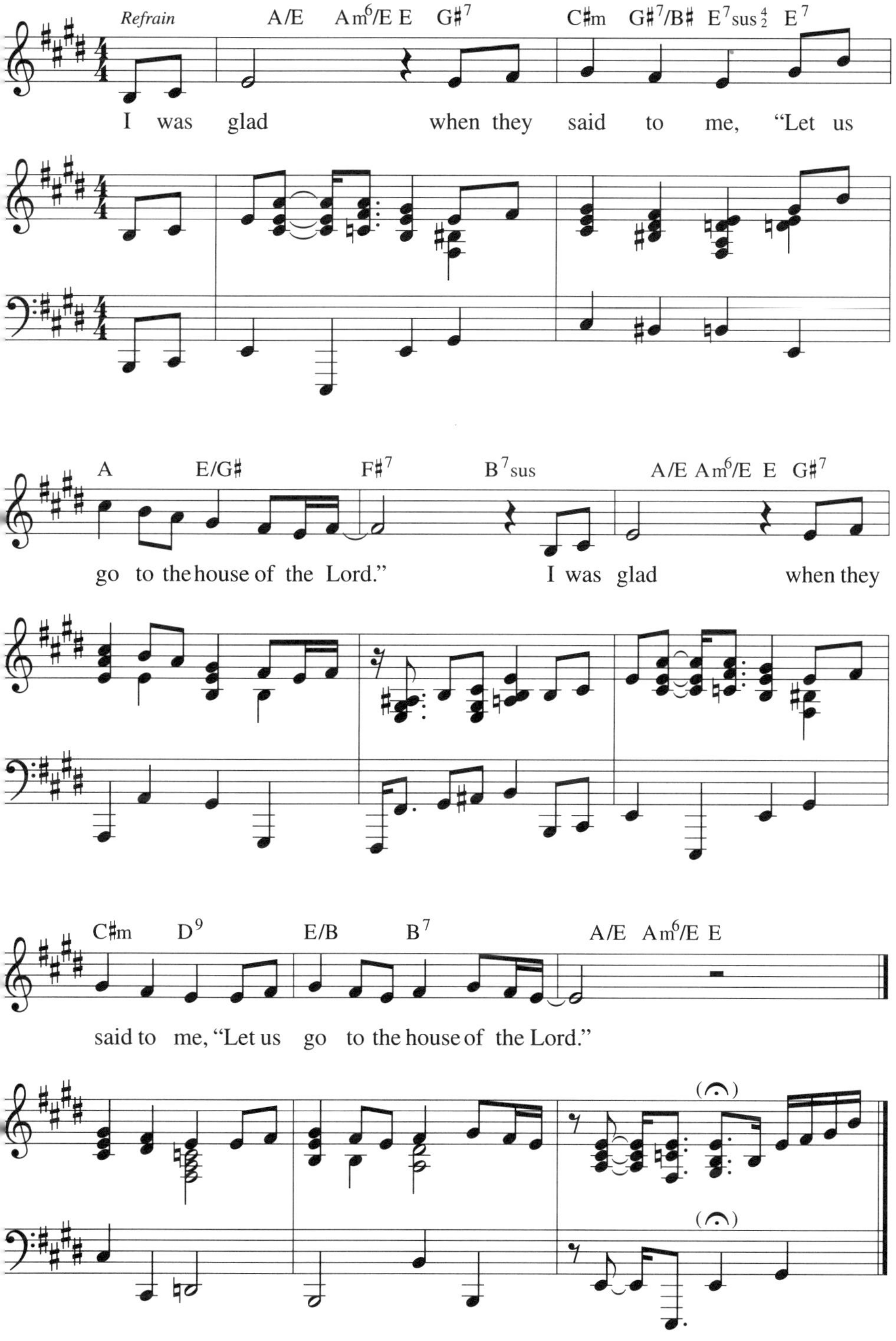
Refrain
A/E Am6/E E G♯7 C♯m G♯7/B♯ E7sus 4 2 E7
I was glad when they said to me, "Let us
A E/G♯ F♯7 B7sus A/E Am6/E E G♯7
go to the house of the Lord." I was glad when they
C♯m D9 E/B B7 A/E Am6/E E
said to me, "Let us go to the house of the Lord."

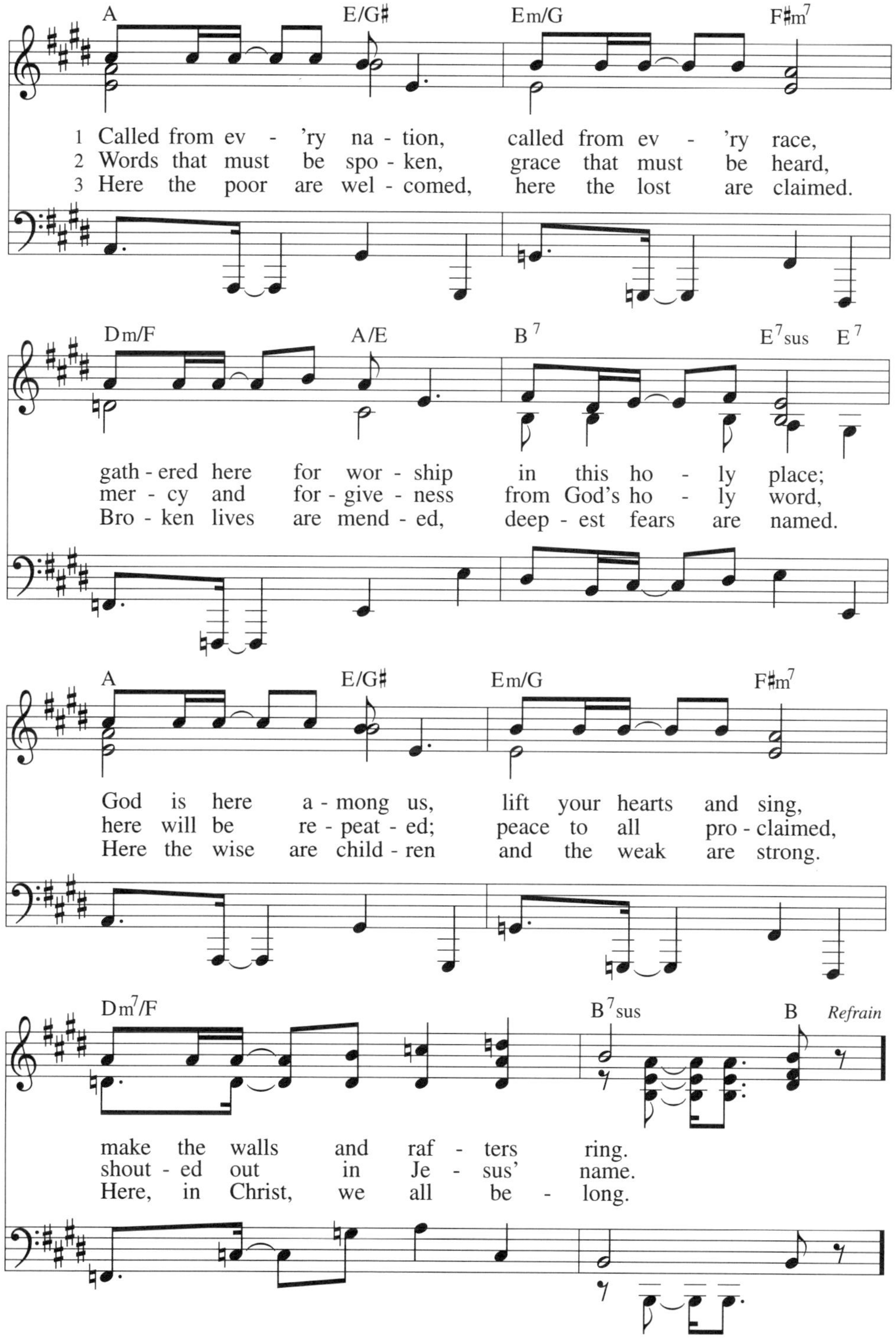
A E/G♯ Em/G F♯m7
1 Called from ev - 'ry na - tion, called from ev - 'ry race,
2 Words that must be spo - ken, grace that must be heard,
3 Here the poor are wel - comed, here the lost are claimed.
Dm/F A/E B7 E7sus E7
gath - ered here for wor - ship in this ho - ly place;
mer - cy and for - give - ness from God's ho - ly word,
Bro - ken lives are mend - ed, deep - est fears are named.
A E/G♯ Em/G F♯m7
God is here a - mong us, lift your hearts and sing,
here will be re - peat - ed; peace to all pro - claimed,
Here the wise are child - ren and the weak are strong.
Dm7/F B7sus B Refrain
make the walls and raf - ters ring.
shout - ed out in Je - sus' name.
Here, in Christ, we all be - long.

Text: Psalm 122:1, refrain; Jay Beech, stanzas
Music: Jay Beech

I was there to hear your borning cry

1 "I was there to hear your born-ing cry, I'll be
2 "When you heard the won-der of the Word I was
3 "In the mid-dle a-ges of your life, not too

there when you are old. I re-joiced the day you
there to cheer you on; you were raised to praise the
old, no lon-ger young, I'll be there to guide you

were bap-tized to see your life un-fold.
liv-ing Lord, to whom you now be-long.
through the night, com-plete what I've be-gun.

I was there when you were but a child, with a
If you find some-one to share your time and you
When the eve-ning gent-ly clos-es in and you

faith to suit you well; in a blaze of light you
join your hearts as one, I'll be there to make your
shut your wea-ry eyes, I'll be there as I have

wan-dered off to find where de-mons dwell."
vers-es rhyme from dusk till ris-ing sun."
al-ways been, with just one more sur-prise."

3rd time to stanza 4

4 "I was there to hear your born-ing cry, I'll be

there when you are old. I re-joiced the day you

were bap-tized to see your life un-fold."

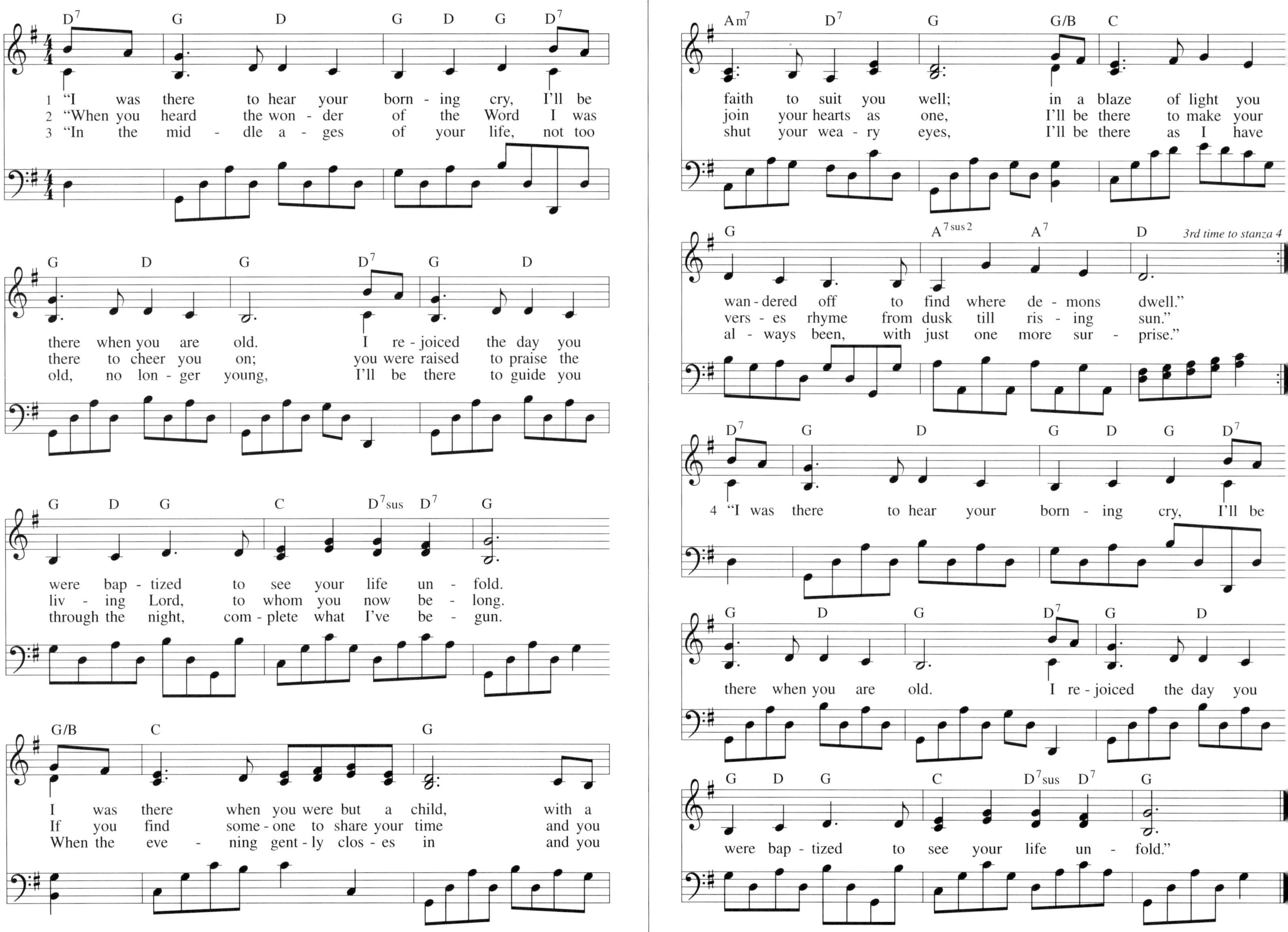

Text and music: John Ylvisaker
Text and music © 1985 John Ylvisaker

Alternate accompaniment

Introduction

Stanzas 1-3

Stanza 4

Music: John Ylvisaker, arr. Richard Webb
Tune © 1985 John Ylvisaker; arr. © 1995 Augsburg Fortress

I will call upon the Lord

Text and music: Michael O'Shields
Text and music © 1981 Sound III and All Nations Music, admin. MCA Music and The Lorenz Corporation

I will celebrate

I will cel - e - brate, sing un - to the Lord;

I will sing to God a new song.

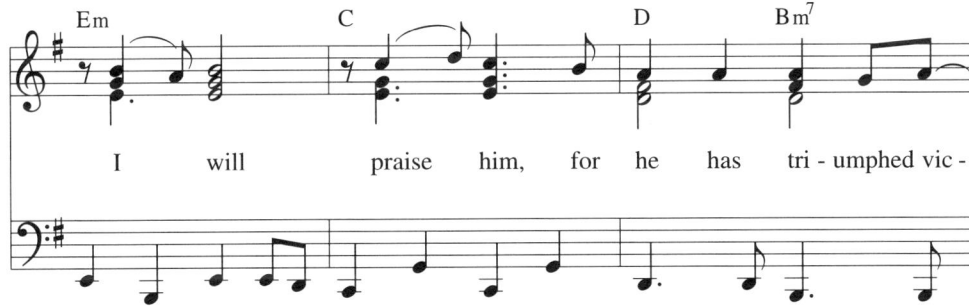

I will praise him, for he has tri - umphed vic -

1. - to - rious - ly. 2. - to - rious - ly.

I will delight

I will de-light in the law of the Lord; I will med - i-tate day and night.

Then, like a tree firm-ly plant - ed, I'll be

ground - ed in your word. Bless - ed

is the one who fol - lows the way of the Lord;

bless - ed is the one.

I will sing, I will sing

1 I will sing, I will sing a song un-to the Lord.
2 We will come, we will come as one be-fore the Lord.
3 If the Son, if the Son shall make . . . you . . . free,
4 They that sow in tears . . . . shall reap . . . in . . joy.
5 Ev - 'ry knee shall bow . . . and ev - 'ry tongue con - fess,
6 In his name, in his name we have the vic-to-ry.

Al - le - lu - ia, glo - ry to the Lord.
Al - le - lu - ia, glo - ry to the Lord.
you . /. shall be free . . . . in - deed.
Al - le - lu - ia, glo - ry to the Lord.
that . . . Je - sus Christ . . . . is . . . Lord.
Al - le - lu - ia, glo - ry to the Lord.

I will sing, I will sing a song un-to the Lord.
We will come, we will come as one be-fore the Lord.
if the Son, if the Son shall make . . . . you . . . free,
They that sow in tears . . . . shall reap . . . . . in . . . joy.
ev - 'ry knee shall bow . . . and ev - 'ry tongue con - fess,
In his name, in his name we have the vic - to - ry.

Refrain

Al - le - lu, al - le - lu - ia, glo - ry to the Lord. Al - le -

I will sing, I will sing a song un-to the Lord.
We will come, we will come as one be-fore the Lord.
if the Son, if the Son shall make . . . . you . . . free,
They that sow in tears . . . . shall reap . . . . in . . . joy.
ev - 'ry knee shall bow . . . and ev - 'ry tongue con - fess,
In his name, in his name we have the vic - to - ry.

lu, al - le - lu - ia, glo - ry to the Lord. Al - le - lu, al - le - lu - ia, glo-

- ry to the Lord. Al - le - lu - ia, glo - ry to the Lord.

Text and music: Max Dyer
Text and music © 1974 CELEBRATION, admin. The Copyright Company

I will sing of the mercies of the Lord

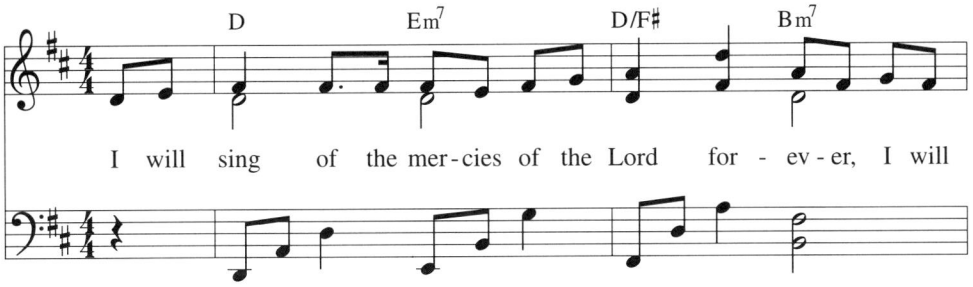

I will sing of the mer-cies of the Lord for - ev - er, I will

faith-ful-ness, thy faith-ful-ness. With my mouth will I make

sing, I will sing. I will sing of the mer - cies of the

D.C. al fine

known thy faith-ful-ness to all gen - er - a - tions.

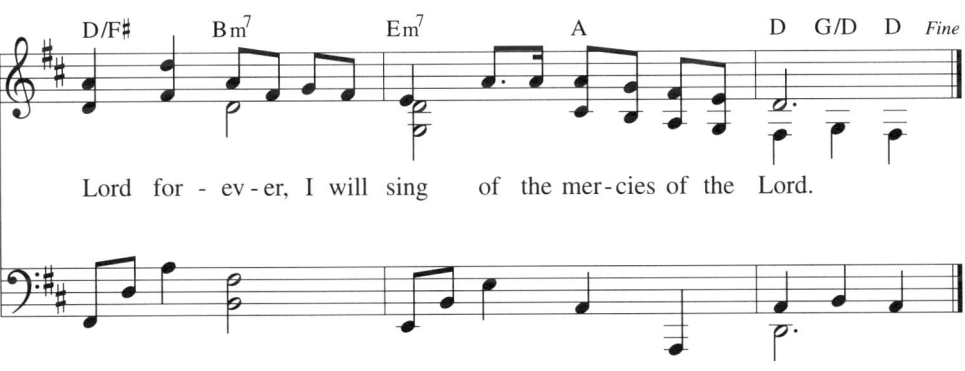

Lord for - ev - er, I will sing of the mer - cies of the Lord.

With my mouth will I make known thy

Text: Psalm 89:1
Music: J. H. Fillmore

In the morning

75

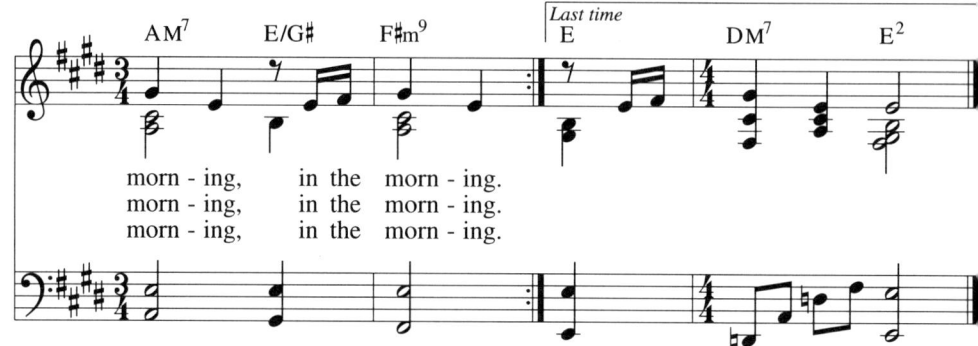

1 In the morn-ing we shall see the
2 In the eve-ning we have said, "If
3 In its cy-cle day-light dawns and

glo - ry of the Lord; rise and sing God's prais-es! In the
on - ly day would come, joy would spring from sor-row." God has
night-time dark-ness parts. Day from day is sev-ered till the

morn-ing we shall see our hope and faith re - stored
kept us through the night, now sha-dows will suc-cumb
Day - star of the morn-ing ri - ses in our hearts.

like the sun God rais - es in the
to the new to - mor - row in the
Day will dawn for - ev - er in the

morn - ing, in the morn - ing.
morn - ing, in the morn - ing.
morn - ing, in the morn - ing.

Text and music: Ben Houge
Text and music © 1999 Augsburg Fortress

Jesus, Lamb of God

76

Je - sus, Lamb of God, wor - thy is your

name; Je - sus, Lamb of God,

wor - thy is your name. name.

Text and music: Dennis Jernigan, refrain of "You are my all in all"
Text and music © 1991 Shepherd's Heart Music, Inc., admin. Word Music, Inc.

Jesus, name above all names

Jesus, remember me

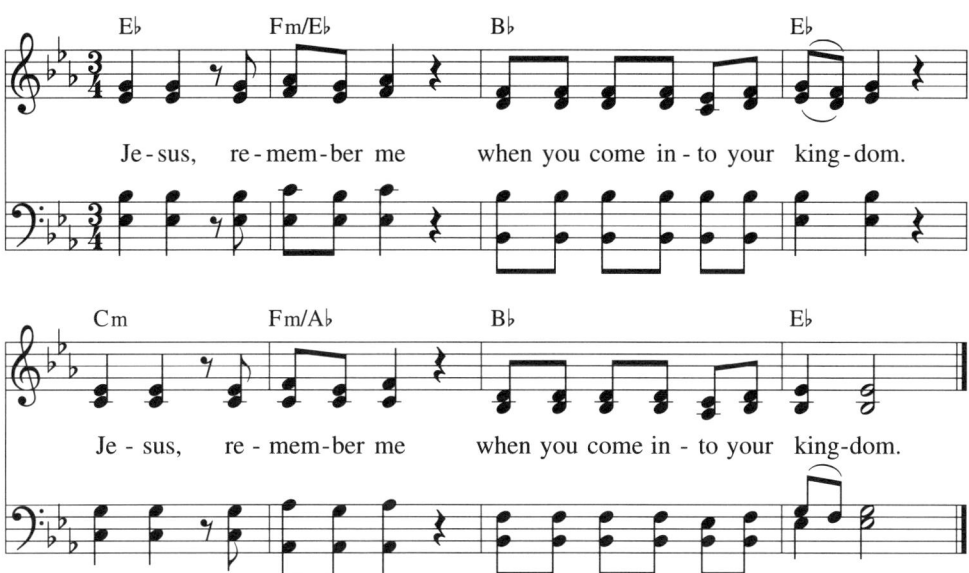

Je - sus, name a - bove all names, beau-ti-ful

Sav - ior, glo-ri-ous Lord, Em-

man - u - el, God is with us, bless-ed Re -

deem - er, liv-ing Word. Word.

Je - sus, re-mem-ber me when you come in - to your king-dom.

Je - sus, re-mem-ber me when you come in - to your king-dom.

Text and music: Naida Hearn
Text and music © 1974 Scripture in Song, a division of Integrity Music, Inc.

Text: Luke 23:42
Music: Jacques Berthier
Music © 1981 Les Presses de Taizé, admin. GIA Publications

Joyous light of glory

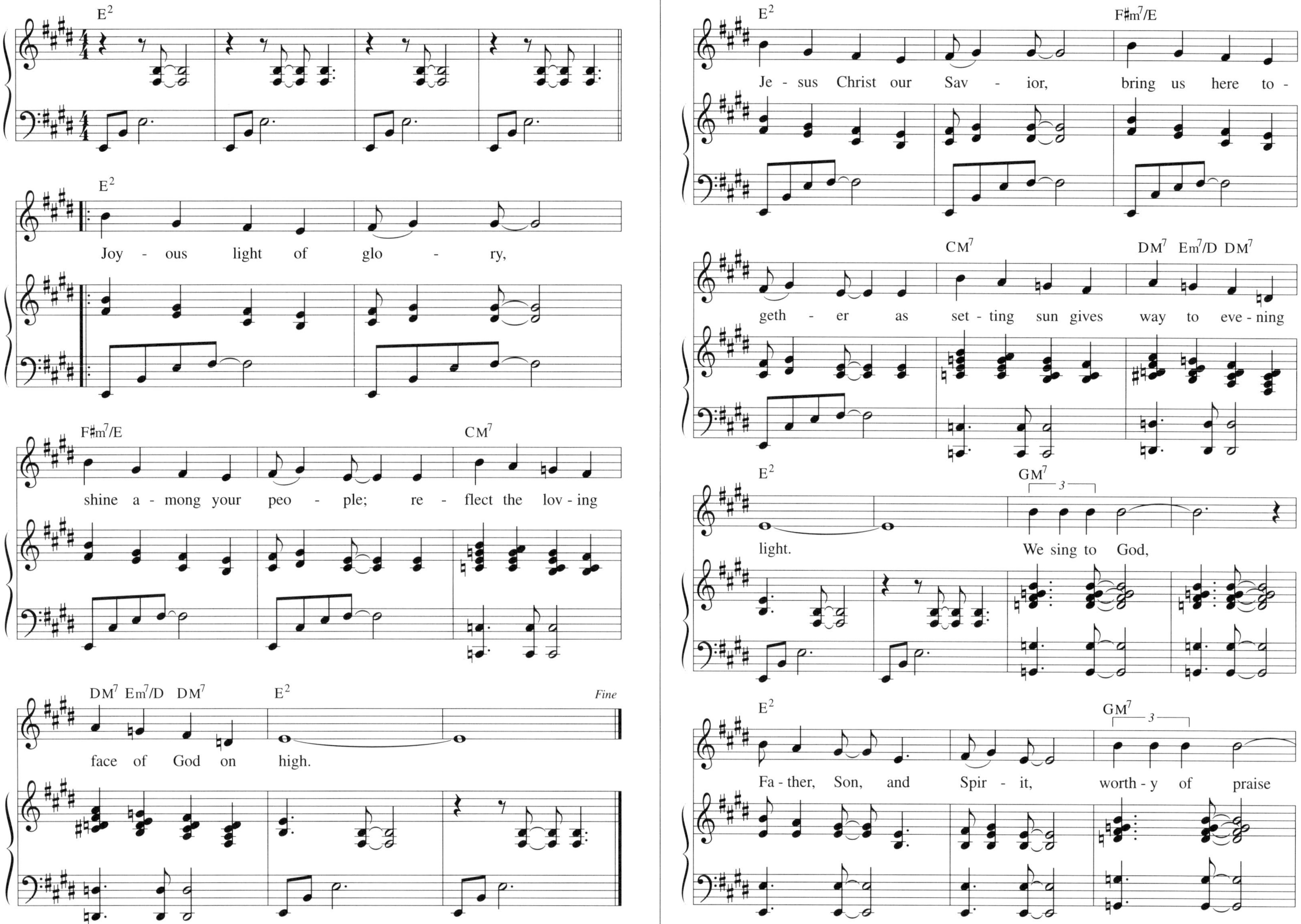
E2
E2
Joy - ous light of glo - ry,
F♯m7/E
CM7
shine a - mong your peo - ple; re - flect the lov - ing
DM7 Em7/D DM7
E2
Fine
face of God on high.
E2
F♯m7/E
Je - sus Christ our Sav - ior, bring us here to -
CM7
DM7 Em7/D DM7
geth - er as set - ting sun gives way to eve - ning
E2
GM7
3
light. We sing to God,
E2
GM7
3
Fa - ther, Son, and Spir - it, worth - y of praise

for - ev - er and ev - er.

O Son of God, you give us life e -

ter - nal; the u - ni - verse pro - claims your

glo - ry.

Text: "Phos hilaron," adapt.
Music: Ralph C. Sappington
Text and music © 1999 Augsburg Fortress

King of kings and Lord of lords: glo - ry, hal - le - lu - jah.

King of kings and Lord of lords: glo - ry, hal - le - lu - jah.

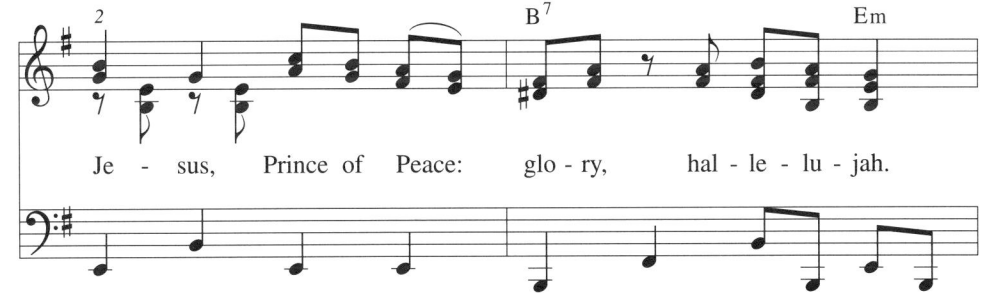

Je - sus, Prince of Peace: glo - ry, hal - le - lu - jah.

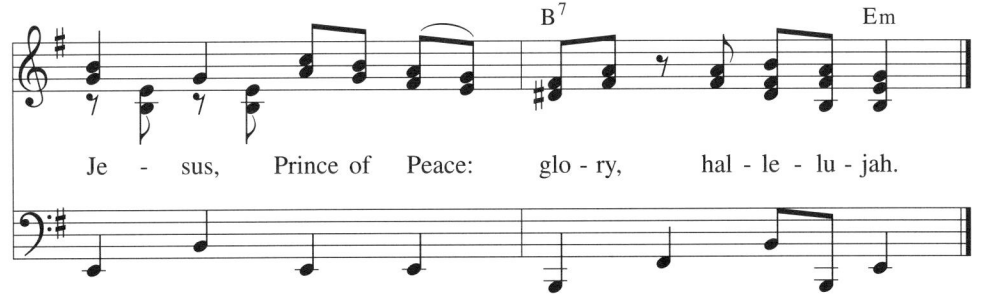

Je - sus, Prince of Peace: glo - ry, hal - le - lu - jah.

*may be sung in canon

Text: Naomi Batya and Sophie Conty
Music: Hebrew traditional
Text and arr. © 1980 Maranatha Praise, Inc., admin. The Copyright Company

81

Kyrie eleison

Ky-ri-e   e-lei-son,   on our world and on   our way.   Ky-ri-e

e-lei-son,   ev-'ry day.

1 For   peace   in   the   world,   for   the
2 That   we   may   live   out   your   im -
3 For   peace   in   our   hearts,   . . .   for
4 For   your   Spir - it   to   guide;   that   you

health of   the   church,   for the   u - ni - ty   of   all;
passioned   re - sponse   to   the   hun - gry   and   the   poor;
peace in   our   homes, ...   for   friends and   fam - i - ly;
cen - ter   our   lives   in   the   wa - ter   and   the   word;

Kyrie eleison = Lord, have mercy

for this   ho - ly   house,   for   all   who   wor - ship and   praise,
that we   may live   out . . . .   truth and   jus - tice and   grace,
for life   and for   love, . . .   for   our   work and   our   play,
that you   nour - ish   our souls . . .   with your   bo - dy and   blood,

let us   pray   to the   Lord,   let us   pray   to the   Lord.

Text and music: Larry Olson
Text and music © 1989 Dakota Road Music

Lamb of God

82

Lamb   of   God,   you   take   a -

Text: "Agnus Dei," tr. English Language Liturgical Consultation
Music: Richard Webb and Daniel Vazquez

Music © 1999 Augsburg Fortress

Lamb of God

Have mercy on me

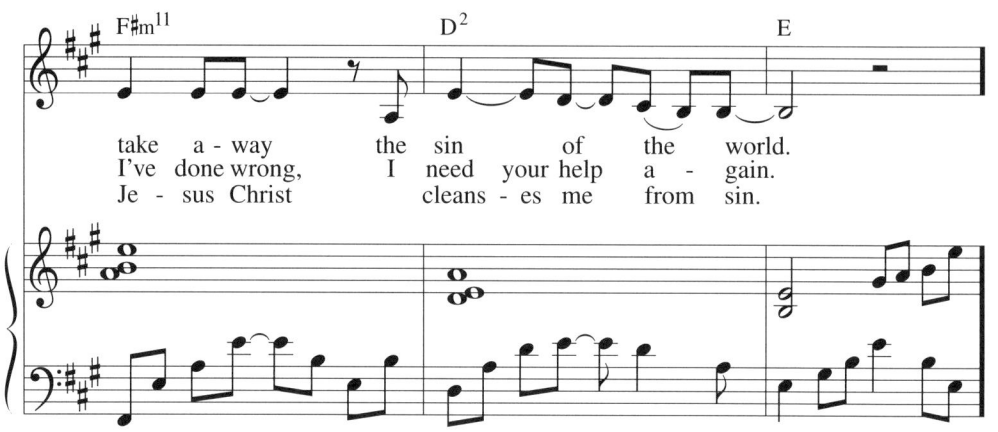

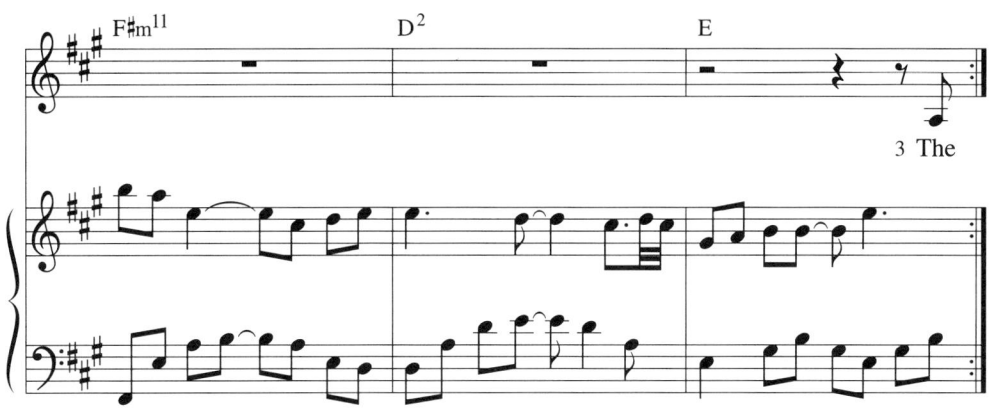

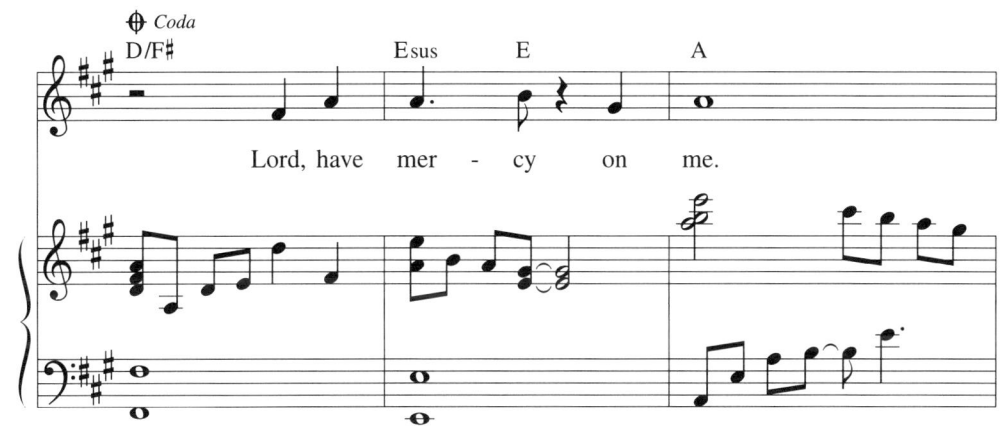

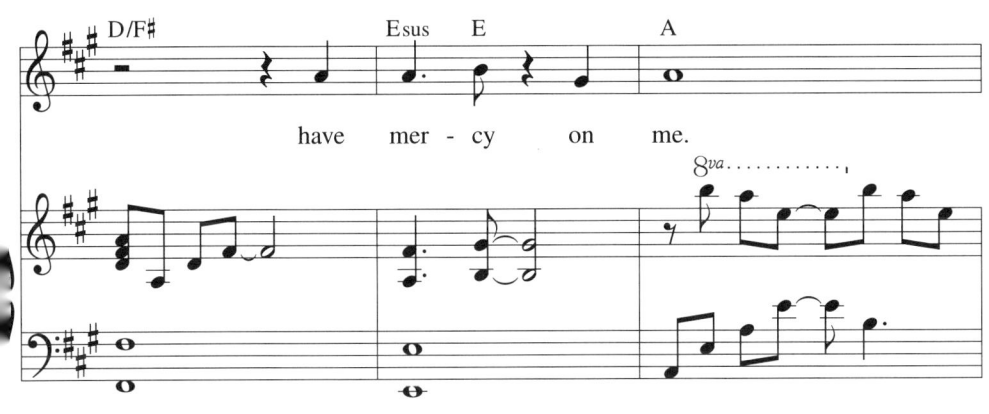

Text and music: Andy Park
Text and music © 1998 Mercy/Vineyard Publishing, admin. Music Services

Lead me, guide me

Lead me, guide me, a - long the way;

Lead me, O Lord, lead me.

for if you lead me, I can - not stray.

1 I am weak and I need thy strength and pow'r
2 Help me tread in the paths of righ - teous - ness,
3 I am lost if you take your hand from me,

Lord, let me walk each day with thee.

to help me o - ver my weak - est hour.
be my aid when Sa - tan and sin op - press.
I am blind with - out ... thy light to see.

Help me through the dark-ness thy face to see.
I am put - ting all . . . . my trust in thee.
Lord, just al - ways let me thy ser - vant be.

Lead me, O Lord, lead me.

Refrain

Text: Doris Akers
Music: Doris Akers; arr. Richard Smallwood

Let justice roll like a river

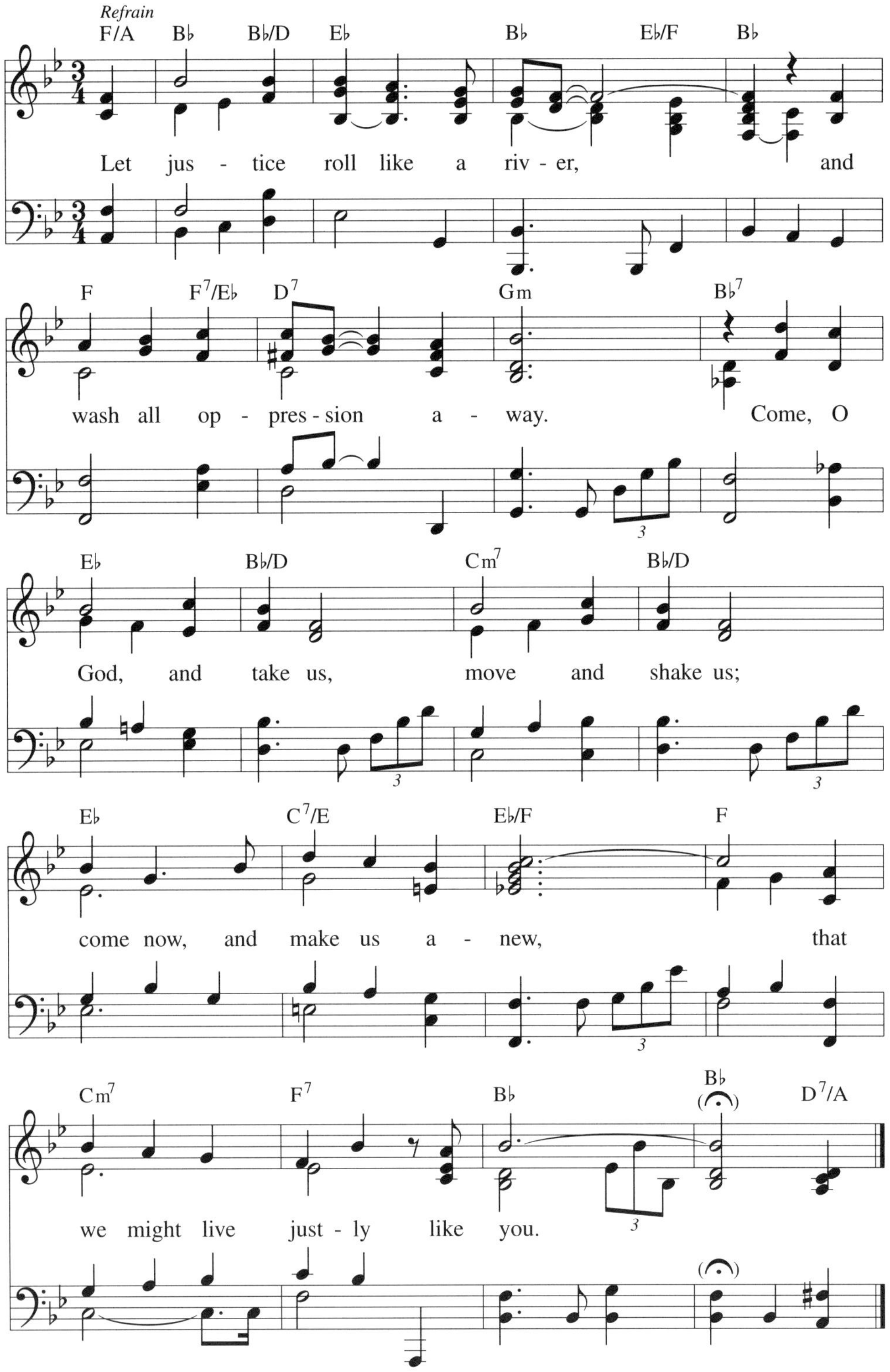
Refrain
Let justice roll like a river, and
wash all oppression away. Come, O
God, and take us, move and shake us;
come now, and make us anew, that
we might live justly like you.

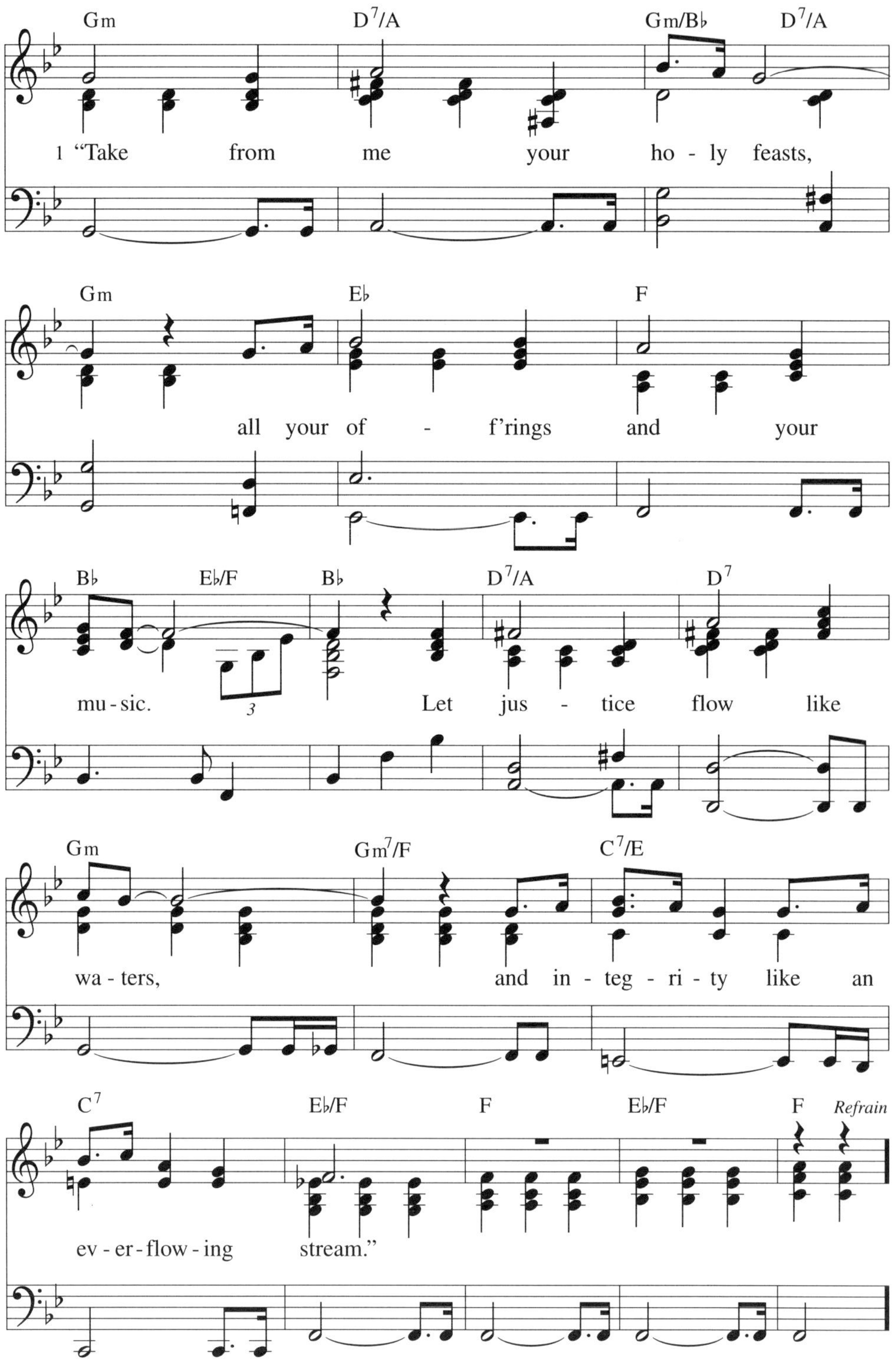
1 "Take from me your holy feasts,
all your off'rings and your
music. Let justice flow like
waters, and integrity like an
ever-flowing stream."
Refrain

Stanzas 2-5

2 How long shall we wait, O God, for the
3 Hear this, all of you who use the poor in your
4 "E - ven now, re - turn to me, let your
5 You have been told the way of life, the

day we beat our swords in - to plows, when your
Lord will turn your laugh - ter to tears, on the
I am gra - cious, gen - 'rous and kind." Come and
act just - ly, to love gent - ly, to

day of your mer - cy to dawn, the
thirst of pow - er and rich - es: the
hearts be bro - ken and hum - ble, for
way of jus - tice and peace: to

Refrain

peace reigns o - ver the earth?
won - drous Day of our God.
seek the mer - cies of God.
walk hum - bly with God.

Text and music: Marty Haugen
Text and music © 1991 GIA Publications

Let my prayer be a fragrant offering

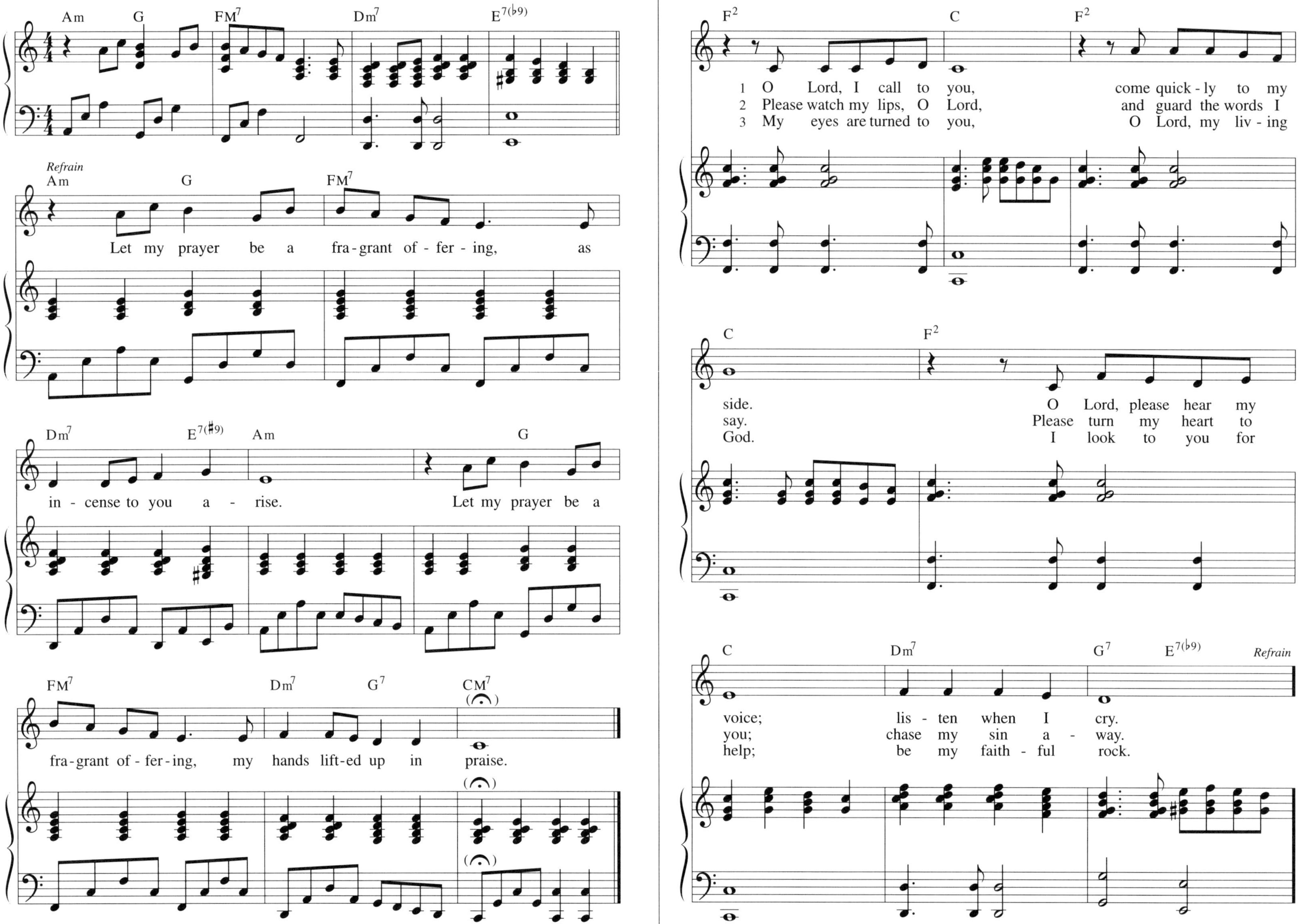
Am G FM7 Dm7 E7(♭9)
Refrain
Am G FM7
Let my prayer be a fra-grant of-fer-ing, as
Dm7 E7(♯9) Am G
in-cense to you a-rise. Let my prayer be a
FM7 Dm7 G7 CM7
fra-grant of-fer-ing, my hands lift-ed up in praise.
F2 C F2
1 O Lord, I call to you, come quick-ly to my
2 Please watch my lips, O Lord, and guard the words I
3 My eyes are turned to you, O Lord, my liv-ing
C F2
side. O Lord, please hear my
say. Please turn my heart to
God. I look to you for
C Dm7 G7 E7(♭9) Refrain
voice; lis-ten when I cry.
you; chase my sin a-way.
help; be my faith-ful rock.

Text: Psalm 141, adapt.
Music: Ralph C. Sappington

Let there be praise

Let there be praise, let there be joy in our hearts.

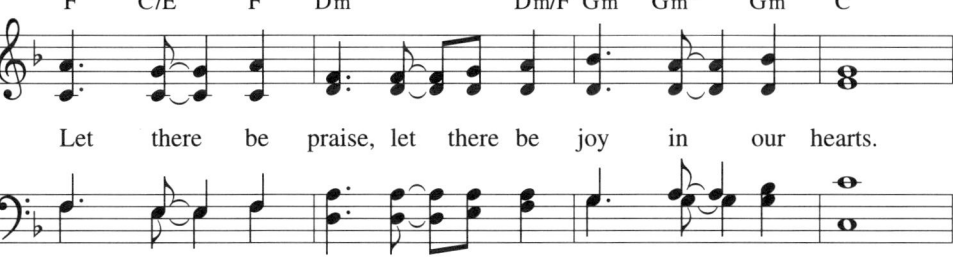

Sing to the Lord, give God the glo - ry. glo - ry.

Let there be praise, let there be joy in our hearts.

For - ev - er - more let his love fill the air, and let there be praise.

Text and music: Melodie Tunney and Dick Tunney
Text and music © 1986 BMG Songs, Inc., Pamela Kay Music, and Charlie Monk Music

Lift up your heads

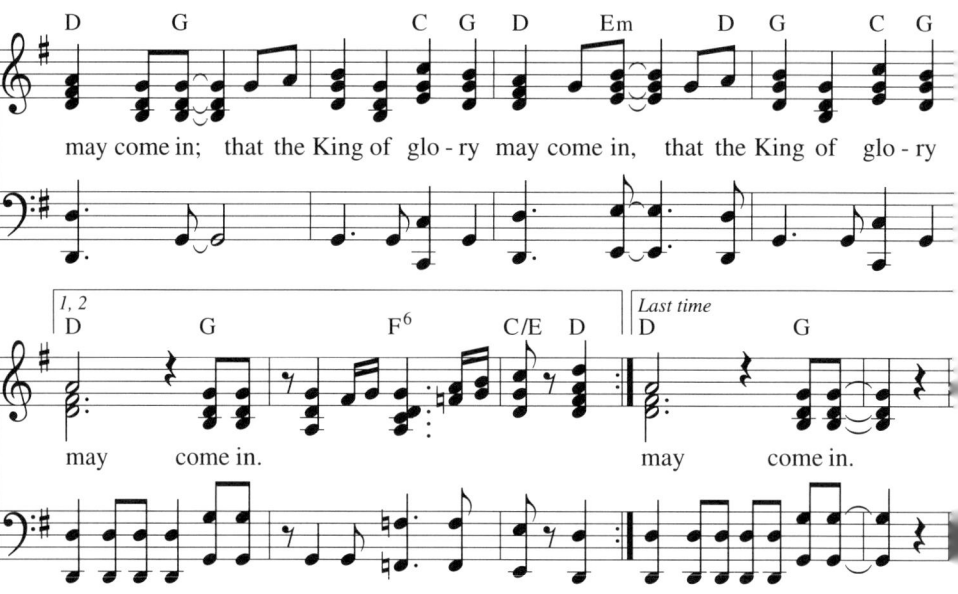

1 Lift up your heads, O you gates; swing wide, you
2 Up from the dead he as-cends, through ev-'ry
3 With trum-pet blast and shouts of joy, all heav-en

ev - er-last-ing doors. Lift up your heads, O you
rank of heav'n-ly pow'r. Let heav'n pre - pare the high-est
greets the ris-en king. With an-gel choirs come line the

gates; swing wide, you ev - er-last-ing doors.
place, throw wide the ev - er-last-ing doors.
way, throw wide the gates and wel-come him.

Refrain

That the King of glo-ry may come in, that the King of glo-ry

may come in; that the King of glo-ry may come in, that the King of glo-ry

1, 2

may come in.

Last time

may come in.

Text and music: Graham Kendrick
Text and music © 1991 Make Way Music, admin. Integrity Music, Inc.

Lord, be glorified

89

1 In my life, Lord, be glo-ri-fied, be glo-ri-fied;
2 In my song, Lord, be glo-ri-fied, be glo-ri-fied;
3 In your church, Lord, be glo-ri-fied, be glo-ri-fied;

in my life, Lord, be glo-ri-fied to - day.
in my song, Lord, be glo-ri-fied to - day.
in your church, Lord, be glo-ri-fied to - day.

Text and music: Bob Kilpatrick
Text and music © 1978 Bob Kilpatrick Music, admin. The Lorenz Corporation

41

Give thanks

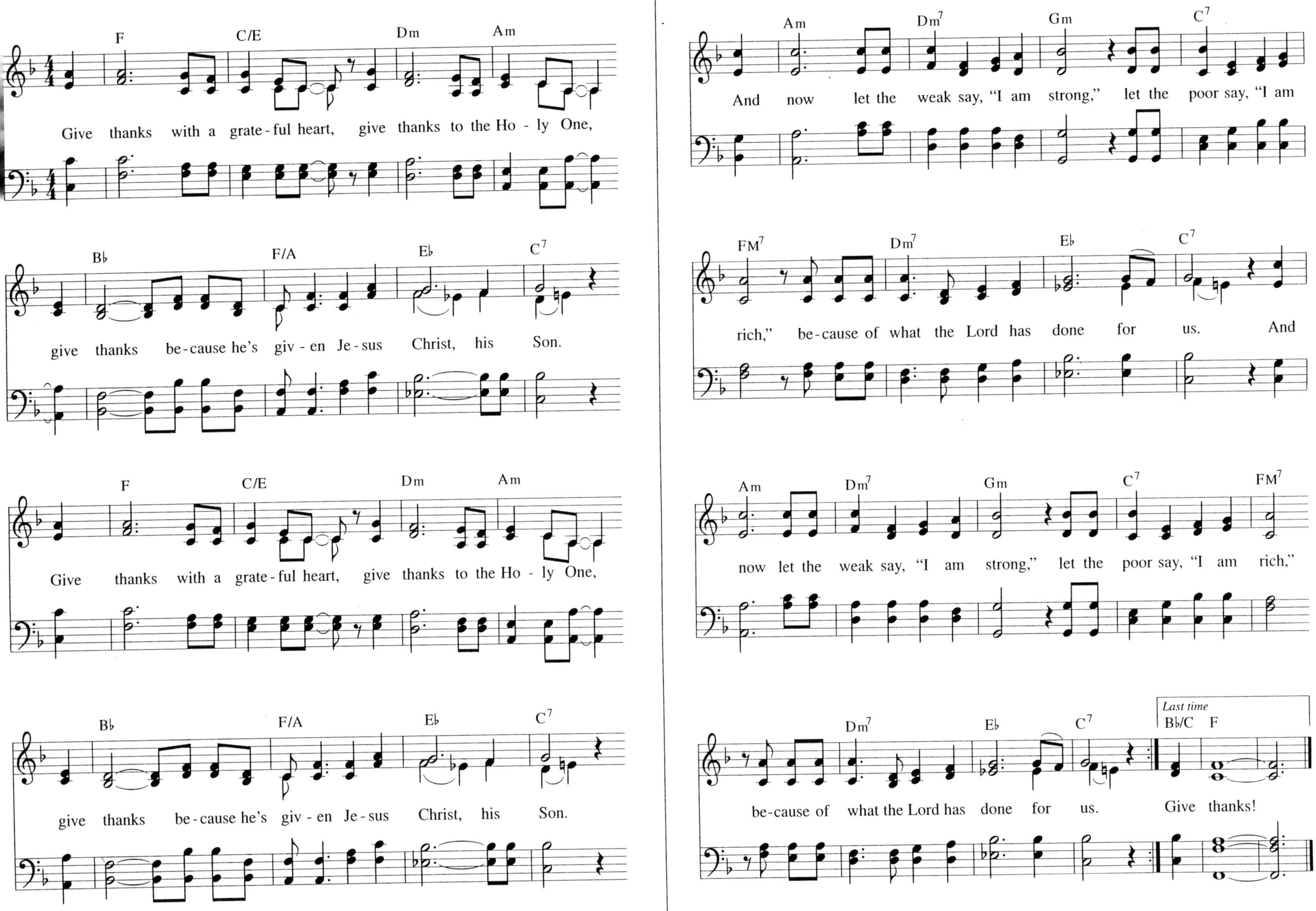
F C/E Dm Am
Give thanks with a grate-ful heart, give thanks to the Ho-ly One,
B♭ F/A E♭ C7
give thanks be-cause he's giv-en Je-sus Christ, his Son.
F C/E Dm Am
Give thanks with a grate-ful heart, give thanks to the Ho-ly One,
B♭ F/A E♭ C7
give thanks be-cause he's giv-en Je-sus Christ, his Son.
Am Dm7 Gm C7
And now let the weak say, "I am strong," let the poor say, "I am
FM7 Dm7 E♭ C7
rich," be-cause of what the Lord has done for us. And
Am Dm7 Gm C7 FM7
now let the weak say, "I am strong," let the poor say, "I am rich,"
Dm7 E♭ C7
be-cause of what the Lord has done for us.
Last time
B♭/C F
Give thanks!

Lord, I lift your name on high

Lord, I lift your name on high, Lord, I love to sing your

prais - es. I'm so glad you're in my life,

I'm so glad you came to save us. You came from heav - en to earth

to show the way, from the earth to the cross, my debt to pay;

from the cross to the grave, from the grave to the sky;

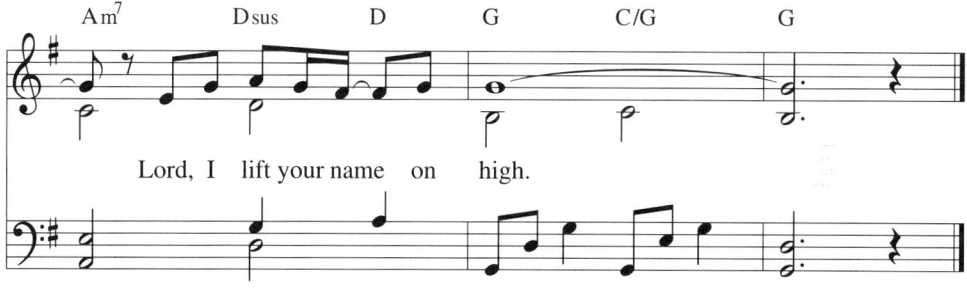

Lord, I lift your name on high.

Text and music: Rick Founds
Text and music © 1989 Maranatha Praise, Inc., admin. The Copyright Company

Lord, listen to your children

On bend - ed knee, with need - y hearts, we

come and pray. Lord, lis - ten to your chil - dren.

With will - ing hearts and o - pen arms, we come and pray.

Lord, lis - ten to your chil - dren. With

sim - ple words of heart - felt thanks, we come. Be-

liev - ing in your prom - is - es, we come. On

bend - ed knee, with need - y hearts, we come and pray. Lord,

lis - ten to your chil - dren, lis - ten to your chil - dren.

Text: Handt Hanson
Music: Handt Hanson; arr. Henry Wiens

Lord, listen to your children praying

Lord, lis-ten to your chil-dren pray-ing, Lord, send your Spir-it in this place;

Lord, lis-ten to your chil-dren pray-ing, send us love, send us pow'r, send us grace.

Text and music: Ken Medema

Lord, my strength

Be my eyes,   be my ears,   be the on -
Ev - 'ry step   that I make,   be the road

1, 3 Lord, my   strength,   Lord, my   rock,
2 Lord, my   strength,   Lord, my   rock,

- ly voice I hear;   guide my soul,   give me sigh
I will take;   be the thoughts   that I keep

lead me   through   the dark;   Lord, my   strength,
you and   you   a - lone;   Lord, my   strength,

help me   walk   with - in   your   light.
and in   ev -   'ry   word I   speak.

Last time to coda

Lord, my   rock,   heal this   wan - d'ring heart.
Lord, my   rock,   lead me   safe - ly home.

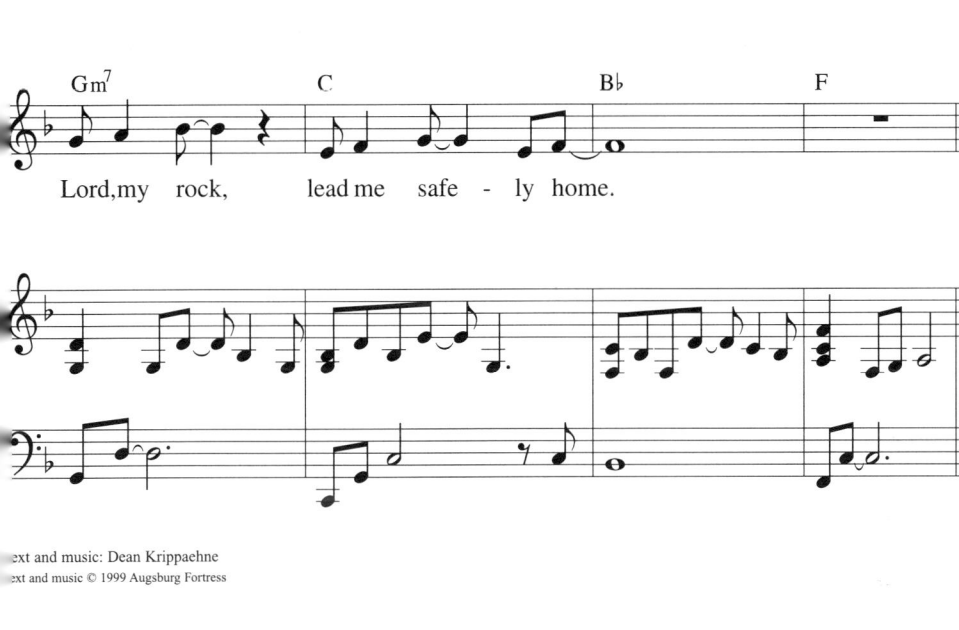

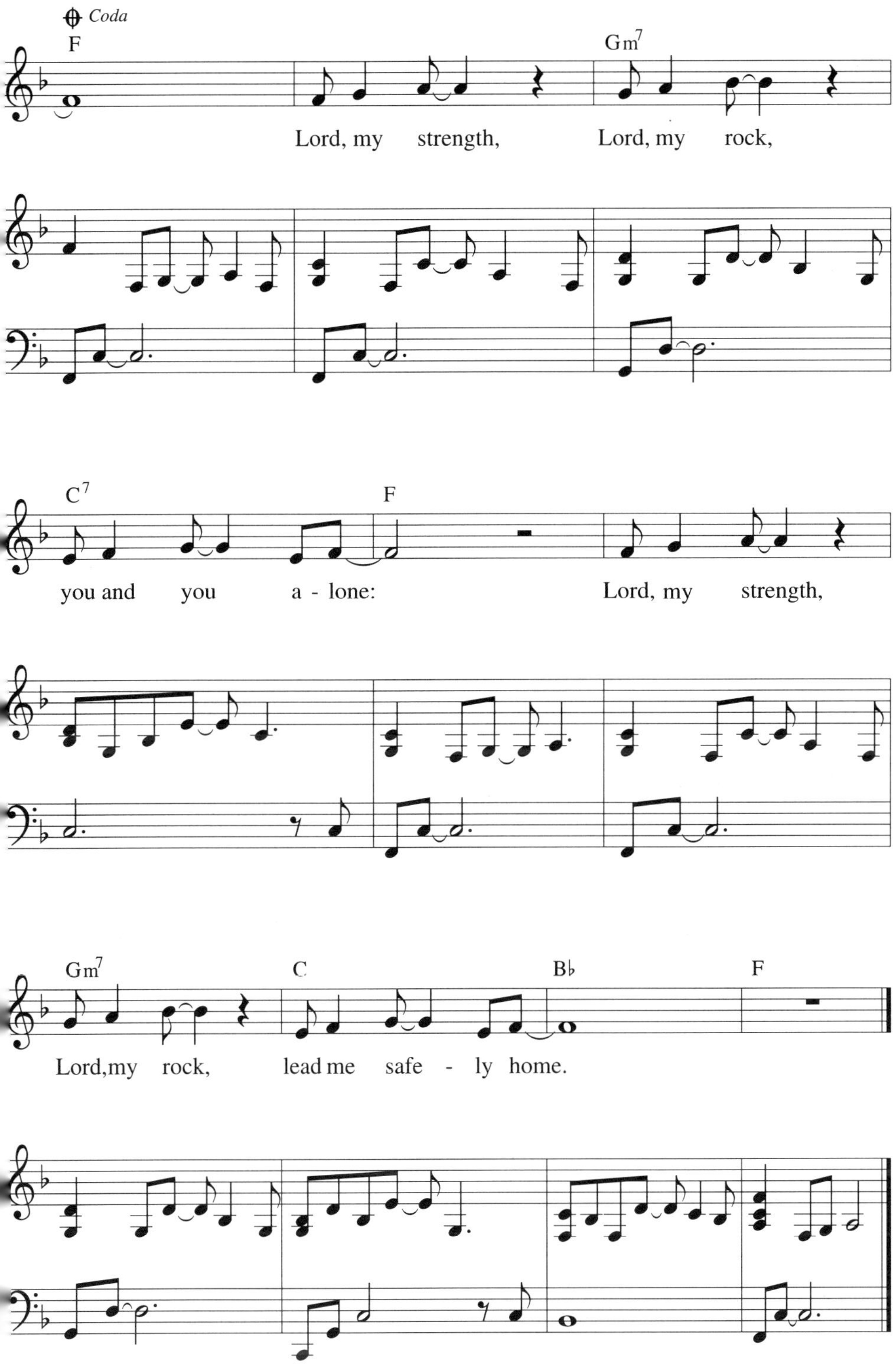
Coda
F
Gm7
Lord, my strength, Lord, my rock,
C7
F
you and you a - lone: Lord, my strength,
Gm7
C
B♭
F
Lord,my rock, lead me safe - ly home.

ext and music: Dean Krippaehne

Majesty

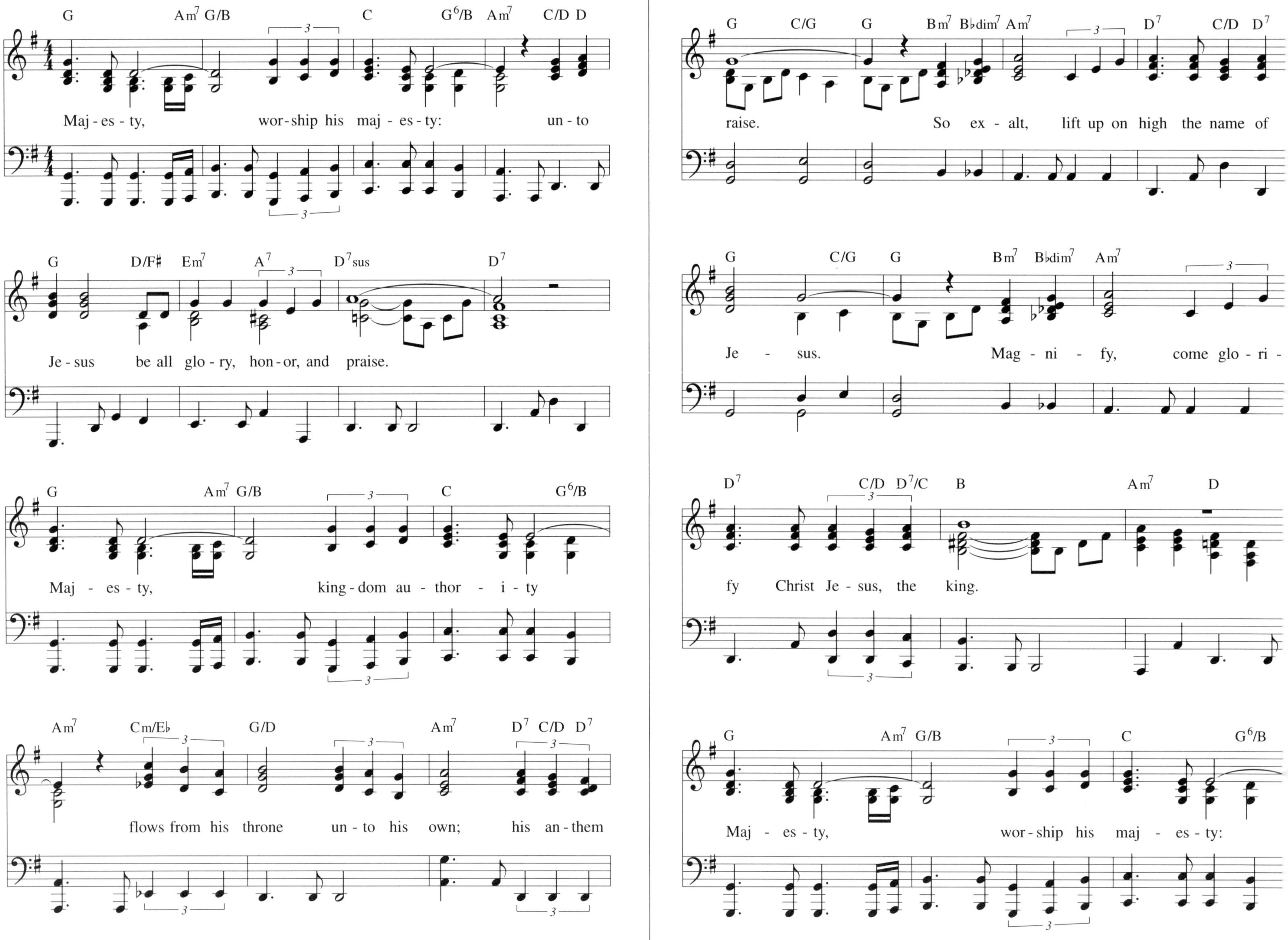
G Am7 G/B C G6/B Am7 C/D D
Maj - es - ty, wor - ship his maj - es - ty: un - to
G D/F♯ Em7 A7 D7sus D7
Je - sus be all glo - ry, hon - or, and praise.
G Am7 G/B C G6/B
Maj - es - ty, king - dom au - thor - i - ty
Am7 Cm/E♭ G/D Am7 D7 C/D D7
flows from his throne un - to his own; his an - them
G C/G G Bm7 B♭dim7 Am7 D7 C/D D7
raise. So ex - alt, lift up on high the name of
G C/G G Bm7 B♭dim7 Am7
Je - sus. Mag - ni - fy, come glo - ri -
D7 C/D D7/C B Am7 D
fy Christ Je - sus, the king.
G Am7 G/B C G6/B
Maj - es - ty, wor - ship his maj - es - ty:

Je - sus who died, now glo - ri - fied, King of all

kings. kings; Je - sus who

died, now glo - ri - fied, King of all kings.

95 Make me a channel of your peace

1 Make me a chan-nel of your peace. Where
2 Make me a chan-nel of your peace. Where
4 Make me a chan-nel of your peace. It

Lord; and where there's doubt, true
light; and where there's sad - ness,

there is ha - tred, let me bring your love;
there's de - spair in life, let me bring hope;
is in par - don - ing that we are par - doned,

faith in you.
ev - er joy. 3 O

where there is in - ju - ry, your par - don,
where there is dark - ness, ... on - ly
in giv - ing of our - selves that we re -

Mas - ter, grant that I may nev - er seek so

Last time to coda

much to be con-soled as to con-sole,

to be un-der-stood as to un-der-

stand, to be loved as to

love with all my soul.

Coda

-ceive, and in dy-ing that we're

born to e-ter-nal life.

Text and music: Sebastian Temple
Text and music © 1967 OCP Publications

Make me a servant

Make me a ser-vant, hum-ble and meek.

Lord, let me lift up those who are weak.

And may the prayer of my heart al-ways be:

Make me a ser-vant, make me a ser-vant,

make me a ser-vant to-day.

Text and music: Kelly Willard
Text and tune © 1982 Willing Heart Music, (admin. Maranatha! Music c/oThe Copyright Company)and Maranatha! Music (admin. The Copyright Company)

May you run and not be weary

May you run and not be wea - ry. May your

heart be filled with song. And may the love of God con-tin-

-ue to give you hope and keep you strong. And may you

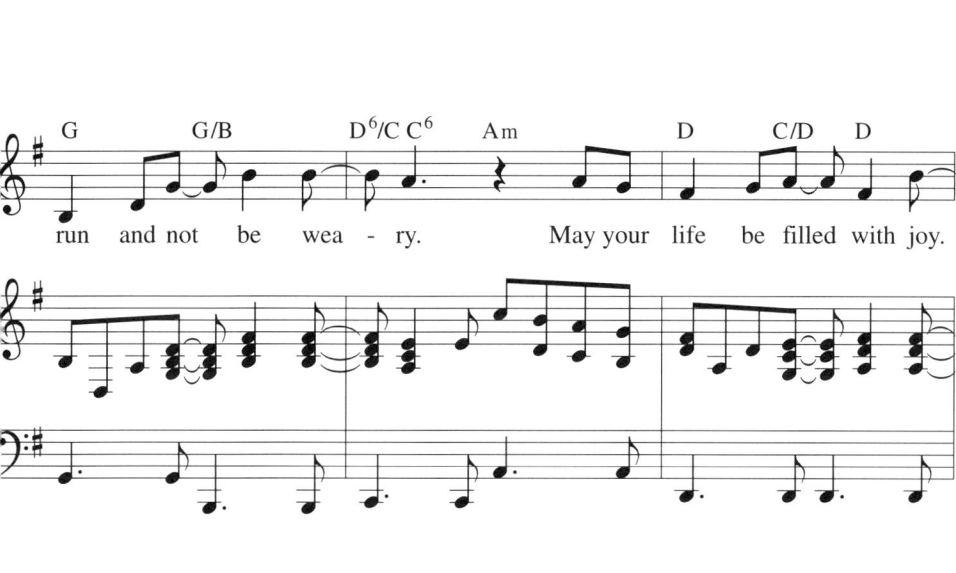

run and not be wea - ry. May your life be filled with joy.

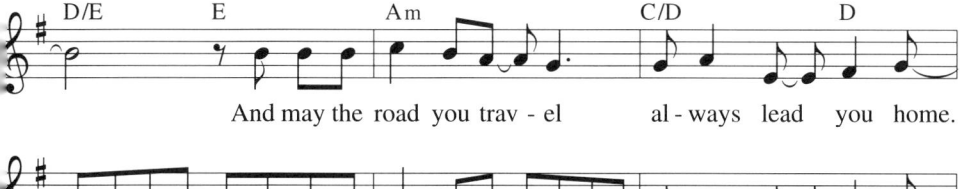

And may the road you trav - el al - ways lead you home.

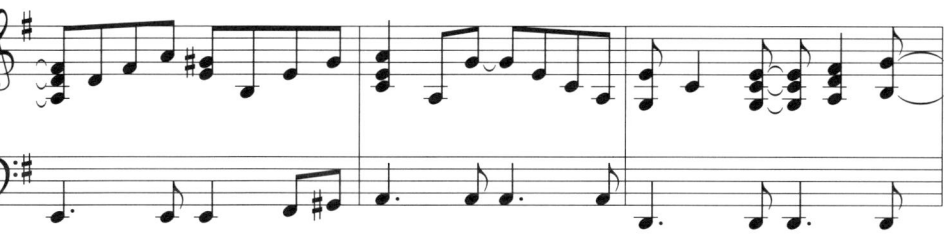

To repeat G C/G | *Last time* G C/G D G

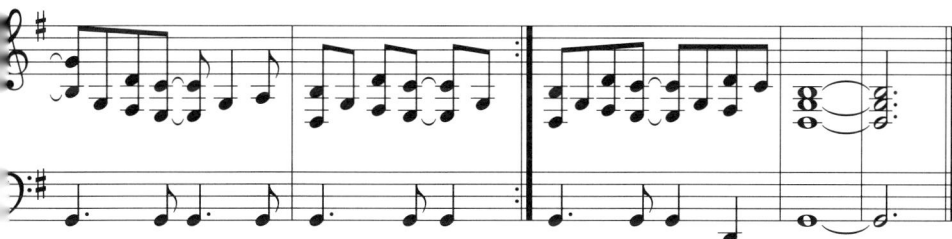

xt: Handt Hanson
usic: Handt Hanson; arr. Henry Wiens
xt and music © 1991 Prince of Peace Publishing, Changing Church, Inc.

Morning has broken

1 Morn-ing has bro - ken like the first morn - ing;
2 Sweet the rain's new fall, sun - lit from heav - en,
3 Mine is the sun - light! Mine is the morn - ing,

black - bird has spo - ken like the first bird.
like the first dew - fall on the first grass.
born of the one light E - den saw play!

Praise for the sing - ing! Praise for the morn - ing!
Praise for the sweet - ness of the wet gar - den,
Praise with e - la - tion, praise ev - 'ry morn - ing,

Praise for them, spring - ing fresh from the Word!
sprung in com - plete - ness where his feet pass.
God's re - cre - a - tion of the new day!

Text: Eleanor Farjeon
Music: Gaelic traditional, arr. Marty Haugen
Text © David Higham Associates, Ltd.
Arr. © 1987 GIA Publications

Mourning into dancing

You've turned my mourn-ing in-to danc-ing a-gain, you've

lift-ed my sor-rows; and I can't stay si-lent, I must

sing, for your joy has come. *Fine*

Where there once was on-ly hurt, you

gave your heal-ing hand; where there

once was on-ly pain, you brought com-fort like a friend

And I feel the sweet-ness of your love pierc-ing my

dark-ness; and I see the bright and morn-ing sun

as it ush-ers in your joy-ful glad-ness. *D.C. al fine*

Text and music: Tommy Walker
Text and music © 1992 Integrity's Praise! Music

Name above all names

Je - sus, Je - sus, name a-bove all names,

the on - ly name by which we must be

saved. Je - sus,

Je - sus, name a-bove all names, the

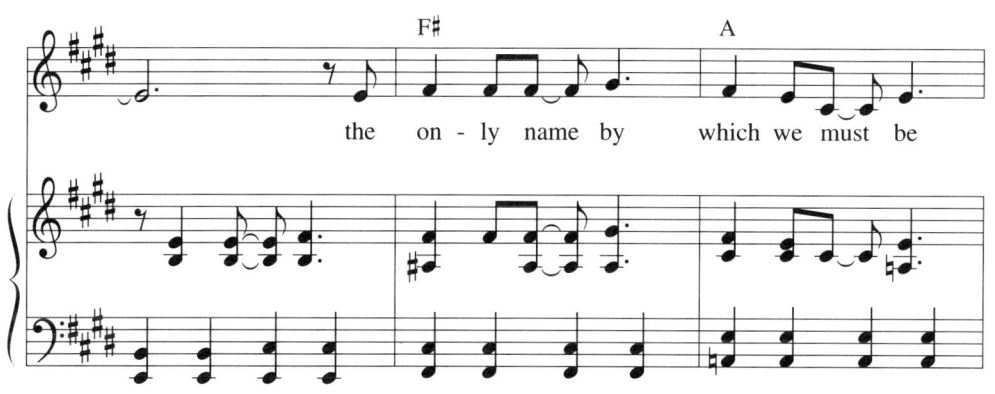

on - ly name by which we must be saved;

the on - ly name by which we must be

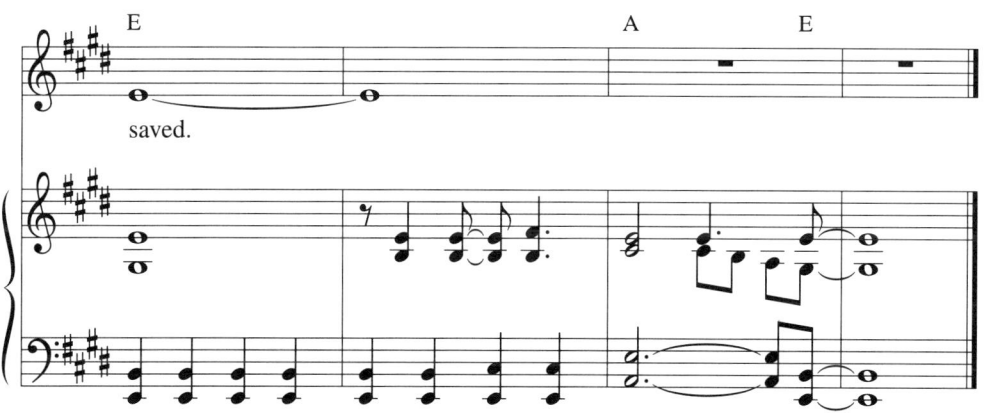

saved.

Text and music: Jay Beech
Text and music © 1988 Jay Beech

Night of silence

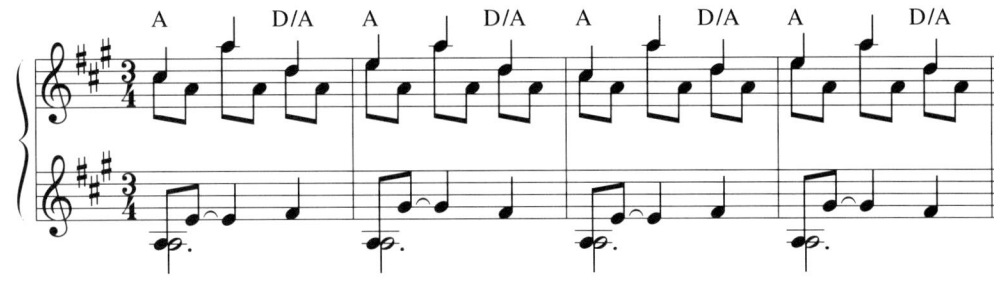

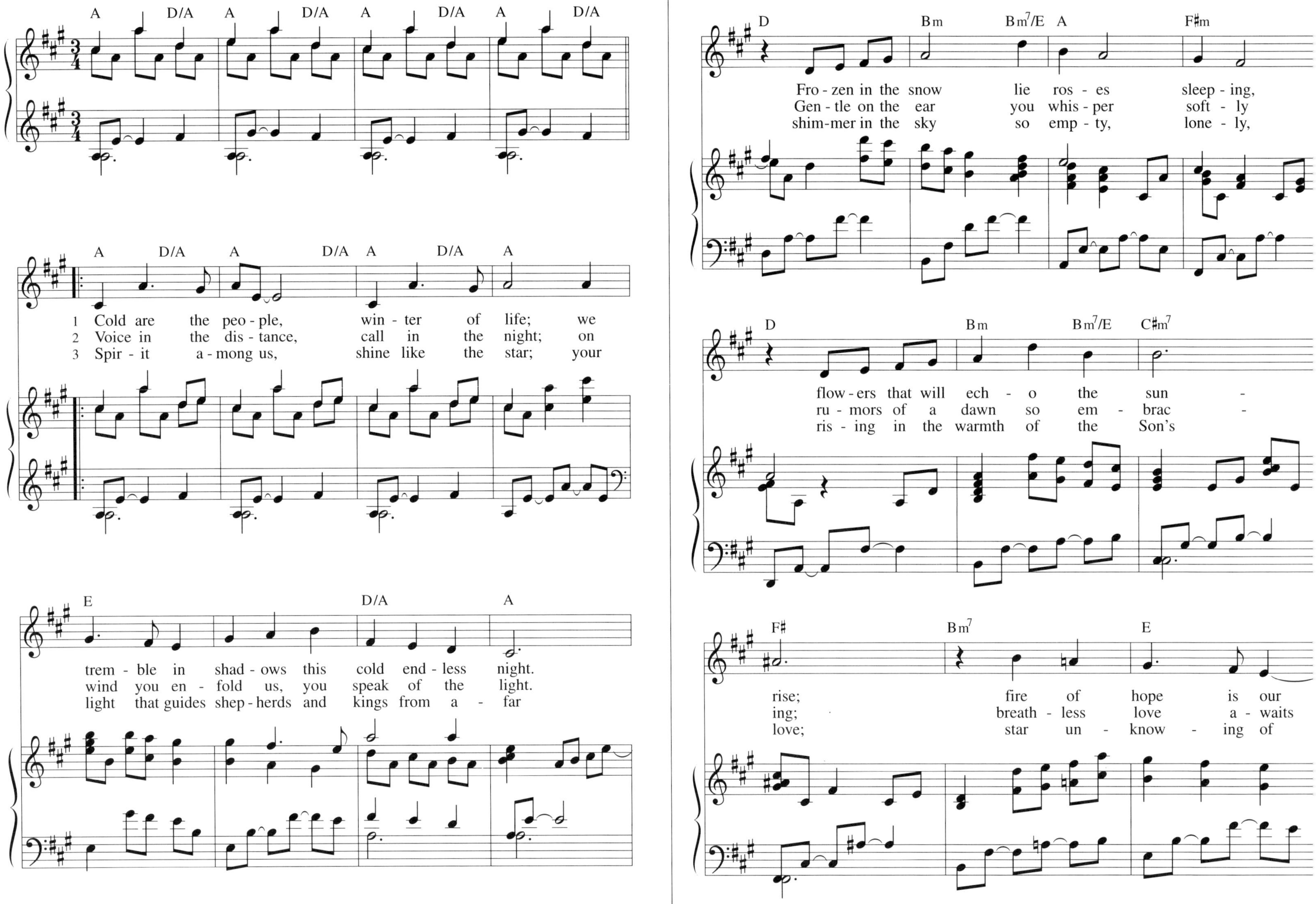

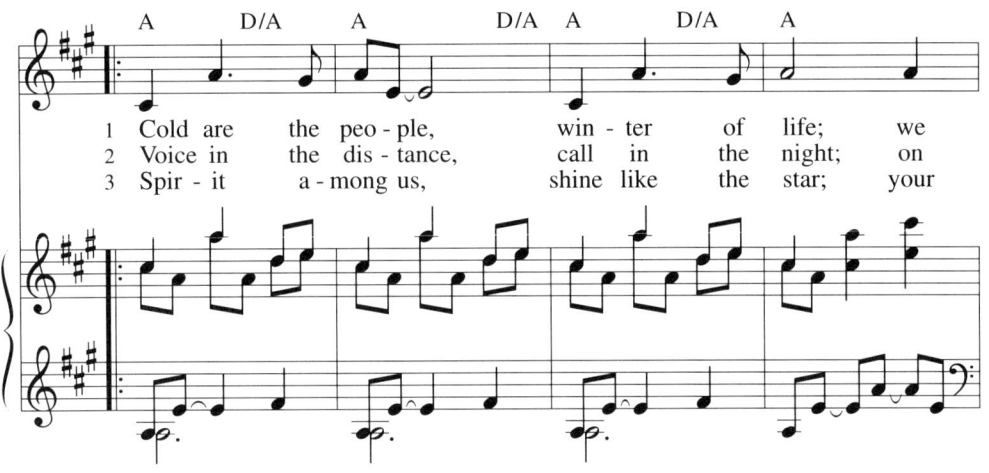

1 Cold are the peo-ple, win-ter of life; we
2 Voice in the dis-tance, call in the night; on
3 Spir-it a-mong us, shine like the star; your

trem-ble in shad-ows this cold end-less night.
wind you en-fold us, you speak of the light.
light that guides shep-herds and kings from a - far

Fro-zen in the snow lie ros-es sleep-ing,
Gen-tle on the ear you whis-per soft-ly
shim-mer in the sky so emp-ty, lone-ly,

flow-ers that will ech - o the sun
ru-mors of a dawn so em - brac -
ris-ing in the warmth of the Son's

rise; fire of hope is our
ing; breath-less love a-waits
love; star un-know-ing of

on - ly   warmth: wea - ry,   its
dark - ened   souls: soon   will   we
night   and   day: Spir - it,   we

flame will be dy - ing soon.
know of the morn - - - ing.
wait for the lov - - ing Son.

Silent night

1 Si - lent night, ho - ly night! All is calm,
2 Si - lent night, ho - ly night! Shep - herds quake
3 Si - lent night, ho - ly night! Son of God,

all is bright   round yon vir - gin moth - er and child.
at the sight;   glo - ries stream from heav - en a - far,
love's pure light   ra - diant beams from your ho - ly face,

Ho - ly In - fant, so ten - der and mild, sleep in heav - en - ly
heav'n - ly hosts . . . sing, al - le - lu - ia! Christ, the Sav - ior, is
with the dawn of re - deem - ing grace, Je - sus, Lord, at your

peace,   sleep in heav - en - ly peace.
born!   Christ, the Sav - ior, is born!
birth,   Je - sus, Lord, at your birth.

"Night of silence" was written to be sung simultaneously with "Silent night." It is suggested that selected voices hum "Silent night" while the remaining voices sing the final stanza of "Night of silence." Likewise, "Silent night" may be sung by the choir and congregation as instruments play "Night of silence."

"Silent night" is included for use with "Night of silence." The harmony and chord symbols above are for use when "Silent night" is sung independently.

Text and music: Daniel Kantor
Text and music © 1984 GIA Publications

Text: Joseph Mohr, tr. John F. Young
Music: Franz Gruber

No longer strangers

1 We once were lost;
2 We once were cut off;
3 We who once were dead,

saved by the prom-ise of God!
spir - it, one bod - y of Christ!
saved us, who raised us to life!

with - out hope, with - out God; but now in Christ
but now we are brought near, for Christ is our
now we . . . live in the light, we fol - low Christ

Refrain

No long - er stran-gers, no long - er lost and a - lone!

Je - sus, we have been found—
peace, . . . we were bro - ken, now whole— one
Je - sus, a - bun - dant in grace— who

No long - er stran-gers,

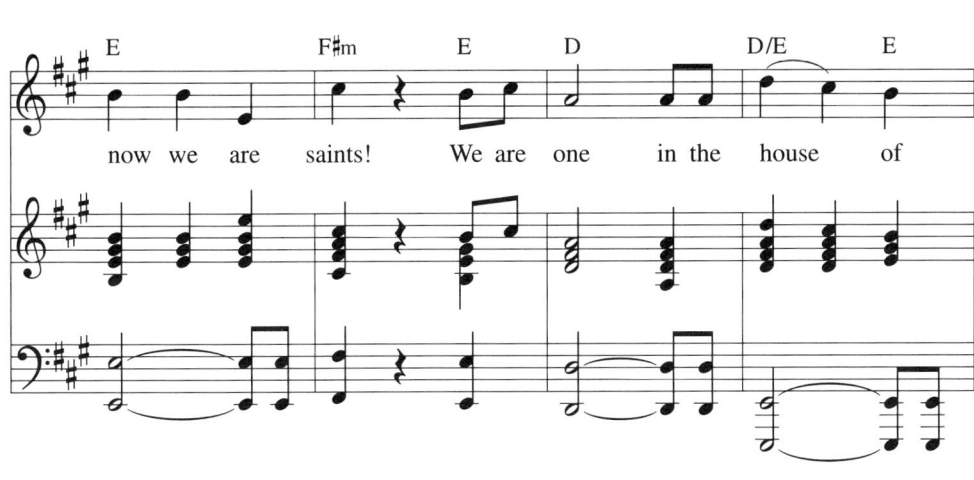

E F♯m E D D/E E
now we are saints! We are one in the house of
A E/A D/A E/A A E/A D/A E/A
D.C.
Last time
A
God!

Text: David Haas
Music: David Haas; arr. Jeanne Cotter

Now God our Father

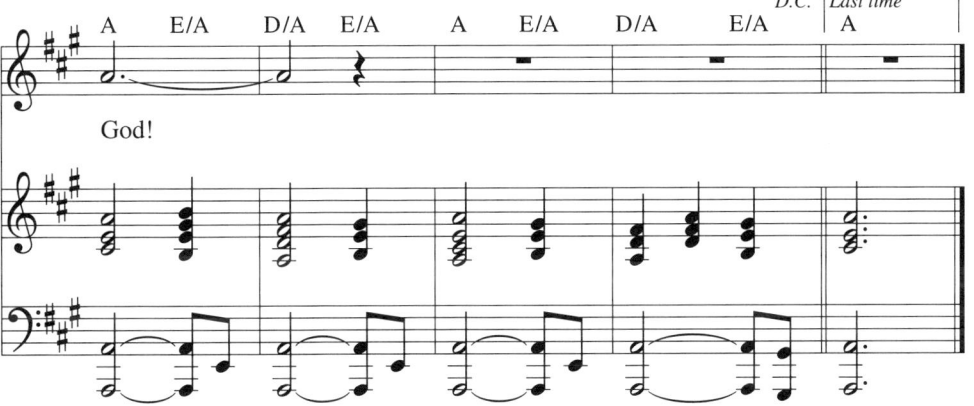

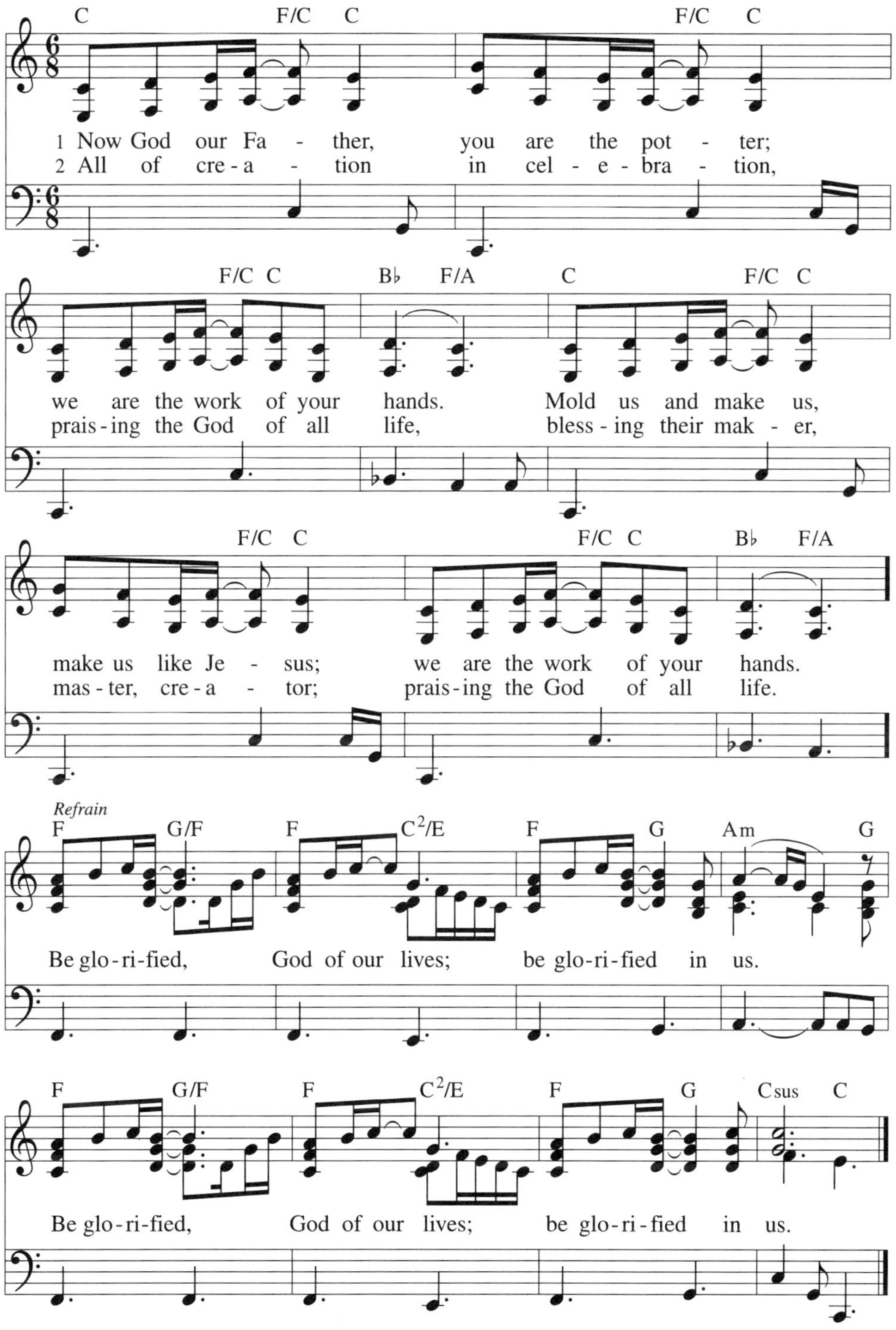
C F/C C F/C C
1 Now God our Fa - ther, you are the pot - ter;
2 All of cre - a - tion in cel - e - bra - tion,
F/C C B♭ F/A C F/C C
we are the work of your hands. Mold us and make us,
prais - ing the God of all life, bless - ing their mak - er,
F/C C F/C C B♭ F/A
make us like Je - sus; we are the work of your hands.
mas - ter, cre - a - tor; prais - ing the God of all life.
Refrain
F G/F F C²/E F G Am G
Be glo - ri - fied, God of our lives; be glo - ri - fied in us.
F G/F F C²/E F G Csus C
Be glo - ri - fied, God of our lives; be glo - ri - fied in us.

Text: Kirk Dearman
Music: Jim Mills

acc different?

Now in this banquet

Refrain

1*

Refrain (stanza 1):

Now in this ban-quet, Christ is our bread;

Advent: God of our jour-neys, day-break to night:

Lent: Lord, you can o-pen hearts that are stone;

here shall all hun-gers be fed.

lead us to jus-tice and light.

live in our flesh and our bone.

Bread that is bro-ken, wine that is poured:

Grant us com-pas-sion, strength for the day,

Lead us to won-der, mys-t'ry and grace,

To stanzas

love is the sign of our Lord.

wis-dom to walk in your way.

one in your lov-ing em-brace.

may be sung in canon

Last time

Lord.

way.

brace.

1* You who have touched us and graced us with

2 Let our hearts burn with the fire of your

love, make us your peo-ple of the

love; o-pen our eyes to the

Refrain

good-ness and light.

glo-ry of God.

stanzas are sung by soloist or choir

3 God who makes the blind to see, God who makes the lame to walk,

bring us danc-ing in-to day, lead your peo-ple in your way.

4 Hope for the hope-less, light for the blind:

"Strong" is your name, Lord, "Gen-tle" and "Kind."

5 Call us to be your light, call us to be your love,

make us your peo-ple a - gain.

6 Come, O Spir-it! Re - new our hearts!

We shall a - rise to be chil-dren of light.

Text and music: Marty Haugen
Text and music © 1986 GIA Publications

Now the day has drawn to a close

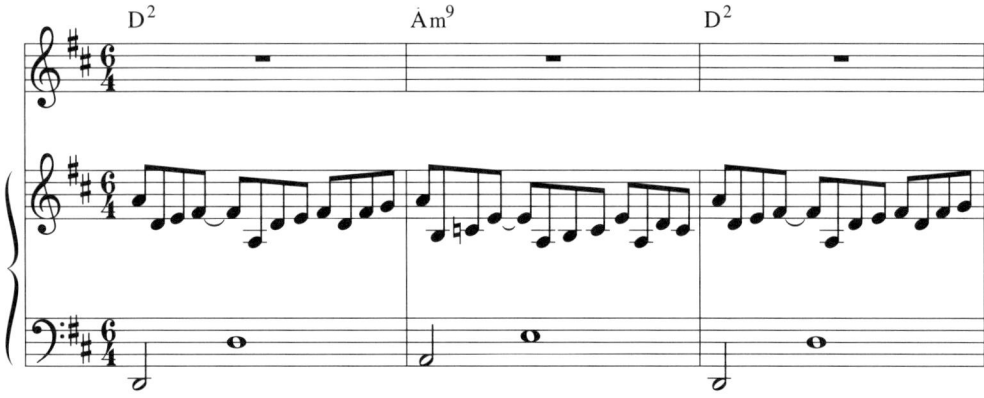

yours.

In our dark - ness, give us you

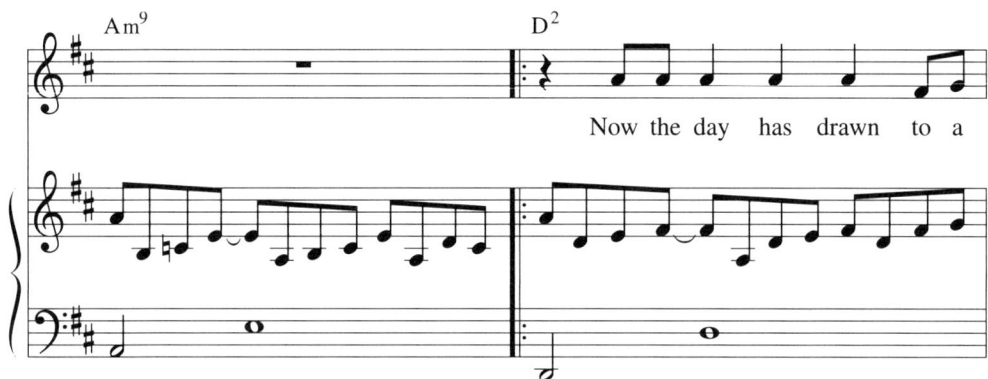

Now the day has drawn to a

light;

let your bright face shine on

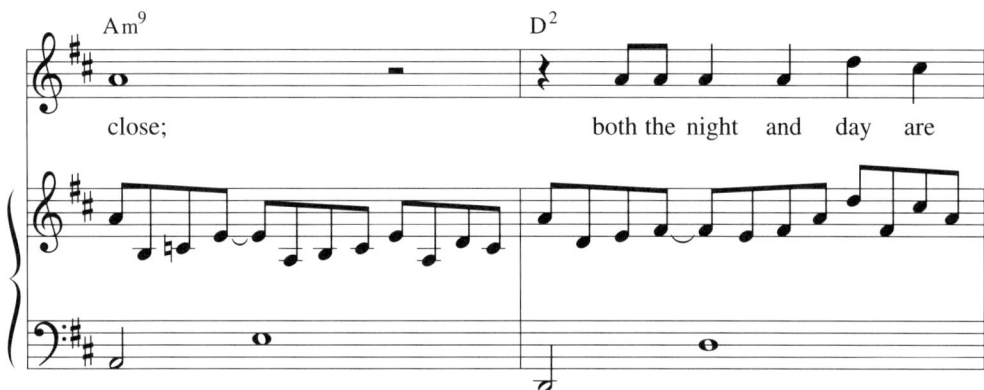

close;

both the night and day are

us.

Be a light un - to our

The phrases of this song may be sung in alternation between leader and congreation.

feet; make the eve - ning shad - ows

flee. A - men

Text and music: Ben Houge

Text and music © 1999 Augsburg Fortress

Now we remain

We hold the death of the Lord deep in our

hearts. Liv - ing, now we re -

main with Je - sus the Christ.

To stanzas / *Last time*

1 Once we were peo - ple a - fraid, lost in the
4 We are the pres - ence of God; this is our

2 Some - thing which we have known, some - thing we've

3 He chose to give of him - self, be - came our

G   D/F♯   Em   Em⁷/D   C   G/B

night.   Then by your cross we were saved;
call: now to be - come bread and wine,

touched,   what we have seen with our eyes,

bread;   bro - ken, that we might live;

Am⁷   G/B   C   *Stanza 4 to coda* ✛   C/D   D   *Refrain*

dead be - came liv - ing, life from your giv - ing.
food for the hun - gry, life for the wea - ry;

this we have heard: life - giv - ing Word.

love be - yond love, pain for our pain.

✛ *Coda*

D   Am⁷   G/B

for to live with the Lord, we must

F   C/E   C/D   D   *Refrain*

die with the Lord.

Text and music: David Haas
Text and music © 1983 GIA Publications

Oh, come, let us sing

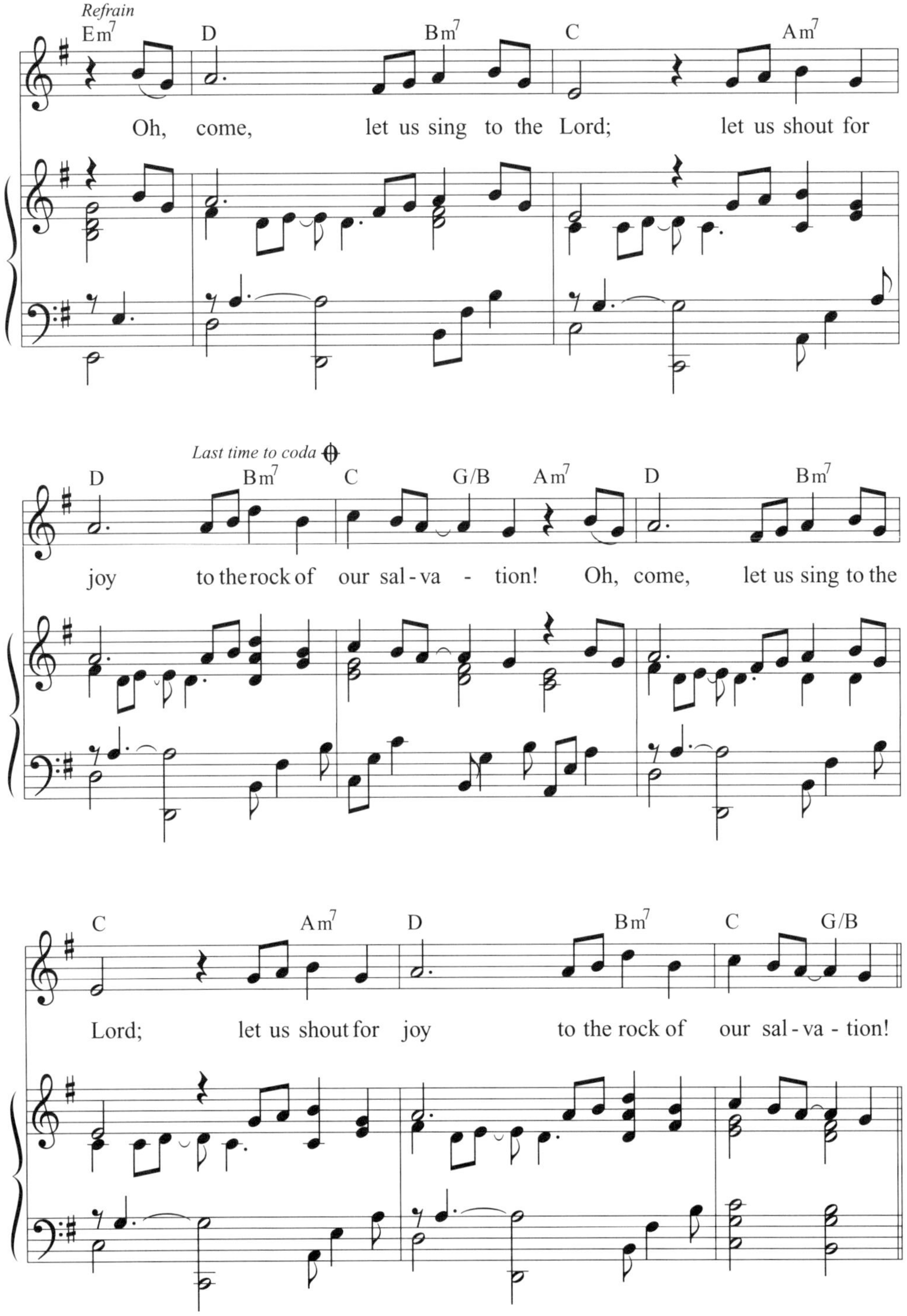
Refrain
Em7 D Bm7 C Am7
Oh, come, let us sing to the Lord; let us shout for
Last time to coda
D Bm7 C G/B Am7 D Bm7
joy to the rock of our sal-va - tion! Oh, come, let us sing to the
C Am7 D Bm7 C G/B
Lord; let us shout for joy to the rock of our sal-va-tion!

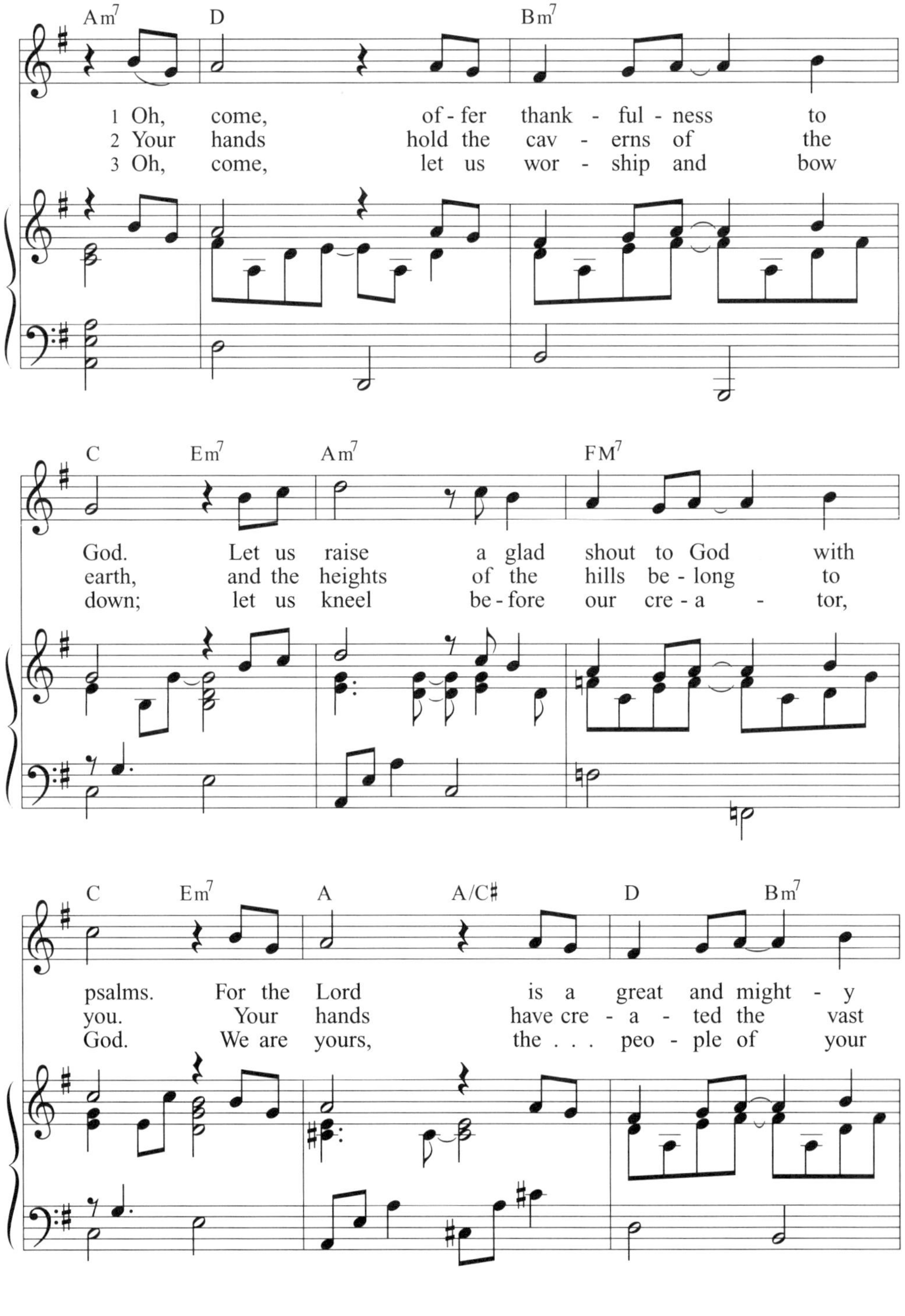
Am7 D Bm7
1 Oh, come, of-fer thank - ful - ness to
2 Your hands hold the cav - erns of the
3 Oh, come, let us wor - ship and bow
C Em7 Am7 FM7
God. Let us raise a glad shout to God with
earth, and the heights of the hills be - long to
down; let us kneel be-fore our cre - a - tor,
C Em7 A A/C# D Bm7
psalms. For the Lord is a great and might - y
you. Your hands have cre - a - ted the vast
God. We are yours, the . . . peo - ple of your

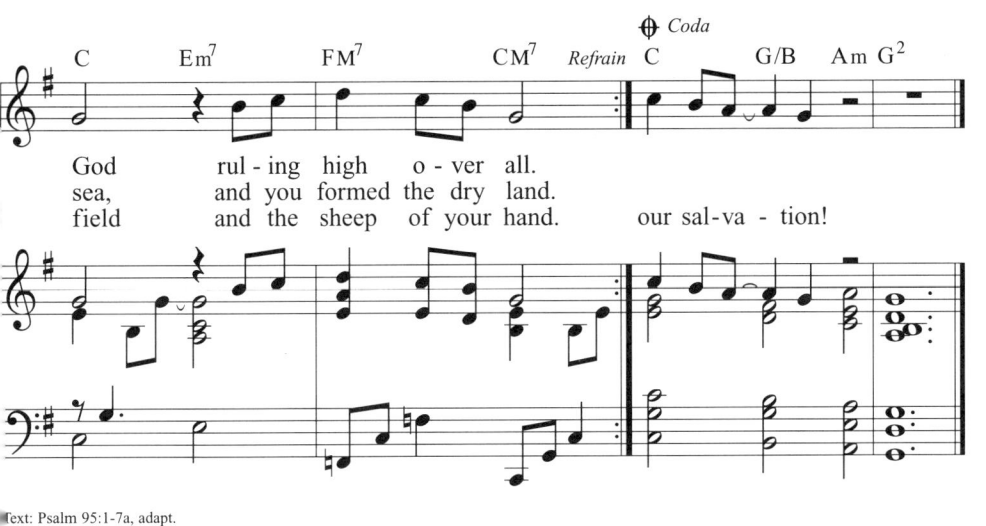

God   rul-ing high o-ver all.
sea,   and you formed the dry land.
field   and the sheep of your hand.   our sal-va - tion!

Text: Psalm 95:1-7a, adapt.
Music: Ben Houge
Text and music © 1999 Augsburg Fortress

108   O Lord, hear our prayer

O   Lord,   hear our   prayer   we of-fer up to

you;   O   Lord,   hear our   prayer.

Text and music: Ralph C. Sappington
Text and music © 1999 Augsburg Fortress

O Lord, my heart is not proud   109

O   Lord,   my heart is not proud,   nor   haugh-ty my

eyes.   I have not gone af-ter things too great, nor mar-vels be-

yond me.   Tru-ly I have set my   soul   in si - lence and

peace;   at rest, as a child in its moth-er's arms,   so   is my

soul.   O   soul,   so   is   my soul.

To repeat / *Last time*

Text: Psalm 131:1-2, tr. The Grail
Music: Margaret Rizza
Text © The Grail, England, admin. A. P. Watt, Ltd.
Music © 1997 Kevin Mayhew

On eagle's wings

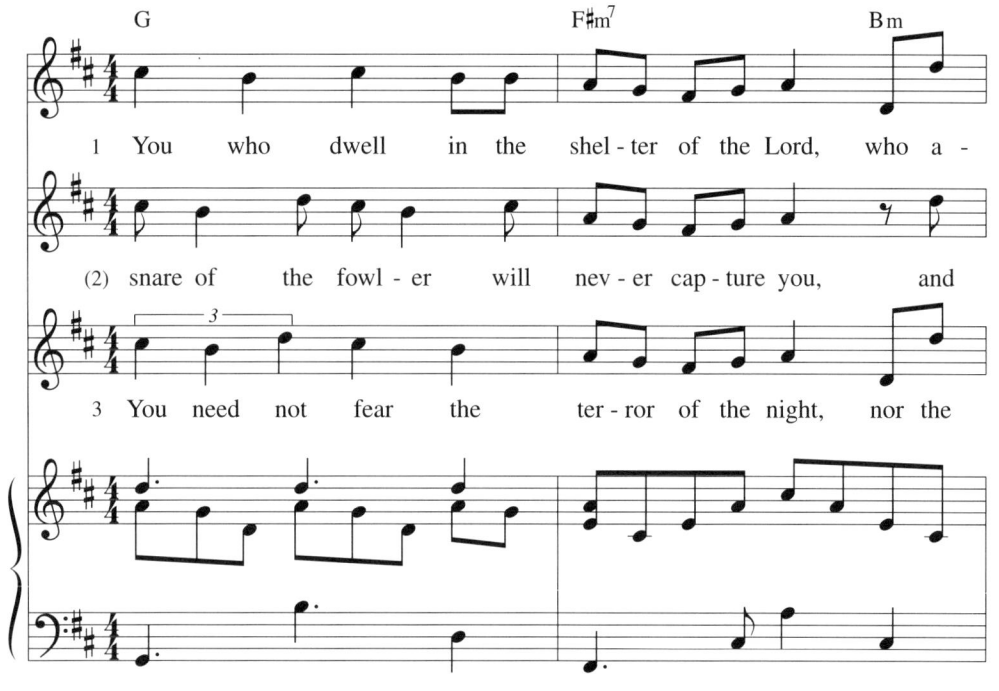

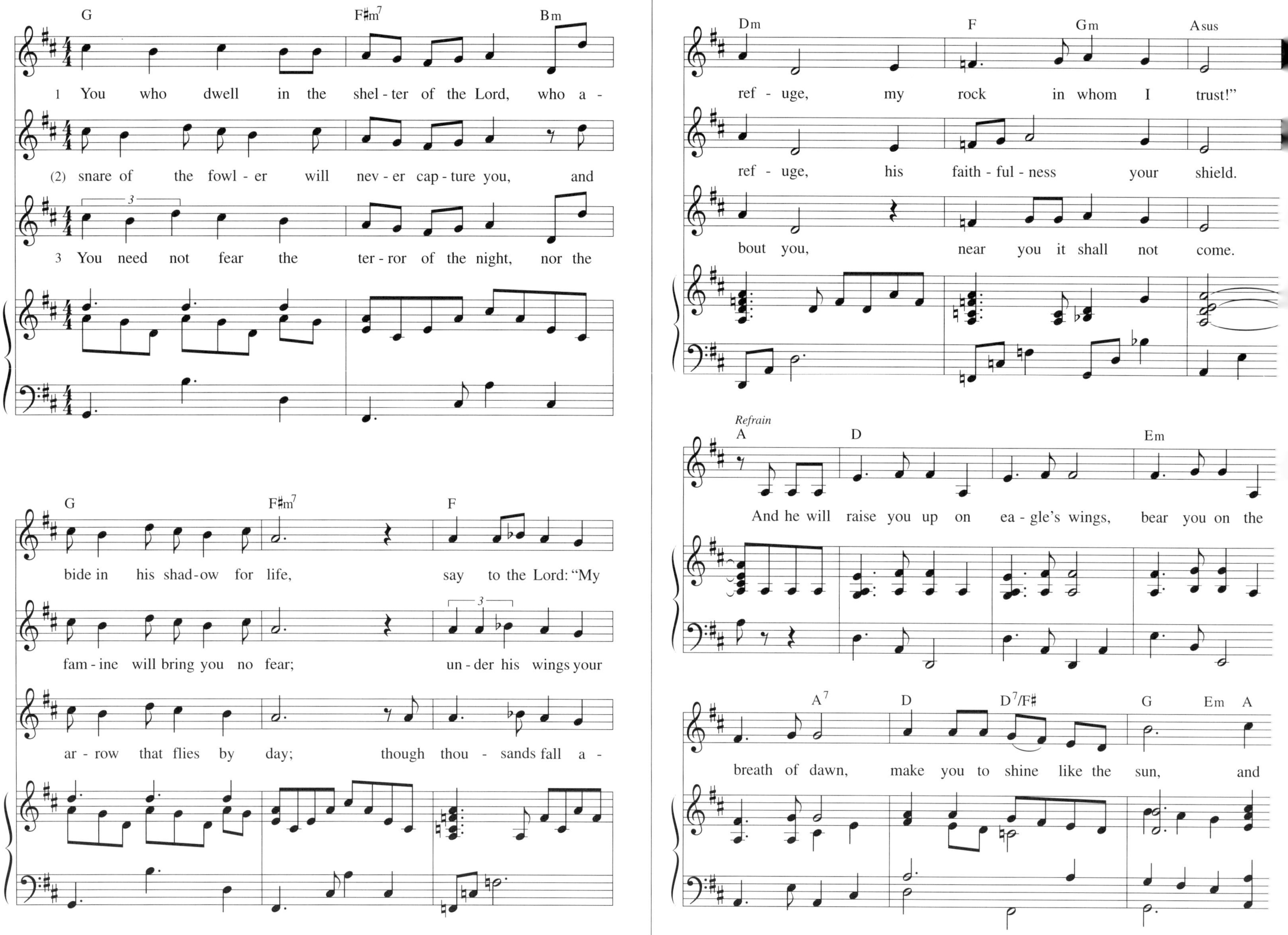

G F♯m7 Bm
1 You who dwell in the shel - ter of the Lord, who a -
(2) snare of the fowl - er will nev - er cap - ture you, and
3 You need not fear the ter - ror of the night, nor the
G F♯m7 F
bide in his shad - ow for life, say to the Lord: "My
fam - ine will bring you no fear; un - der his wings your
ar - row that flies by day; though thou - sands fall a -
Dm F Gm Asus
ref - uge, my rock in whom I trust!"
ref - uge, his faith - ful - ness your shield.
bout you, near you it shall not come.
Refrain
A D Em
And he will raise you up on ea - gle's wings, bear you on the
A7 D D7/F♯ G Em A
breath of dawn, make you to shine like the sun, and

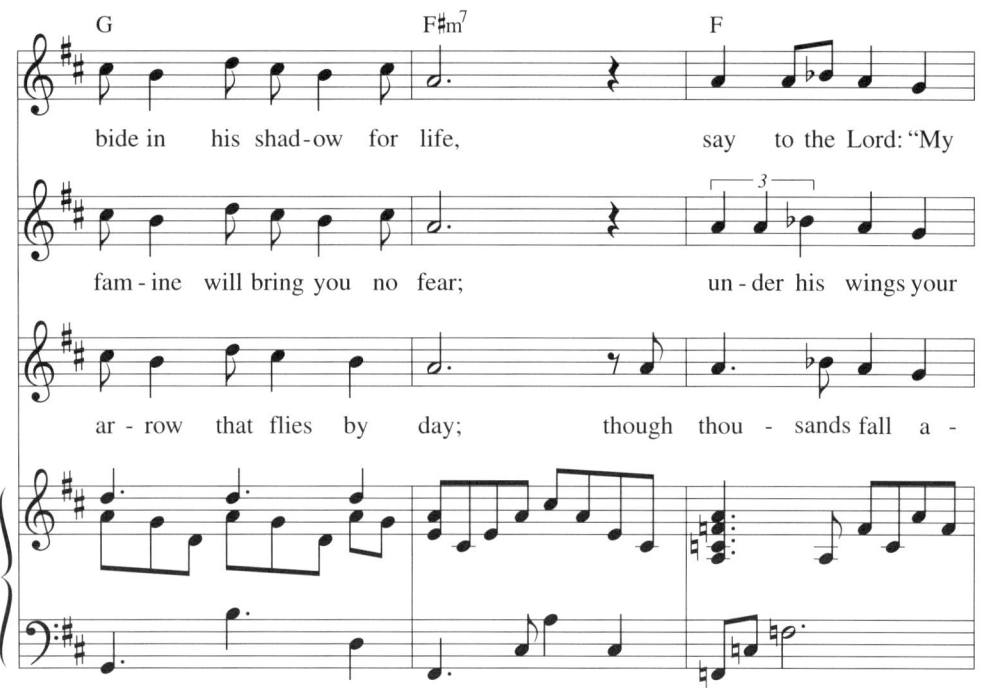

hold you in the palm of his hand.

bear you up, lest you dash your foot a-gainst a stone.

To stanzas

2 The 4 For to his an-gels he's giv-en a com-mand to

Coda

And hold you, hold you in the

guard you in all of your ways; up - on their hands they will

palm of his hand.

Text and music: Michael Joncas
Text and music © 1979, 1991 New Dawn Music

One bread, one body

One bread, one bod-y, one Lord of all;

we are one bod - y in this one Lord.

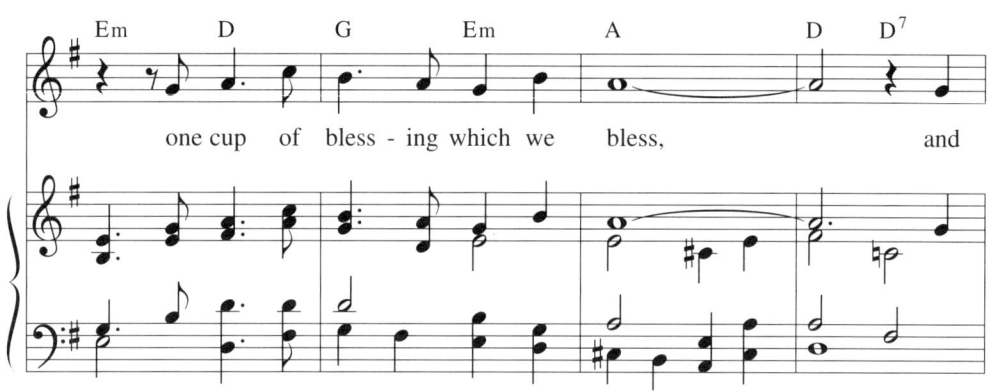

one cup of bless - ing which we bless, and

1 Gen - tile or Jew, ser - vant or free,
2 Man - y the gifts, man - y the works,
3 Grain for the fields, scat - tered and grown,

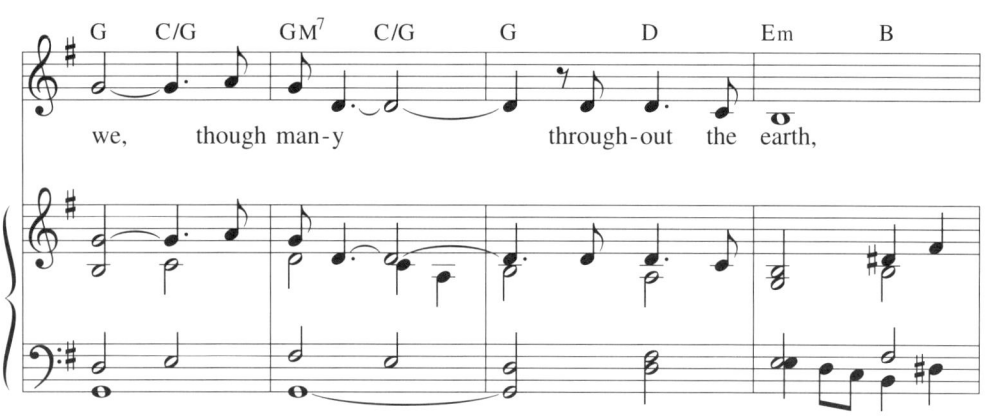

we, though man-y through-out the earth,

wom-an or man, no more.
one in the Lord of all.
gath-ered to one for all.

Text and music: John Foley
Text and music © 1978 John B. Foley and New Dawn Music

Only by grace

On-ly by grace can we en - ter, on-ly by grace can we stand;

not by our hu - man en - deav - or,

but by the blood of the Lamb. In - to your pres - ence you call

us, you call us to come.

In-to your pres - ence you draw us, and now by your grace we come,

now by your grace we come.

Lord, if you mark our trans-gres - sions, who would stand?

Thanks to your grace we are cleansed by the blood of the Lamb.

Fine

D.C. al fine

Text and music: Gerrit Gustafson
Text and music © 1990 Integrity's Hosanna! Music

Open our eyes, Lord

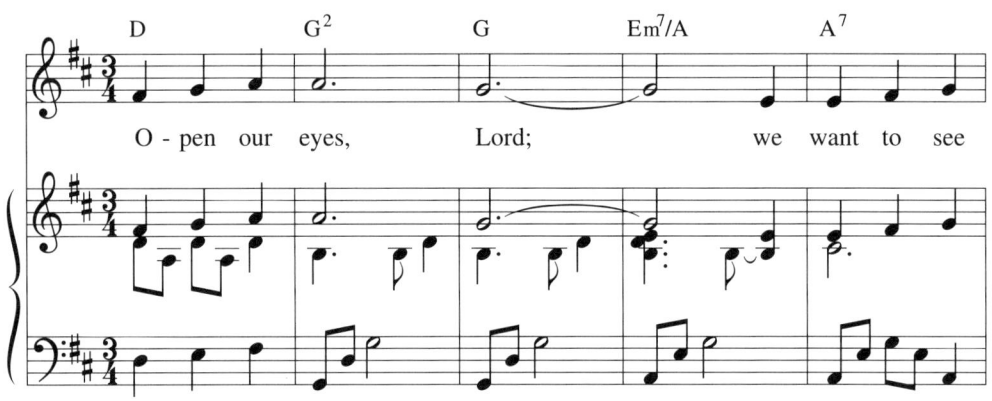

D G2 G Em7/A A7
O - pen our eyes, Lord; we want to see
G/D D A/C♯ Bm D/A GM9
Je - sus, to reach out and touch
Em A7 G/D D2 D
him, and say that we love him.

DM7 A/G G Em7 A7
O - pen our ears, Lord, and help us to
G/D D A Bm7 D/A GM9
lis - ten. O - pen our eyes,
Em7 A7 Em/D D
Lord, we want to see Je - sus.

Text and music: Bob Cull

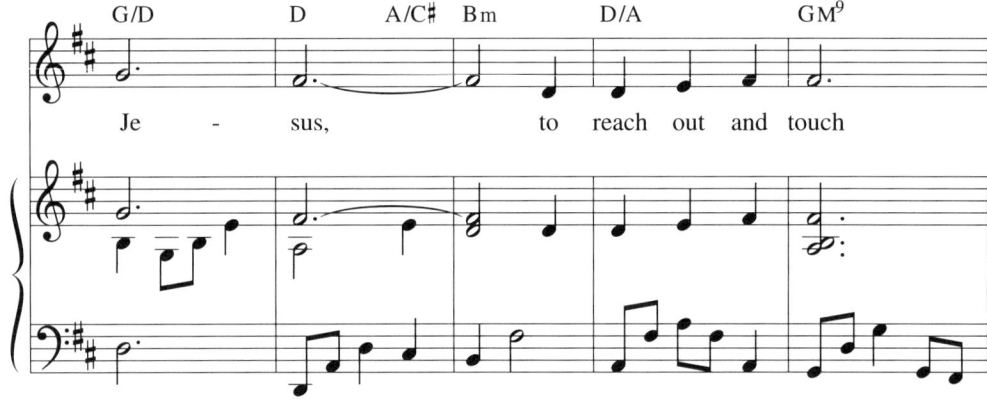

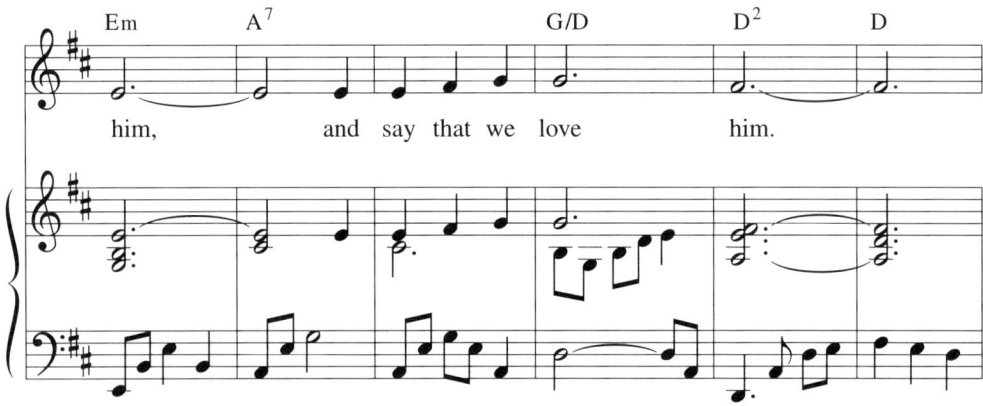

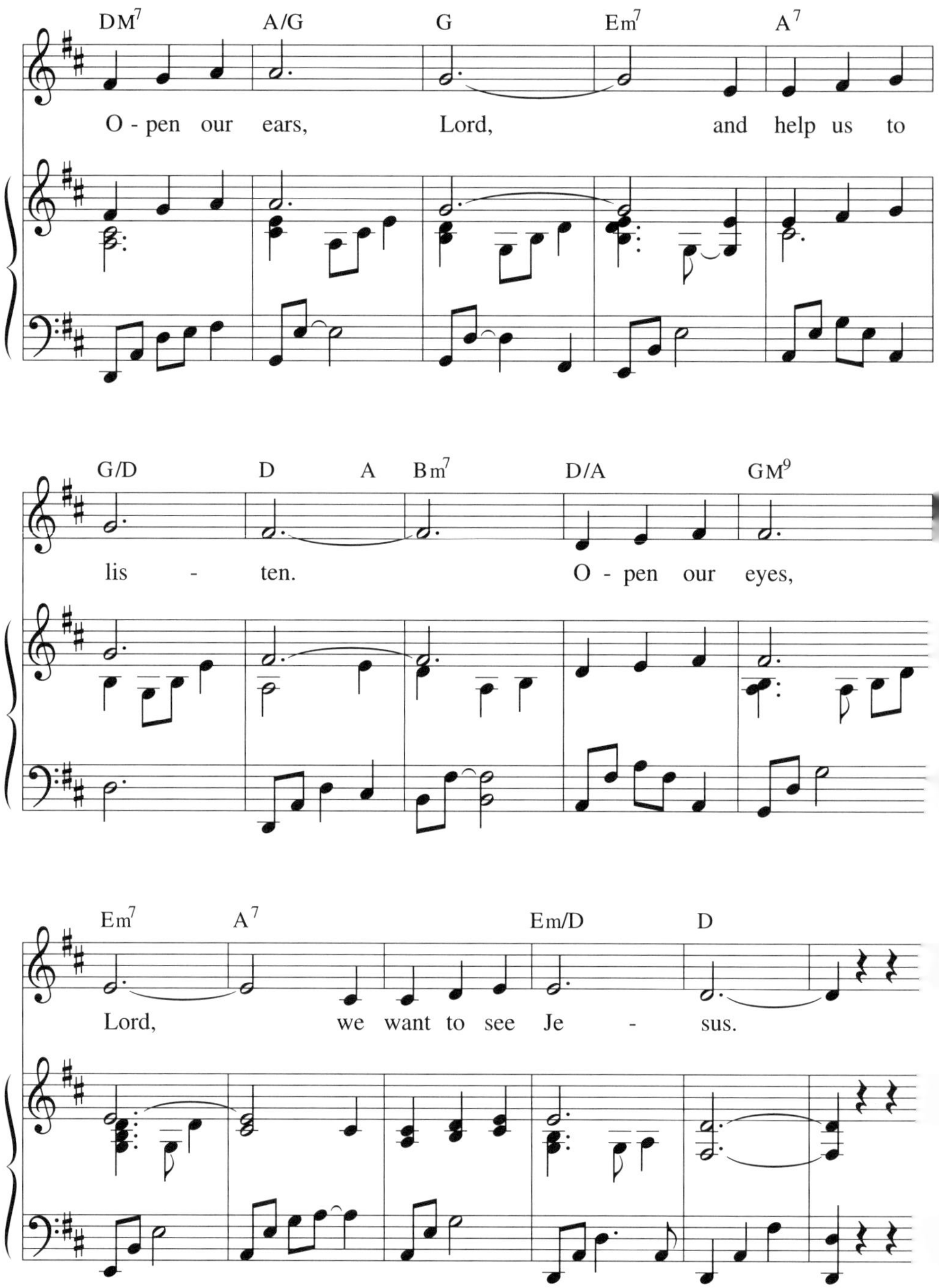

Our confidence is in the Lord

Our con-fi-dence is in the Lord, the source of our sal-va-tion.

Rest is found in God a-lone, the au-thor of cre-a-tion.

We will not fear the e - vil day, be-cause we have a ref-

- uge; in ev-'ry cir-cum-stance we say,

our hope is built on Je - sus. God is our for-tress, we will

nev-er be shak-en. God is our for-tress, we will nev-er be shak-en.

God is our for-tress,we will nev-er be shak-en. God is our for-tress, we will

nev-er be shak-en. We will put our trust in God.

To repeat

We will put our trust in God.

Last time

God.

Text and music: Noel Richards and Tricia Richards

Text and music © 1989 Kingsway's Thankyou Music, admin. EMI Christian Music Publishing

Out in the wilderness

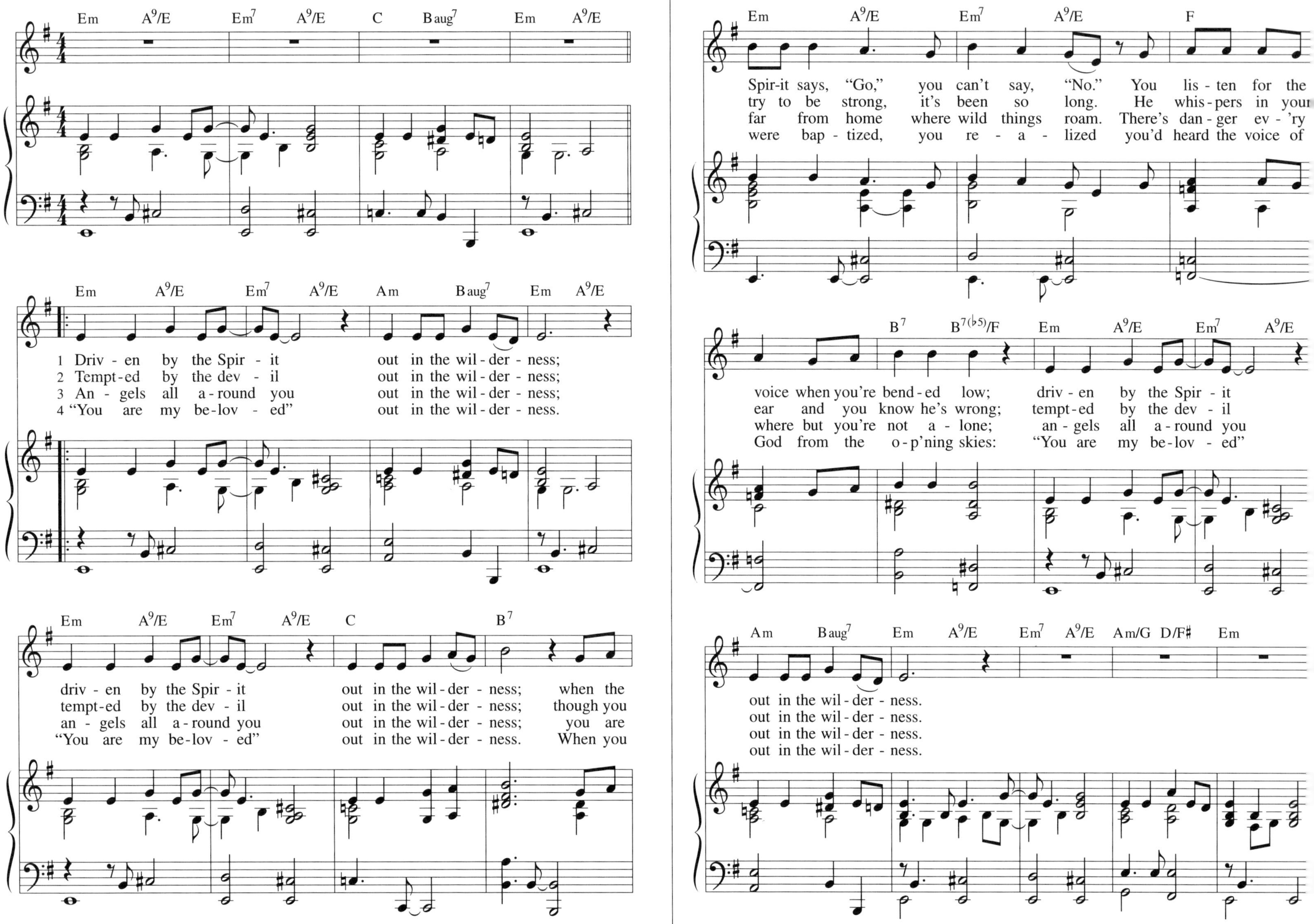

Spir-it says, "Go," you can't say, "No." You lis - ten for the
try to be strong, it's been so long. He whis-pers in your
far from home where wild things roam. There's dan - ger ev - 'ry
were bap - tized, you re - a - lized you'd heard the voice of

1 Driv - en by the Spir - it out in the wil - der - ness;
2 Tempt - ed by the dev - il out in the wil - der - ness;
3 An - gels all a - round you out in the wil - der - ness;
4 "You are my be - lov - ed" out in the wil - der - ness.

voice when you're bend - ed low; driv - en by the Spir - it
ear and you know he's wrong; tempt - ed by the dev - il
where but you're not a - lone; an - gels all a - round you
God from the o - p'ning skies: "You are my be - lov - ed"

driv - en by the Spir - it out in the wil - der - ness; when the
tempt - ed by the dev - il out in the wil - der - ness; though you
an - gels all a - round you out in the wil - der - ness; you are
"You are my be - lov - ed" out in the wil - der - ness. When you

out in the wil - der - ness.
out in the wil - der - ness.
out in the wil - der - ness.
out in the wil - der - ness.

Text and music: Jay Beech
Text and music © 1999 Jay Beech

Praise, praise, praise the Lord

Praise, praise, praise the Lord! Praise God's ho - ly name. Al - le -lu - ia!

Praise, praise, praise the Lord! Praise God's ho - ly name. Al - le -lu - ia!

Praise God's ho - ly name. Al - le-lu - ia! Praise God's ho - ly name. Al - le-lu - ia!

Praise God's ho - ly name. Al - le-lu - ia! Praise God's ho - ly name. Al - le-lu - ia!

This song may be repeated, adding a vocal part on each repetition:
melody (alto) alone; melody + tenor; melody + lower parts; all voices.

Text: traditional; collected by Elaine Hanson
Music: Cameroon processional; arr. Ralph M. Johnson
Text and music © 1994 earthsongs

Praise the name of Jesus

Praise the name of Je - sus, praise the name of

Je - sus; he's my rock, he's my for - tress,

he's my de - liv - er - er, in him will I trust.

Praise the name of Je - sus.

Text and music: Roy Hicks Jr.
Text and music © 1976 Latter Rain Music, admin. EMI Christian Music Publishing

Praise to you, O Christ, our Savior

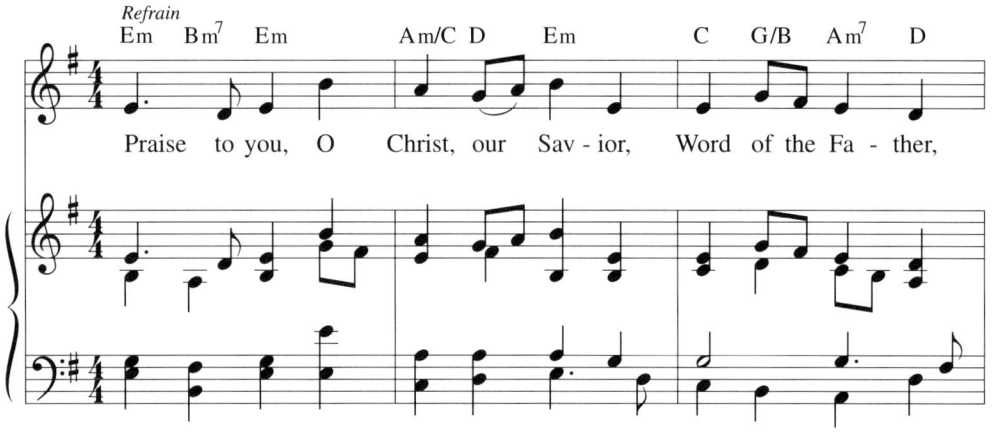

Refrain

Praise to you, O Christ, our Sav-ior, Word of the Fa-ther,

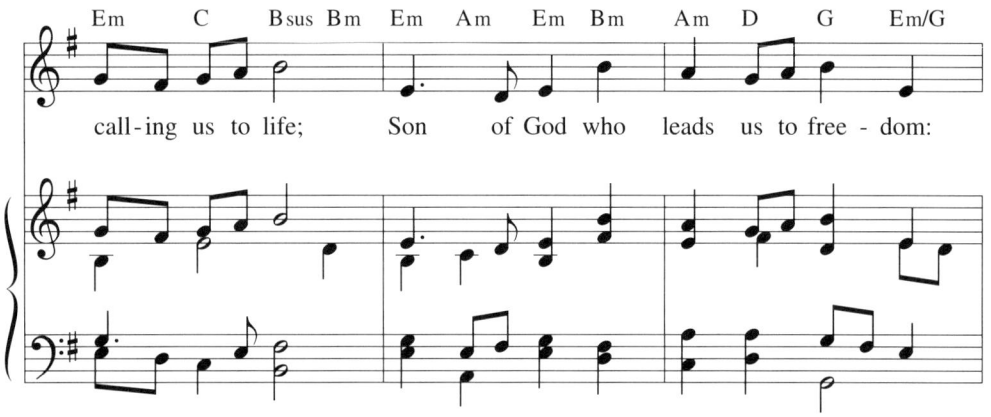

call-ing us to life; Son of God who leads us to free-dom:

To stanzas / *Last time*

glo-ry to you, Lord Je-sus Christ! Christ!

1 You are the Word who calls us out of dark-ness;
2 You are the one whom proph-ets hoped and longed for;
3 You are the Word who calls us to be ser-vants;
4 You are the Word who binds us and u-nites us;

You are the Word who leads us in-to light; you are the Word who
You are the one who speaks to us to-day; you are the one who
You are the Word whose on-ly law is love; you are the Word made
You are the Word who calls us to be one; you are the Word who

brings us through the des-ert: glo-ry to you, Lord Je-sus Christ!
leads us to our fu-ture: glo-ry to you, Lord Je-sus Christ!
flesh who lives a-mong us: glo-ry to you, Lord Je-sus Christ!
teach-es us for-give-ness: glo-ry to you, Lord Je-sus Christ!

Text and music: Bernadette Farrell
Text and music © 1986 Bernadette Farrell, admin. OCP Publications

Praise to you, O God of mercy

1 Praise to you, O God of mer-cy! Thanks be to you for-
2 From of old you loved and sought us! Thanks be to you for-
3 Praise to you, O God of mer-cy! Thanks be to you for-

ev – er! Rais – ing high the weak and low – ly:
ev – er! Truth and jus – tice you have taught us:
ev – er! Rais – ing high the weak and low – ly:

Last time to coda

thanks be to you for – ev – er!
thanks be to you for – ev – er!
thanks be to you for –

Strong is your faith – ful-ness, strong is your love, re –

D.C. al coda

mem – b'ring your cov-e-nant of life with us.

Coda

ev – er! Thanks be to you for – ev – er!

Text and music: Marty Haugen
Text and music © 1990 GIA Publications

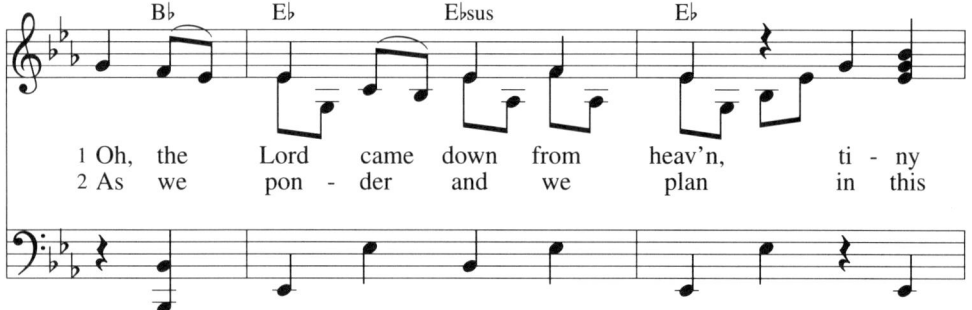

1 Oh, the Lord came down from heav'n, ti - ny
2 As we pon - der and we plan in this

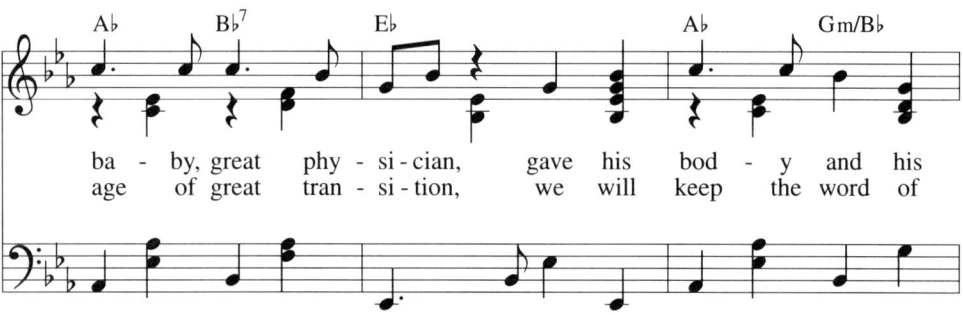

ba - by, great phy - si - cian, gave his bod - y and his
age of great tran - si - tion, we will keep the word of

blood to live out a ho - ly mis - sion.
God at the heart of each de - ci - sion.

His dis - ci - ples, they went out to ful -
Praise the Fa - ther, Lord of love; praise the

fill the great com - mis - sion, with a seed of faith so
Christ, in glor - y ris - en; praise the Spir - it, by whose

small, learned a dif - f'rent kind of fish - in'.
pow'r we will share the gifts we're giv - en—

Will we go?
as we go.

Refrain
And we'll all share the vi - sion, who in

Christ we all shall be. Come, re - joice in the

mis - sion of a new com - mu - ni - ty.

In this place where we ga - ther, Je - sus,

still our rest - less souls; to your Spir - it we will

lis - ten. We will go.

Last time
go.

Text: Dan Bielenberg
Music: Appalachian traditional, adapt. and arr. Dori Erwin Collins
Text and music © 1999 Augsburg Fortress

Seed, scattered and sown

Refrain

Seed, scat-tered and sown; wheat, gath-ered and

land; wine, work of our hands;

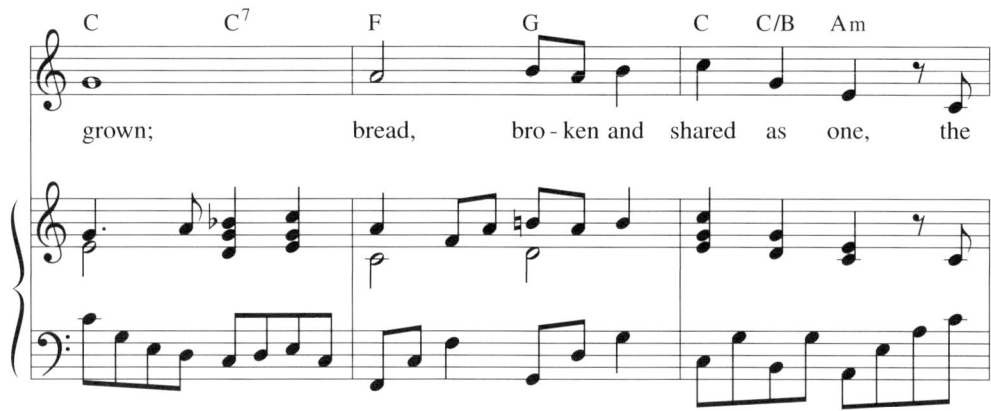

grown; bread, bro-ken and shared as one, the

one cup that is shared by all; the Liv - ing Cup, the

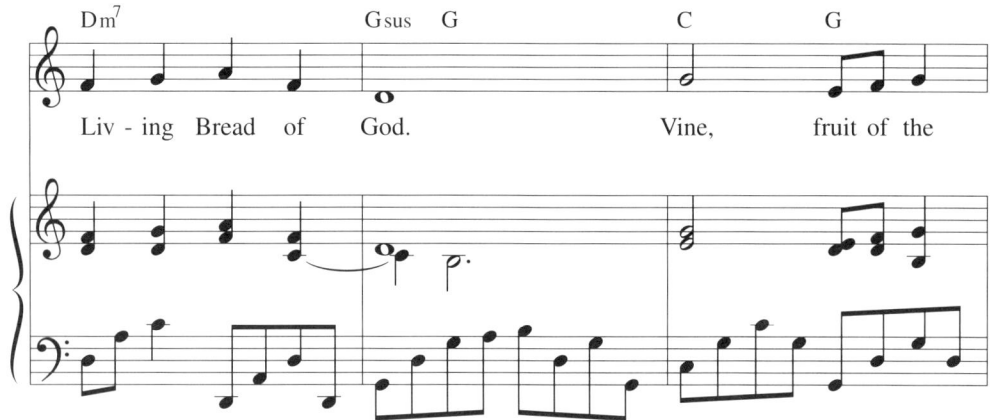

Liv - ing Bread of God. Vine, fruit of the

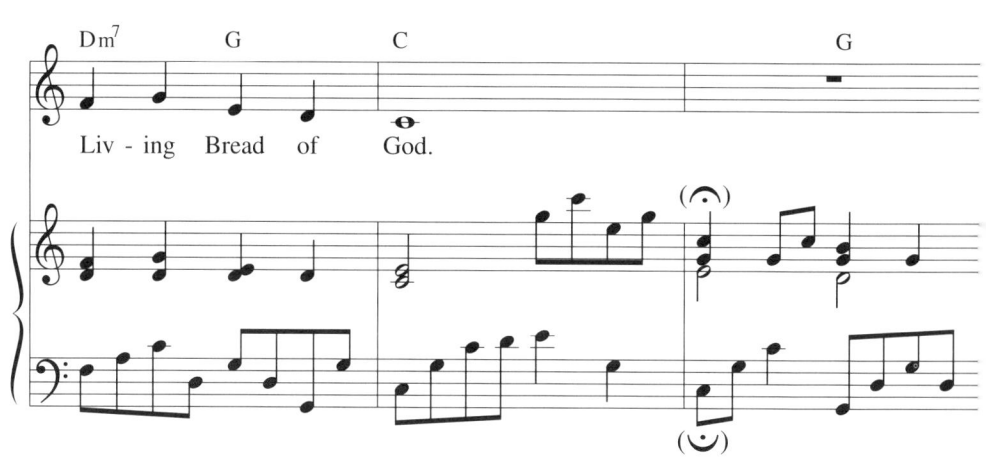

Liv - ing Bread of God.

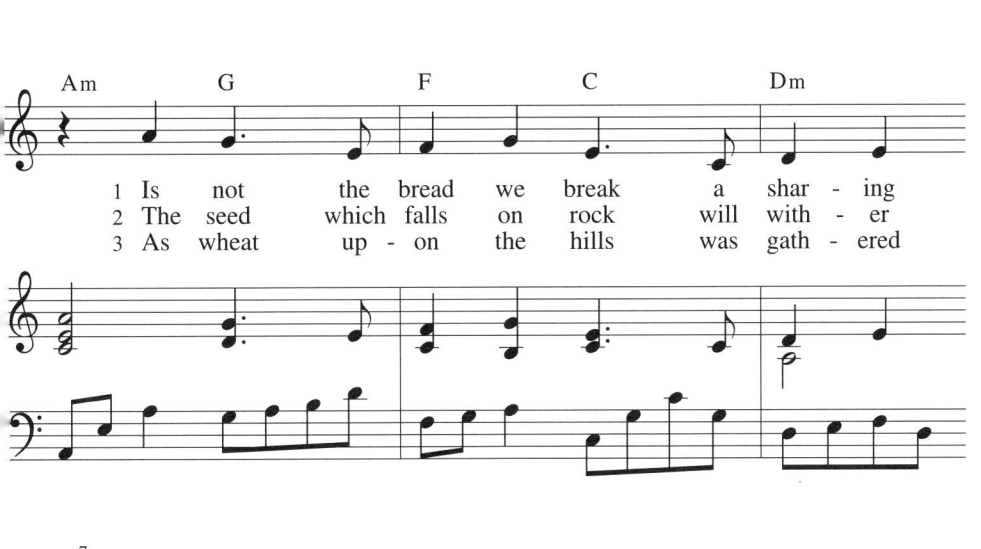

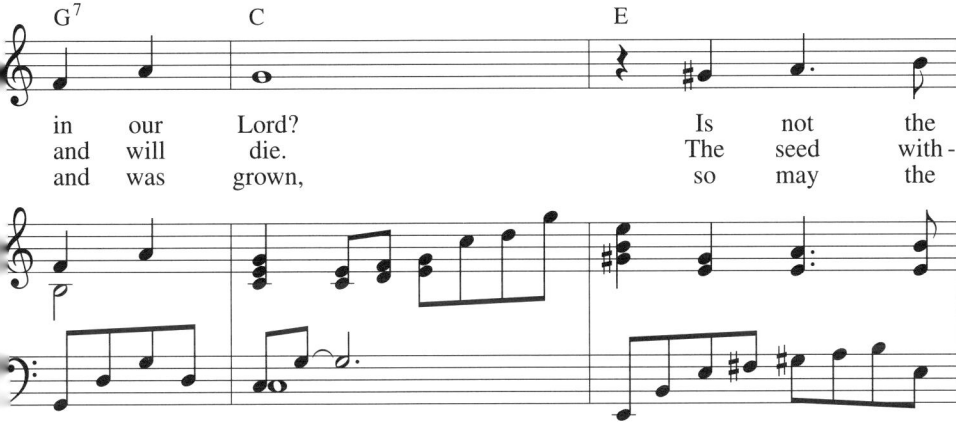

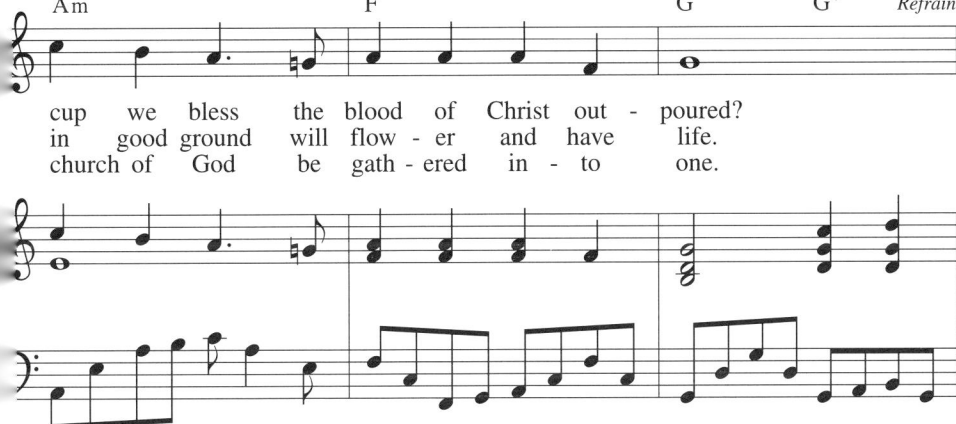

Am G F C Dm
1 Is not the bread we break a shar - ing
2 The seed which falls on rock will with - er
3 As wheat up - on the hills was gath - ered
G7 C E
in our Lord? Is not the
and will die. The seed with-
and was grown, so may the
Am F G G7 Refrain
cup we bless the blood of Christ out - poured?
in good ground will flow - er and have life.
church of God be gath - ered in - to one.

xt: Dan Feiten
isic: Dan Feiten; arr. Eric Gunnison and R. J. Miller

Seek ye first

122

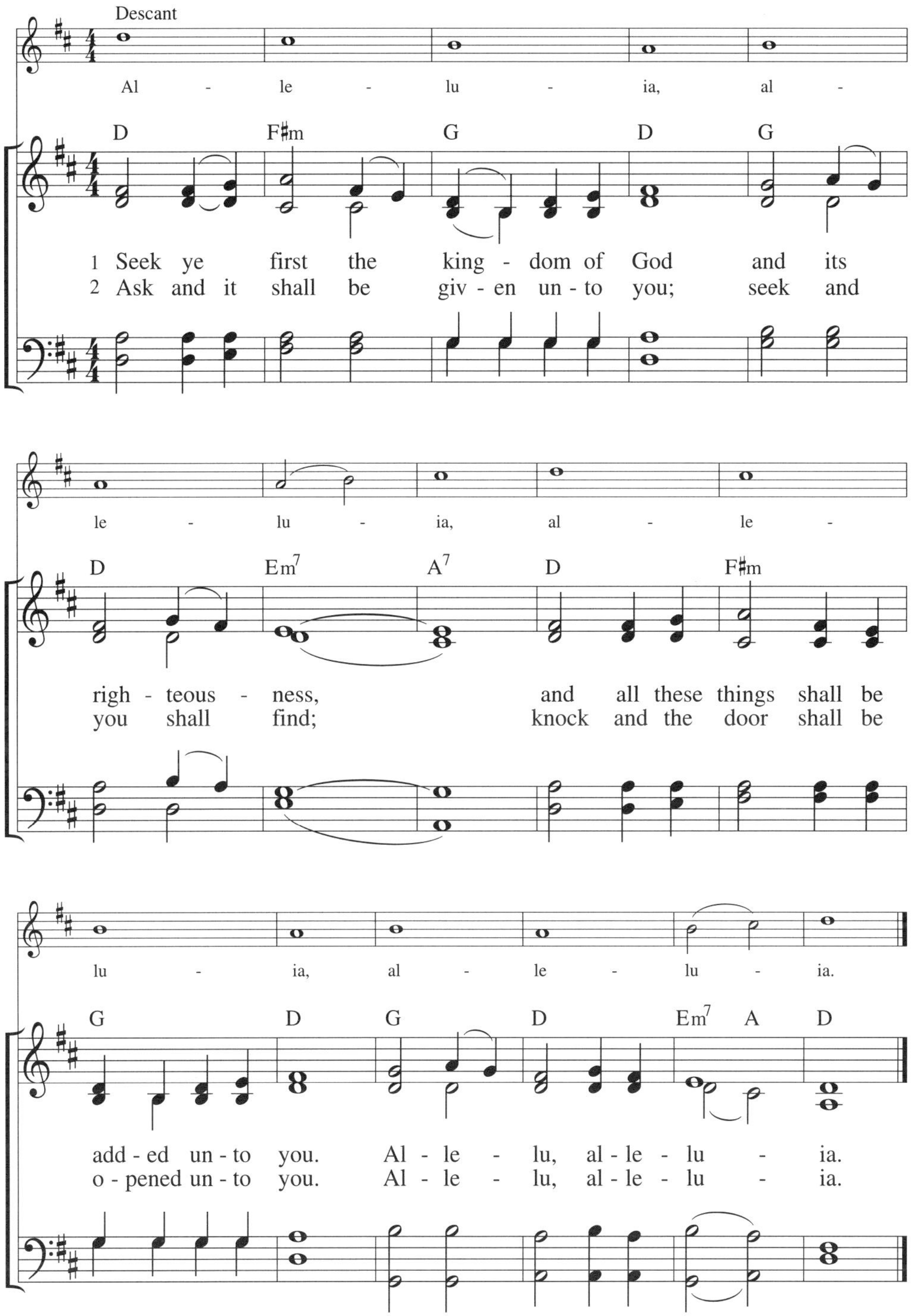

Descant
Al - le - lu - ia, al -
D F♯m G D G
1 Seek ye first the king - dom of God and its
2 Ask and it shall be giv - en un - to you; seek and
le - lu - ia, al - le -
D Em7 A7 D F♯m
righ - teous - ness, and all these things shall be
you shall find; knock and the door shall be
lu - ia, al - le - lu - ia.
G D G D Em7 A D
add - ed un - to you. Al - le - lu, al - le - lu - ia.
o - pened un - to you. Al - le - lu, al - le - lu - ia.

Text: Matthew 6:33, 7:7; adapt. Karen Lafferty
Music: Karen Lafferty

Shine, Jesus, shine

Refrain

Shine, Je-sus, shine, fill this land with the Fa-ther's glo-ry;

blaze, Spir-it, blaze, set our hearts on fire.

Flow, riv-er, flow, flood the na-tions with grace and mer-cy;

send forth your Word, Lord, and let there be light!

To stanzas | *Last time*

1 Lord, the light of your love is shin-ing, in the midst of the
2 As we gaze on your king-ly bright-ness, so our fac-es dis-

dark - ness, shin-ing; Je-sus, light of the world, shine up-on us,
play your like - ness, ev - er chang-ing from glo - ry to glo - ry,

set us free by the truth you now bring us.
mir - rored here, may our lives tell your sto - ry.

Shine on me, shine on me:
Shine on me, shine on me:

Refr

Text and music: Graham Kendrick
Text and music © 1989 Make Way Music, Ltd., admin. Integrity's Hosanna! Music

Shout to the Lord

My Je - sus, my Sav - ior, Lord, there is none like you.

All of my days I want to praise the won - ders of your might - y love. My com - fort, my shel - ter,

tow - er of ref - uge and strength; let ev - 'ry breath,

all that I am nev - er cease to wor - ship you.

Shout to the Lord, all the earth; let us sing

pow - er and maj - es - ty, praise to the King.

Moun - tains bow down and the seas will roar at the sound of your

name. I sing for joy at the work of your hands; for -

ev - er I'll love you, for - ev - er I'll stand.

Noth - ing com - pares to the prom - ise I have in you.

Text and music: Darlene Zschech
Text and music © 1993 Darlene Zschech/Hillsongs Australia, admin. Integrity Music, Inc.

Sing a new song

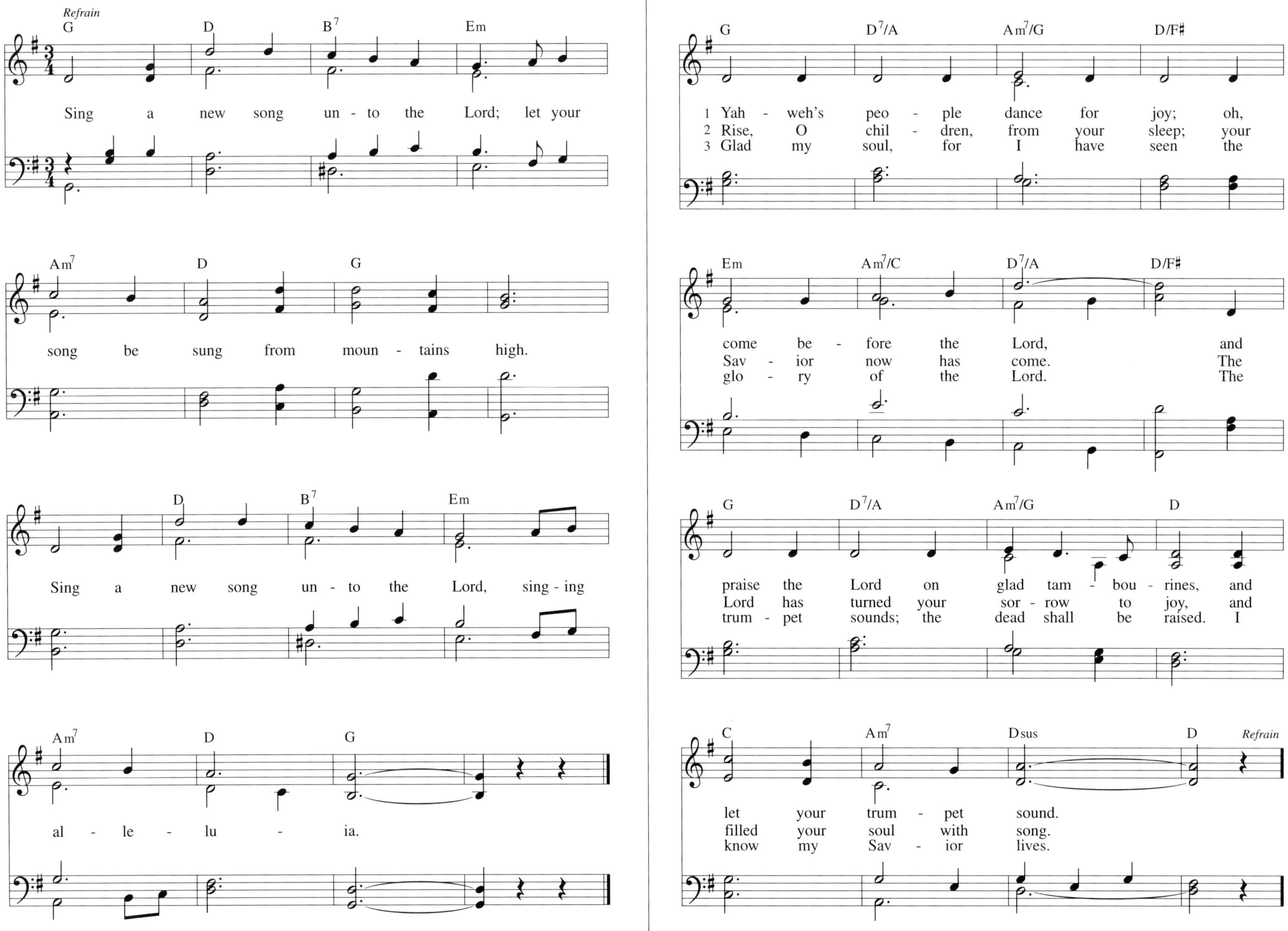

Sing a new song un-to the Lord; let your

1 Yah - weh's peo - ple dance for joy; oh,
2 Rise, O chil - dren, from your sleep; your
3 Glad my soul, for I have seen the

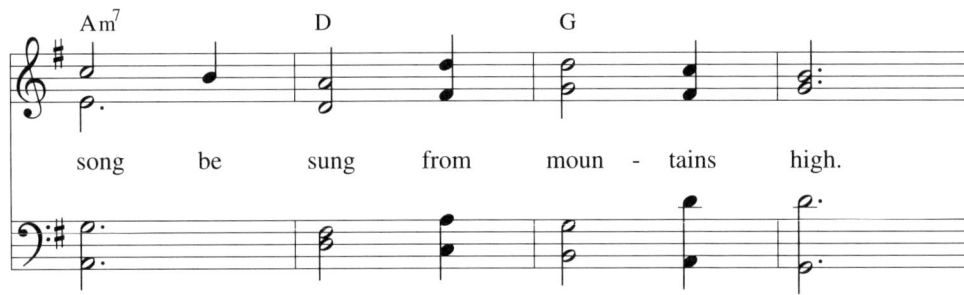

song be sung from moun - tains high.

come be - fore the Lord, and
Sav - ior now has come. The
glo - ry of the Lord. The

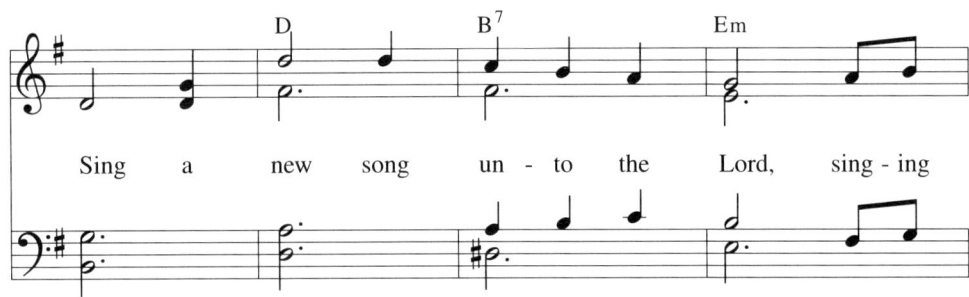

Sing a new song un-to the Lord, sing-ing

praise the Lord on glad tam - bou - rines, and
Lord has turned your sor - row to joy, and
trum - pet sounds; the dead shall be raised. I

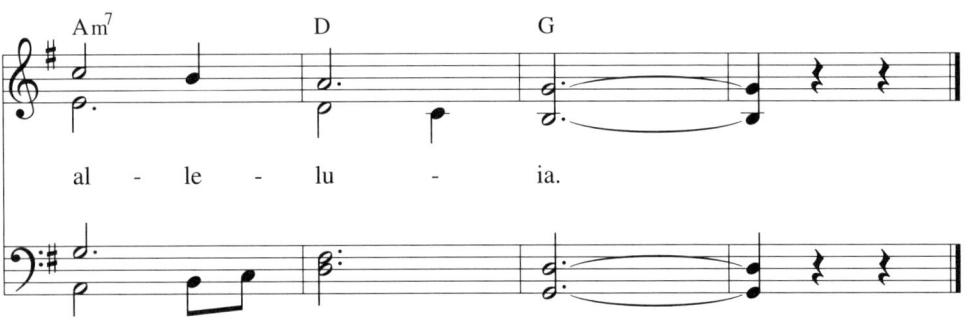

al - le - lu - ia.

let your trum - pet sound.
filled your soul with song.
know my Sav - ior lives.

Text and music: Daniel Schutte
Text and music © 1972, 1974 Daniel Schutte, admin. New Dawn Music

Sing out, earth and skies

Leader

1 Come, O God of all the earth: come to us, O
2 Come, O God of wind and flame: fill the earth with
3 Come, O God of flash-ing light: twin-kling star and
4 Come, O God of snow and rain: show-er down up -
5 Come, O Jus-tice, come, O Peace: come and shape our

Leader

Righ - teous One; come, and bring our love to birth:
righ - teous - ness; teach us all to sing your name:
burn - ing sun; God of day and God of night:
on the earth; come, O God of joy and pain:
hearts a - new; come and make op - pres - sion cease:

All

in the glo - ry of your Son.
may our lives your love con - fess.
in your light we all are one.
God of sor - row, God of mirth.
bring us all to life in you.

Refrain

Sing out, earth and skies! Sing of the God who

loves you! Raise your joy - ful cries!

Dance to the life a - round you!

Text and music: Marty Haugen
Text and music © 1985 GIA Publications

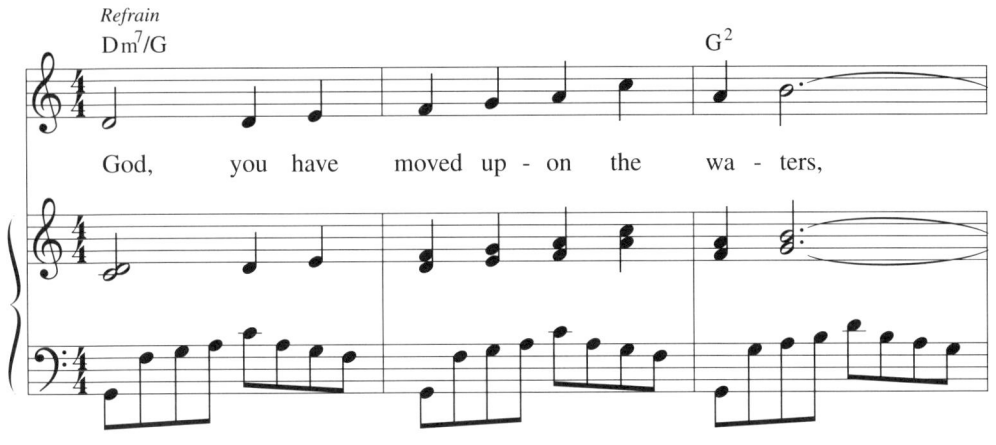

127 Song over the waters

Refrain
Dm7/G
G2
God, you have moved up - on the wa - ters,
Dm7/G
you have sung in the rush of wind and
G2
Dm7/G
flame; and in your love you have
G2
called us sons and daugh - ters: make us
Dm7/G
Last time to coda
G2
peo - ple of the wa - ter and your name.
Am7
1 Come fill our wait - ing hearts with the
2 Give us a thirst for love, give us a
3 You are the breath of life, you are the
4 Come, o - pen ev - 'ry heart, come now and
L.H.

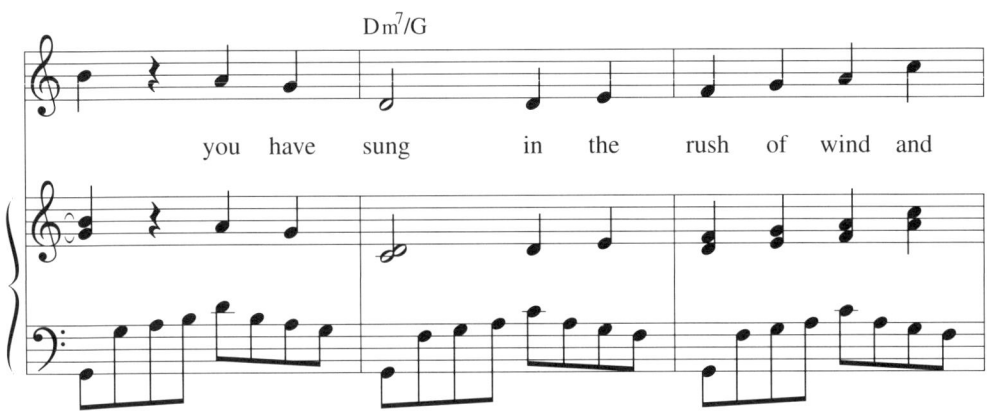

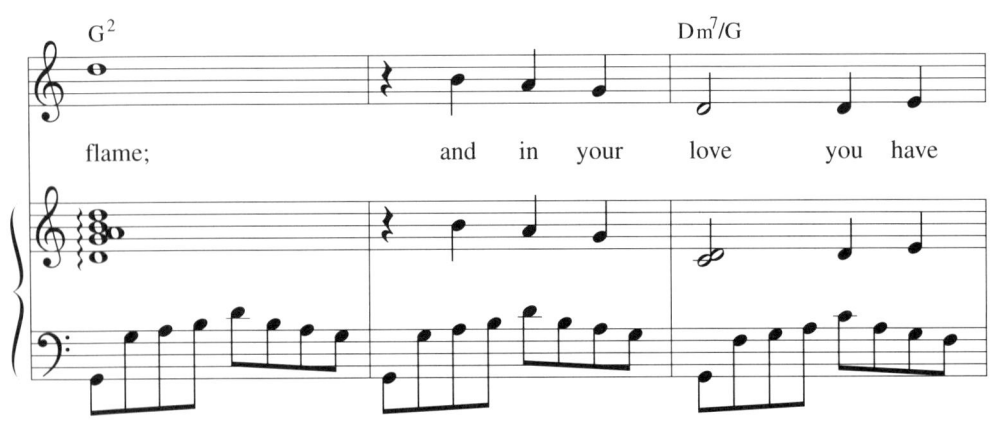

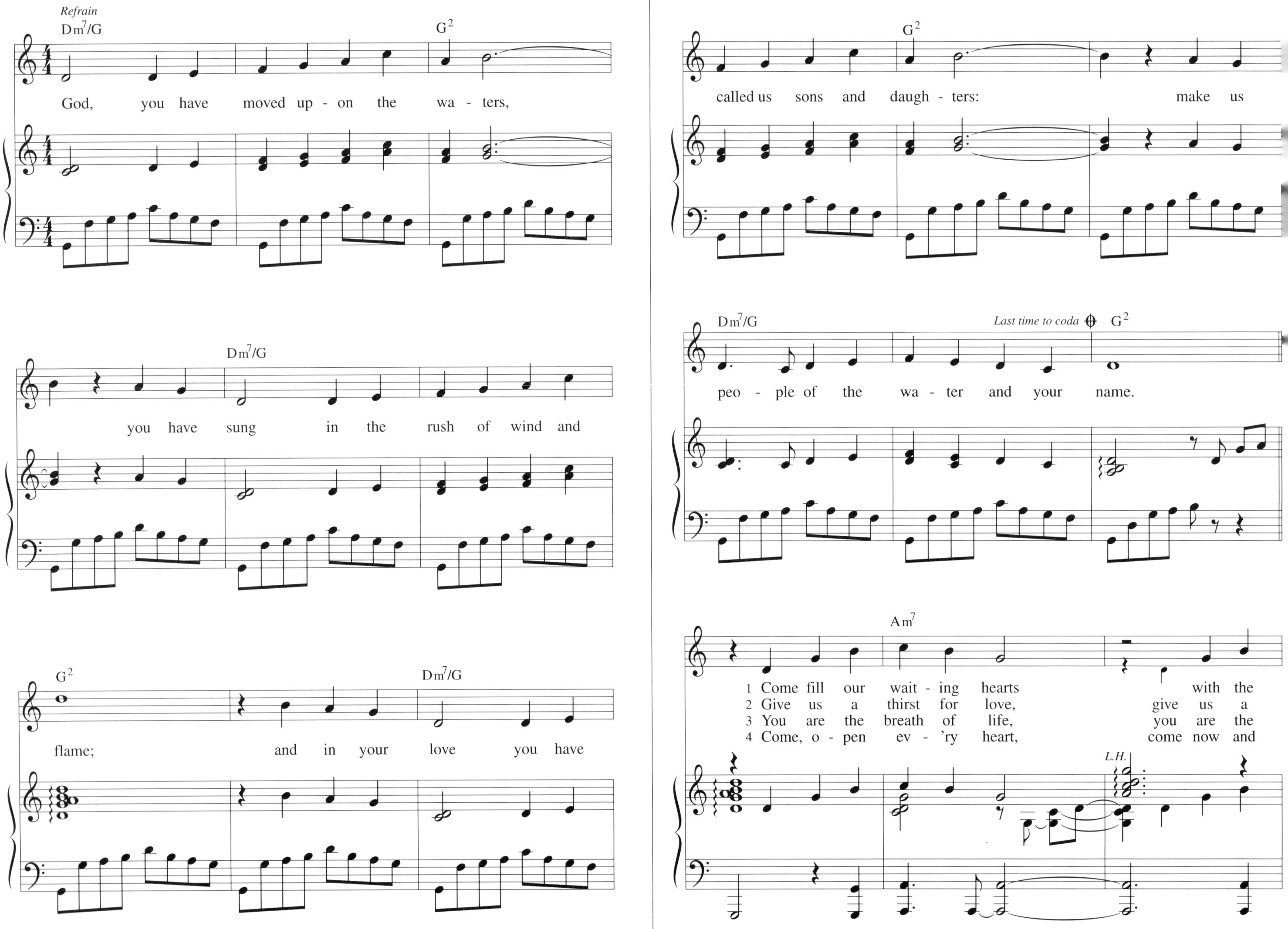

spir - it of Je - sus, let us shine with your
hun - ger for jus - tice, make us one with the
hope of the hope - less, come and fill us with
wake us to won - der, make us ves - sels of

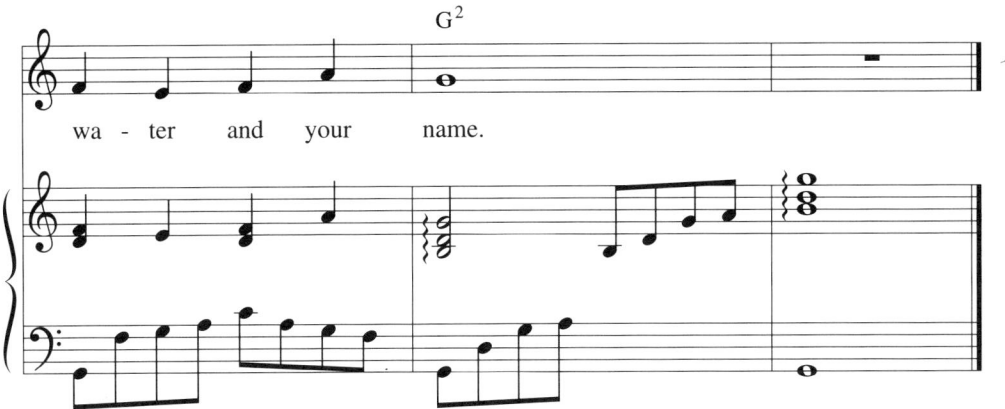

wa - ter and your name.

E♭   Dm7   G2   *Refrain*

light and peace.
mind of Christ.
light and peace.
light and peace.

Coda
G2   Dm7/G

name.   Make us peo - ple of the

Text and music: Marty Haugen
Text and music © 1987 GIA Publications

128 Soon and very soon

1 Soon and ver-y soon
2 No more cry-in' there,
3 No more dy-in' there,
4 Soon and ver-y soon

we are goin' to see the King,

soon and ver-y soon
no more cry-in' there,
no more dy-in' there,
soon and ver-y soon

we are goin' to see the King,

soon and ver-y soon
no more cry-in' there,
no more dy-in' there,
soon and ver-y soon

we are goin' to see the King.

Hal-le-lu-jah, hal-le-lu-jah, we're goin' to see the King!

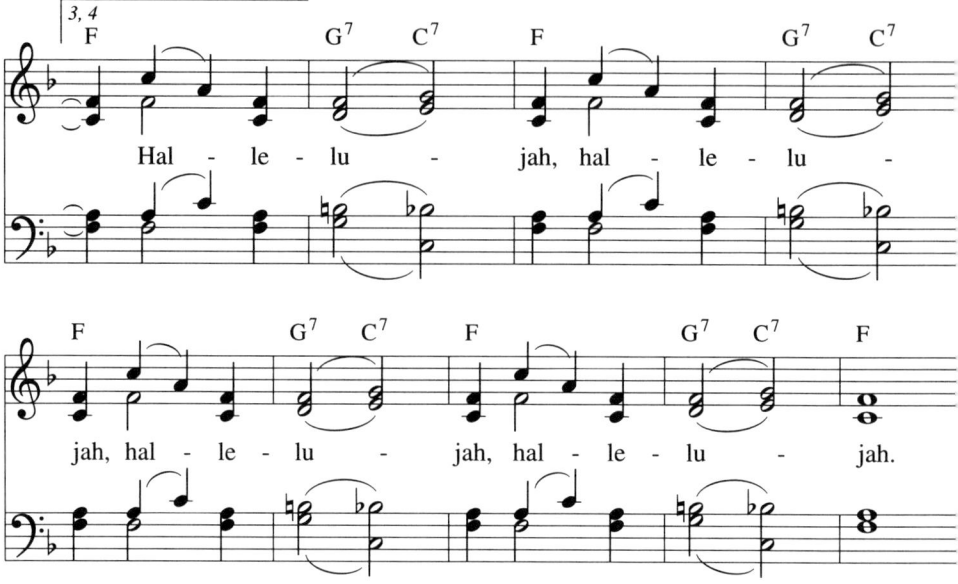

Hal - le - lu - jah, hal - le - lu -

jah, hal - le - lu - jah, hal - le - lu - jah.

Text and music: Andraé Crouch
Text and music © 1976 Bud John Songs, Inc./Crouch Music, admin. EMI Christian Music Publishing

Spirit of the living God

129

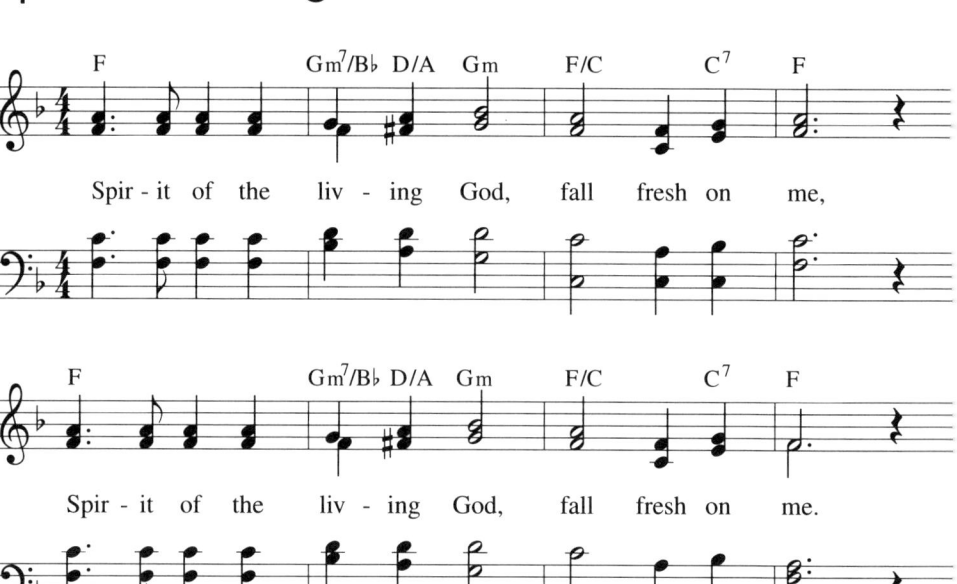

Spir - it of the liv - ing God, fall fresh on me,

Spir - it of the liv - ing God, fall fresh on me.

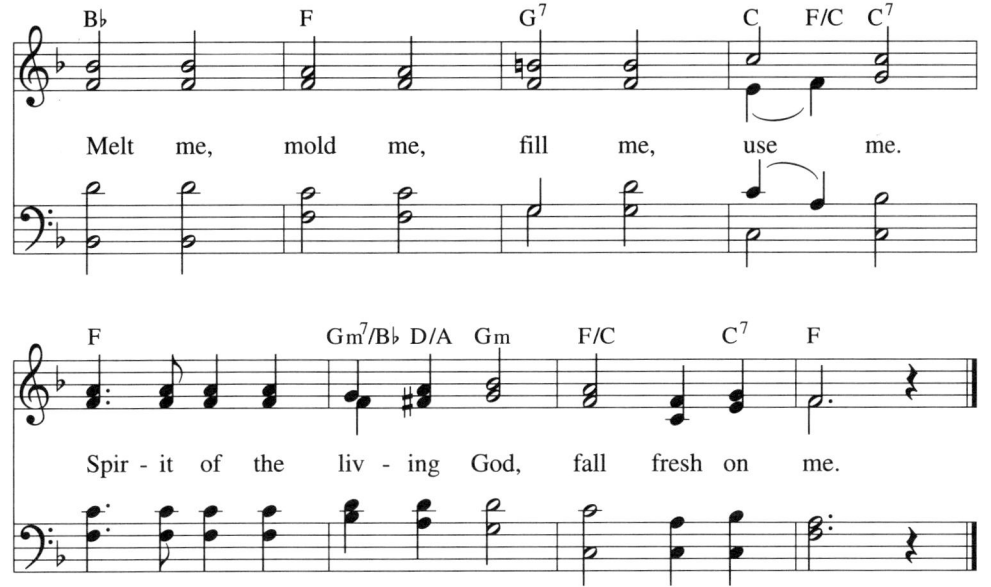

Text and music: Daniel Iverson
Text and music © 1935 Birdwing Music, admin. EMI Christian Music Publishing

130

Spirit song

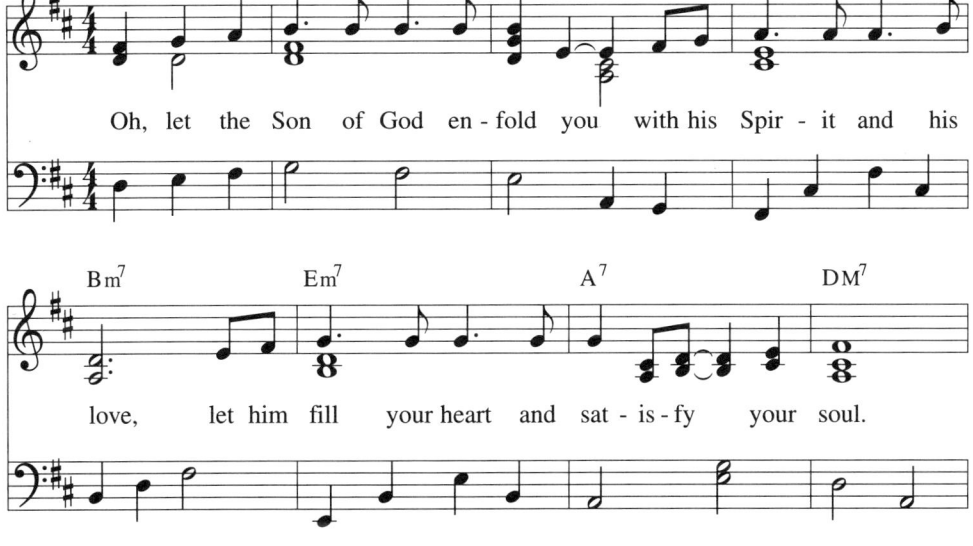

Text and music: John Wimber
Text and music © 1979 Mercy/Vineyard Publishing, admin. Music Services

Stand in the congregation

1 I will stand in the con-gre-ga - tion and I will ex-
2 I will stand in the con-gre-ga - tion and I will...
3 We will join as a con-gre-ga - tion and we will ex-

alt you; I will stand in the con-gre-ga-
praise your name; I will stand in the con-gre-ga-
alt you; we will join as a con-gre-ga-

- tion and I will ex - alt you. Let the
- tion and I will... praise your name. With your
- tion and we will ex - alt you. We will

chil-dren of your sal-va - tion lift their prais - es too!
peo-ple in ev-'ry na - tion I will shout this praise!
sing... as all cre-a - tion lifts the song a - new!

Hal - le - lu - jah!

Hal-le-lu - jah! Hal-le-lu - jah!

Hal-le-lu - jah! Hal-le-lu - jah!

Let the chil-dren of your sal-va - tion lift their prais-es too!

Hal - le - lu - jah!

Text and music: Bill Batstone
Text and music © 1988 Maranatha Praise, Inc., admin. The Copyright Company

Step by step

O God, you are my God, and I will ev-er praise

step by step you'll lead me, and I will fol-low you all of my

you. O God, you are my God, and

days. O days, and I will fol-low you all of my

I will ev-er praise you. I will seek you in the morn-

days, and I will fol-low you all of my days, and

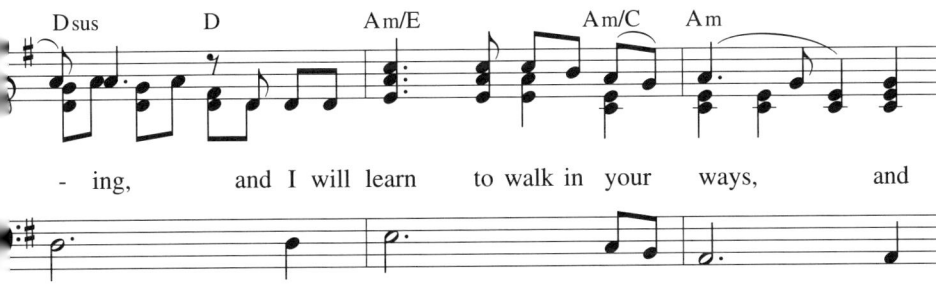

- ing, and I will learn to walk in your ways, and

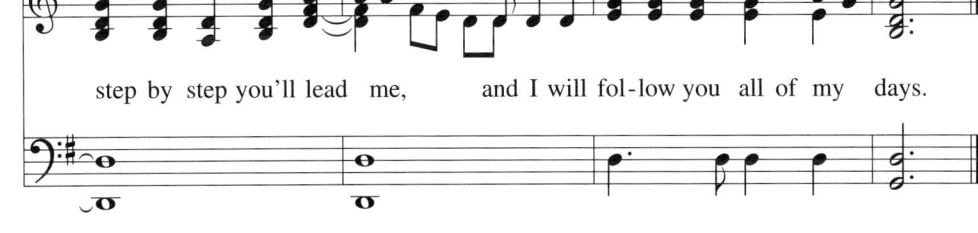

step by step you'll lead me, and I will fol-low you all of my days.

Text: Beaker
Music: Beaker; arr. Nylea Butler-Moore

That Christ be known

1 That Christ be known, we share in Word and wa - ter; with ev - 'ry
2 To make Christ known, we say the Word in sto - ry; with ev - 'ry
3 In hope we serve; we give our - selves in glad - ness; with ev - 'ry

sign of love and grace the faith is shown. We break the
tell - ing of our hope the faith is shown. We speak the
sac - ri - fi - cial act the faith is shown. We use our

bread and pass the cup for each and all, and in the
gos - pel, free and clear to each and all, and in the
gifts, em - brace the gifts of each and all, and in the

pres - ence of this love, the Christ is known.
mes - sage of God's love, the Christ is known.
liv - ing of our love, the Christ is known.

That we may be filled

Word and Spir-it bless us; through bread and wine re-fresh us that

Not as we ought but as we are a-ble, we

we may be filled, that we may be filled with

of-fer our thanks as we come to your ta-ble. Through

love.

Text: Handt Hanson and Paul Murakami
Music: Handt Hanson and Paul Murakami; arr. Henry Wiens
Text and music © 1991 Prince of Peace Publishing, Changing Church, Inc.

The church song

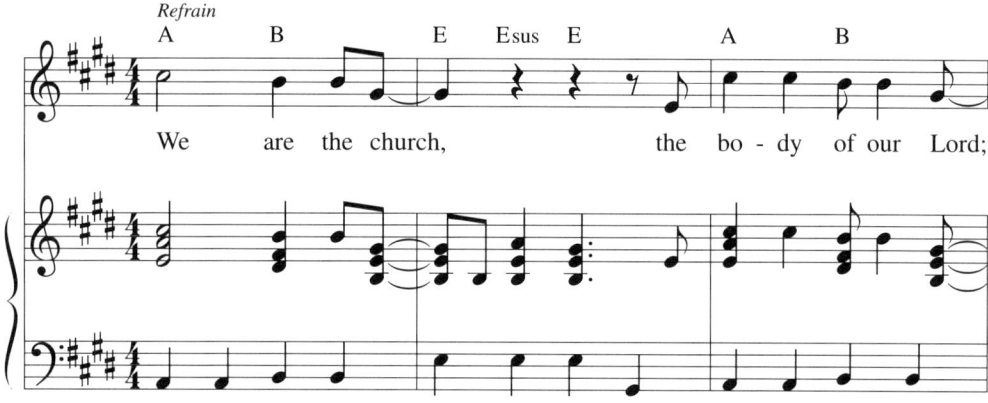

We are the church, the bo-dy of our Lord; we are all God's chil-dren.

To stanzas We have been re-stored. *Last time* We have been re-stored.

1 The church is not a build-ing when
2 You can go to wor-ship but you
3 The church is not a busi-ness, a com
4 The church, it is the peo-ple

peo-ple go to pray; it's not made out of stic
can-not go to church; you can't find a build-ing that
mit-tee or a board; it's not a cor-por-a
liv-ing out their lives, called, en-light-ened, san

and stones, it's not made out of clay.
a-live no mat-ter how you search.
-tion for the busi-ness of the Lord.
-ti-fied for the work of Je-sus Christ.

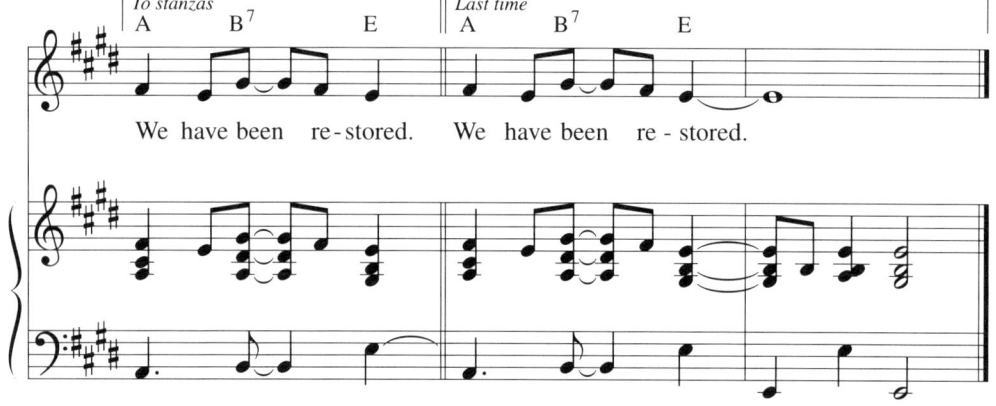

Text and music: Jay Beech
Text and music © 1988 Jay Beech

Refrain

The King of glo-ry comes, the na-tion re-joic-es.

O-pen the gates be-fore him, lift up your voic-es.

1 Who is the King of glo-ry; how shall we call him?
2 In all of Gal-i-lee, in cit-y or vil-lage,
3 Sing then of Da-vid's Son, our Sav-ior and broth-er;
4 He gave his life for us, the pledge of sal-va-tion;
5 He con-quered sin and death; he tru-ly has ris-en,

He is Em-man-u-el, the prom-ised of ag-es.
he goes a-mong his peo-ple, cur-ing their ill-ness.
in all of Gal-i-lee was nev-er an-oth-er.
he took up-on him-self the sins of the na-tion.
and he will share with us his heav-en-ly vi-sion.

: Willard F. Jabusch
sic: Israeli traditional, arr. *Worship & Praise*
© 1968, 1995 Willard F. Jabusch, admin. OCP Publications
© 1999 Augsburg Fortress

The summons

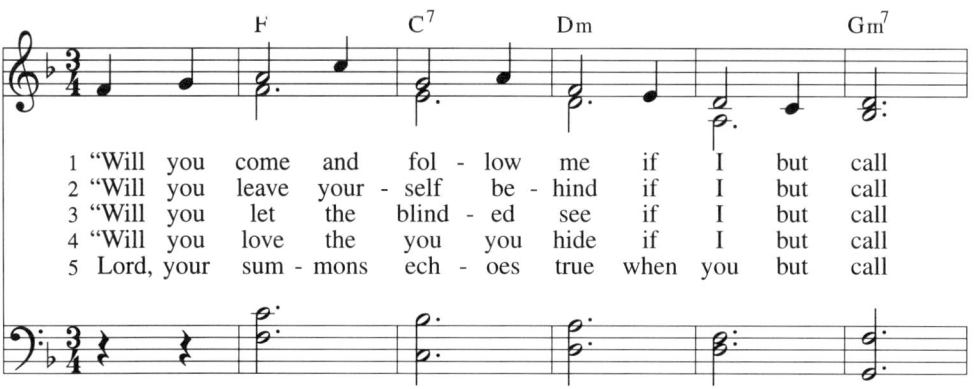

1 "Will you come and fol - low me if I but call
2 "Will you leave your - self be - hind if I but call
3 "Will you let the blind - ed see if I but call
4 "Will you love the you you hide if I but call
5 Lord, your sum - mons ech - oes true when you but call

Will you let my love be shown, will you let my
Will you risk the hos - tile stare, should your life at -
Will you kiss the lep - er clean, and do such as
Will you use the faith you've found to re - shape the
In your com - pa - ny I'll go where your love and

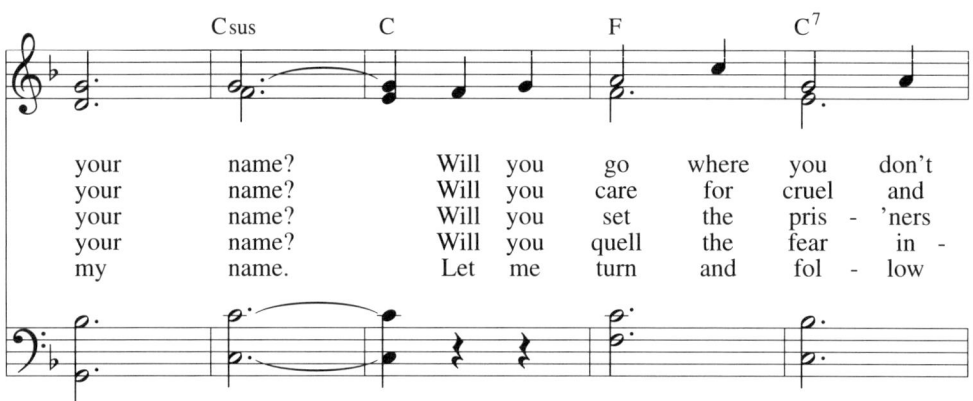

your name? Will you go where you don't
your name? Will you care for cruel and
your name? Will you set the pris - 'ners
your name? Will you quell the fear in -
my name. Let me turn and fol - low

name be known, will you let my life be
tract or scare? Will you let me an - swer
this un - seen, and ad - mit to what I
world a - round, through my sight and touch and
foot - steps show. Thus I'll move and live and

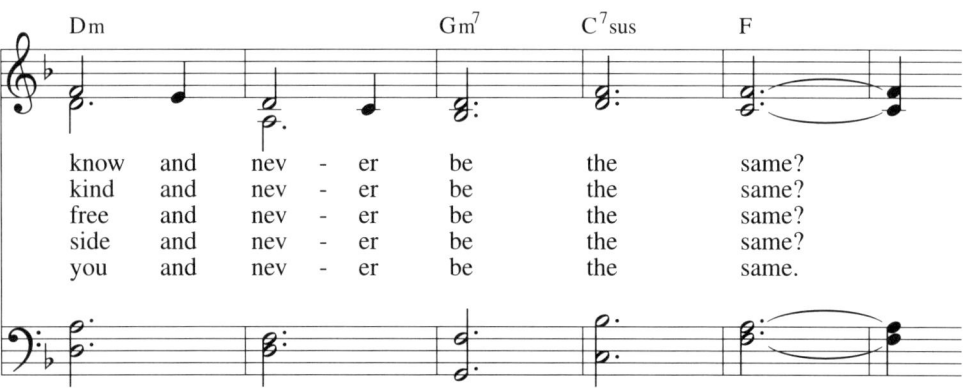

know and nev - er be the same?
kind and nev - er be the same?
free and nev - er be the same?
side and nev - er be the same?
you and nev - er be the same.

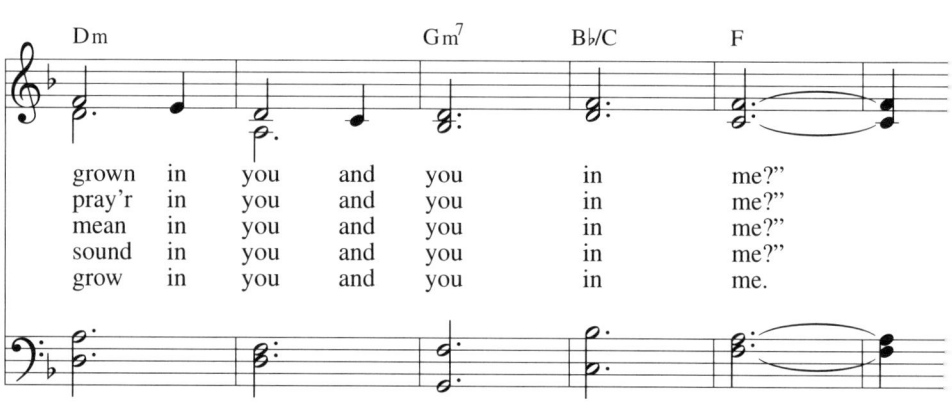

grown in you and you in me?"
pray'r in you and you in me?"
mean in you and you in me?"
sound in you and you in me?"
grow in you and you in me.

Text: John Bell
Music: Scottish traditional; arr. John Bell
Text and arr. © 1987 Iona Community, admin. GIA Publications

The trees of the field

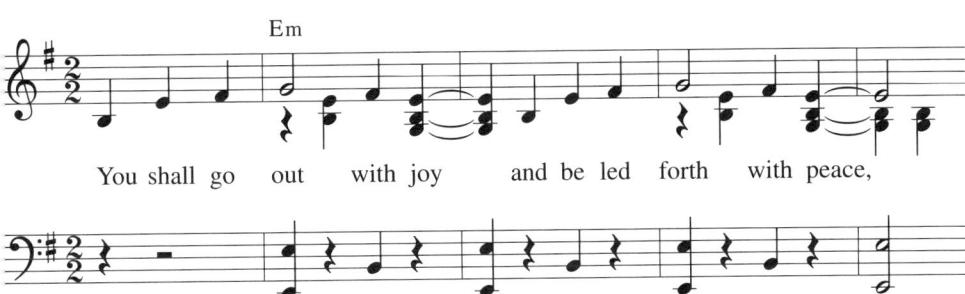

You shall go out with joy and be led forth with peace,

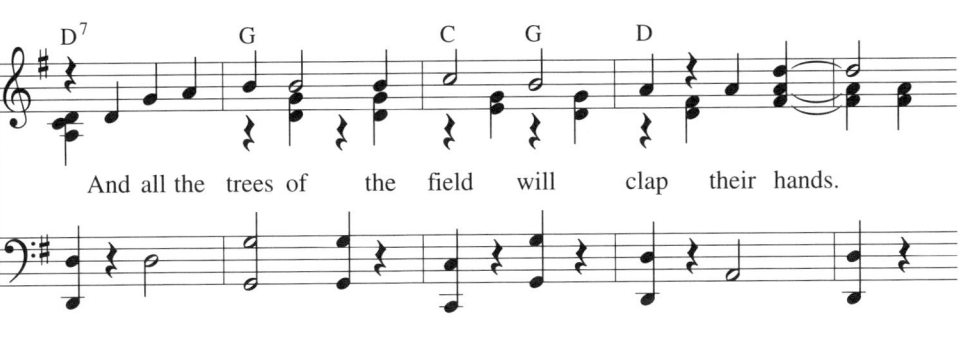

And all the trees of the field will clap their hands.

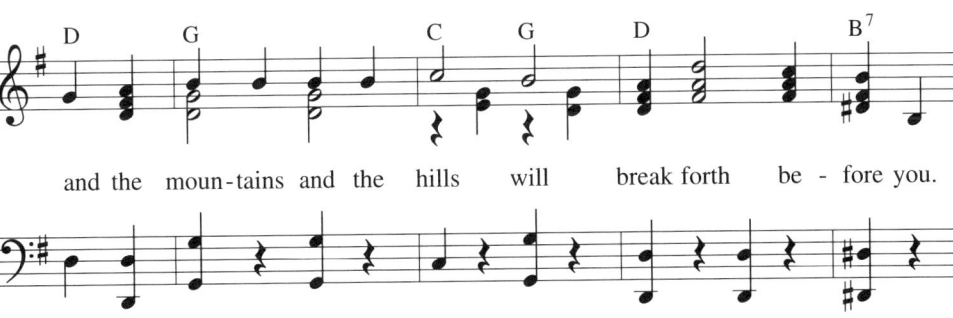

and the moun-tains and the hills will break forth be - fore you.

The trees of the field will clap their hands.

There'll be shouts of joy and all the trees of the field

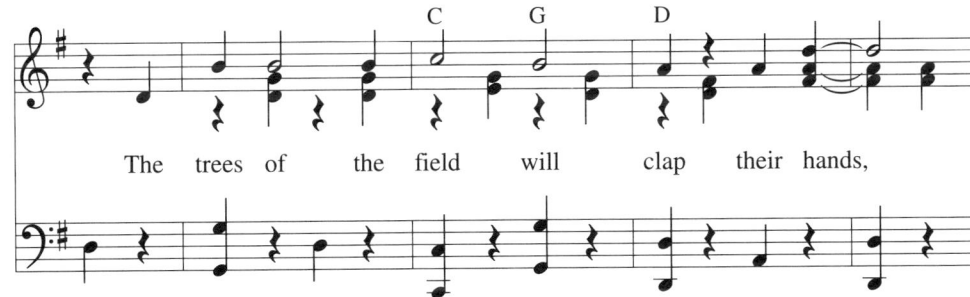

The trees of the field will clap their hands,

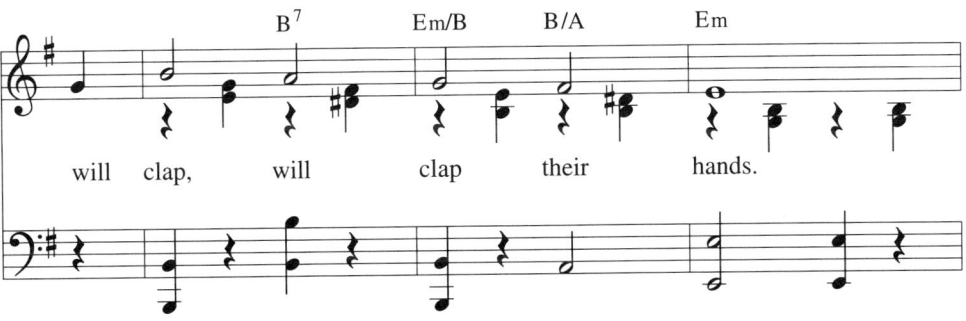

will clap, will clap their hands.

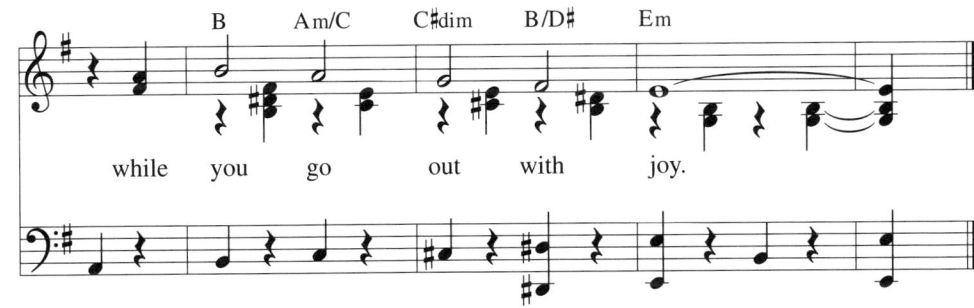

while you go out with joy.

Text: Steffi Geiser Rubin
Music: Stuart Dauermann

139 The trumpets sound, the angels sing

1 The trum-pets sound, the an - gels sing,
2 Ta - bles are la - den with good things;
3 The hun-gry heart he sat - is - fies,

the feast is read - y to be - gin.
oh, taste the peace and joy he brings.
of - fers the poor his par - a - dise.

The gates of heav'n are o - pen wide,
He'll fill you up with love di - vine;
Now hear all heav'n and earth ap - plaud

and Je - sus wel - comes you in - side.
he'll turn your wa - ter in - to wine.
the a - maz - ing good - ness of the Lord.

Refrain

Sing with thank - ful - ness songs of pure de - light.

Come and rev - el in heav - en's love and light.

Take your place at the ta - ble of the King.

The feast is read - y to be - gin;

Last time

the feast is read - y to be - gin.

Text and music: Graham Kendrick
Text and music © 1989 Make Way Music, admin. Integrity Music, Inc.

There is a Redeemer

1 There is a Re - deem - er, Je - sus, God's own Son,
2 Je - sus, my Re - deem - er, name a - bove all names,
3 When I stand in glo - ry, I will see his face;

pre - cious Lamb of God, Mes - si - ah, Ho - ly One.
pre - cious Lamb of God, Mes - si - ah, hope for sin - ners slain.
there I'll serve my king for - ev - er, in that ho - ly place.

Refrain

Thank you, O my Fa - ther, for giv - ing us your Son and

send - ing your Spir - it till the work on earth is done.

Text and music: Keith Green

Text and music © 1982 Birdwing Music/Cherry Lane Music Publishing Co., Inc., admin. by EMI Christian Music Publishing

This is the day

This is the day, this is the day that the Lord has made, that the

Lord has made; we will re - joice, we will re - joice and be

glad in it, and be glad in it. This is the day that the

Lord has made; we will re - joice and be glad in it.

This is the day, this is the day that the Lord has made.

Text: Psalm 118:24
Music: Les Garrett
Music © 1967, 1980 Scripture in Song, a division of Integrity Music, Inc.

Refrain

This is the feast of vic - to - ry for our God. Al - le - lu - ia.

This is the feast of vic - to - ry. This is the feast of vic -

- to - ry for our God. Al - le - lu -

- ia, al - le - lu - ia.

1 Wor - thy is Christ, the Lamb who was slain, whose blood set us free to be peo -

- ple of God. Pow - er, rich - es, wis - dom, and strength,

hon - or and bless - ing, and glo - ry are his.

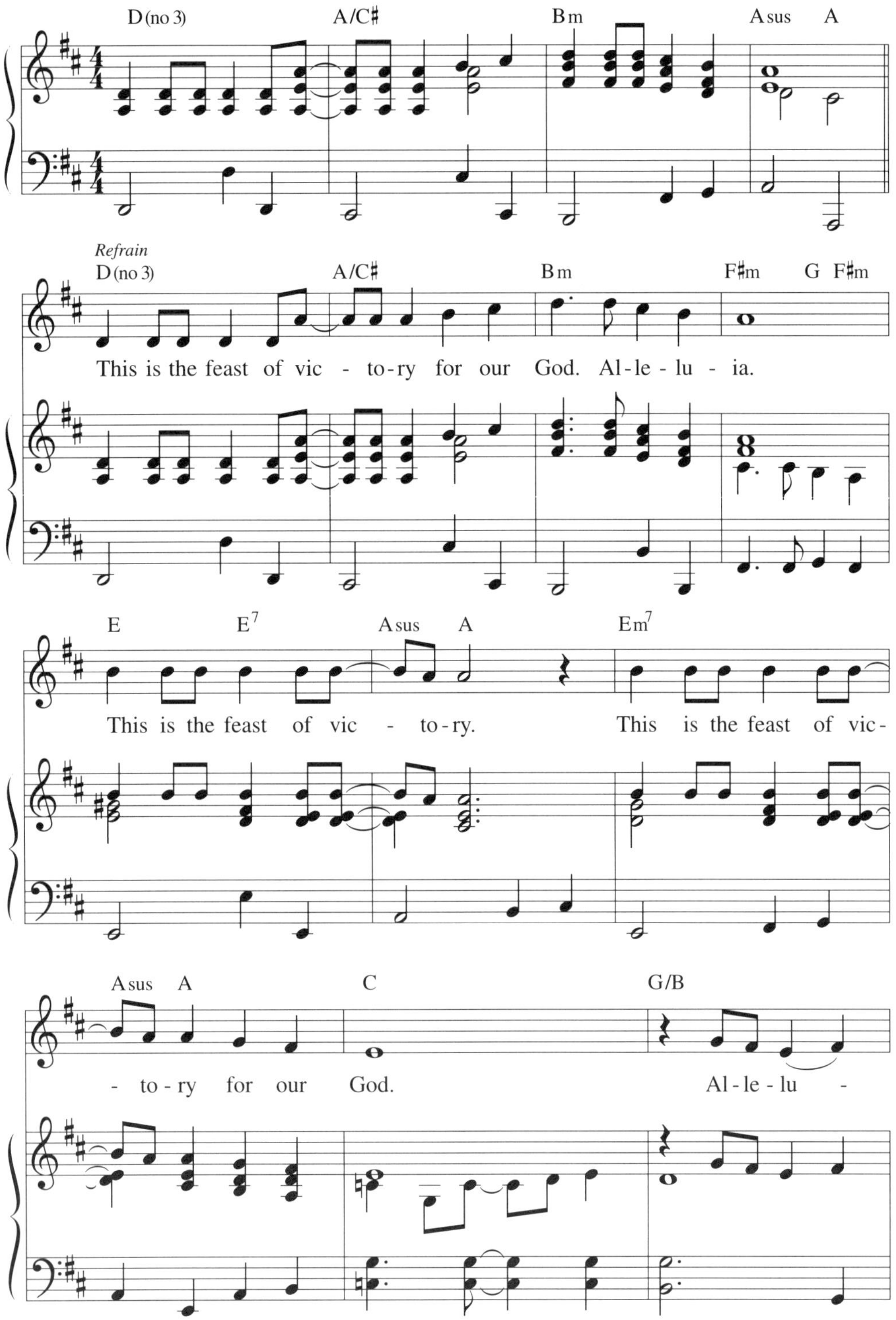

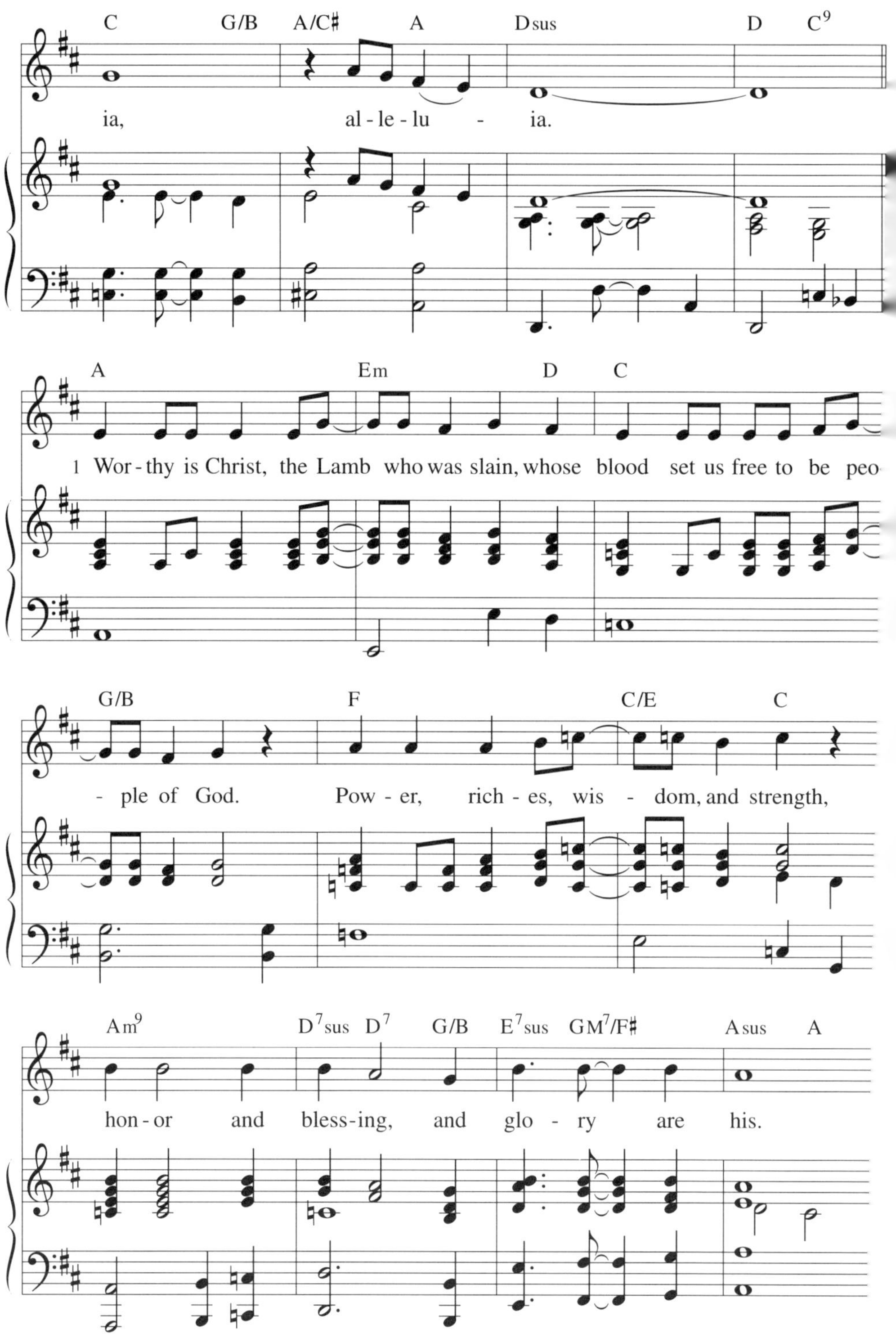

Refrain
D(no 3) A/C♯ Bm F♯m G F♯m
This is the feast of vic - to-ry for our God. Al-le-lu - ia.
E E7 Asus A Em7
This is the feast of vic - to-ry. This is the feast of vic-
Asus A C G/B
- to-ry for our God. Al-le-lu -
C G/B A/C♯ A Dsus D C9
ia, al-le-lu - ia.

A Em C
2 Sing with all the peo - ple of God, and join in the hymn of all cre -
G/B C G/B F C/E C
a - tion: Bless-ing, hon - or, glo - ry, and might
Am9 Dsus D G/B Am7
be to God and the Lamb for - ev - er and
Esus E/F♯ G♯m7(♭5) Asus A7
ev - er. A - men.

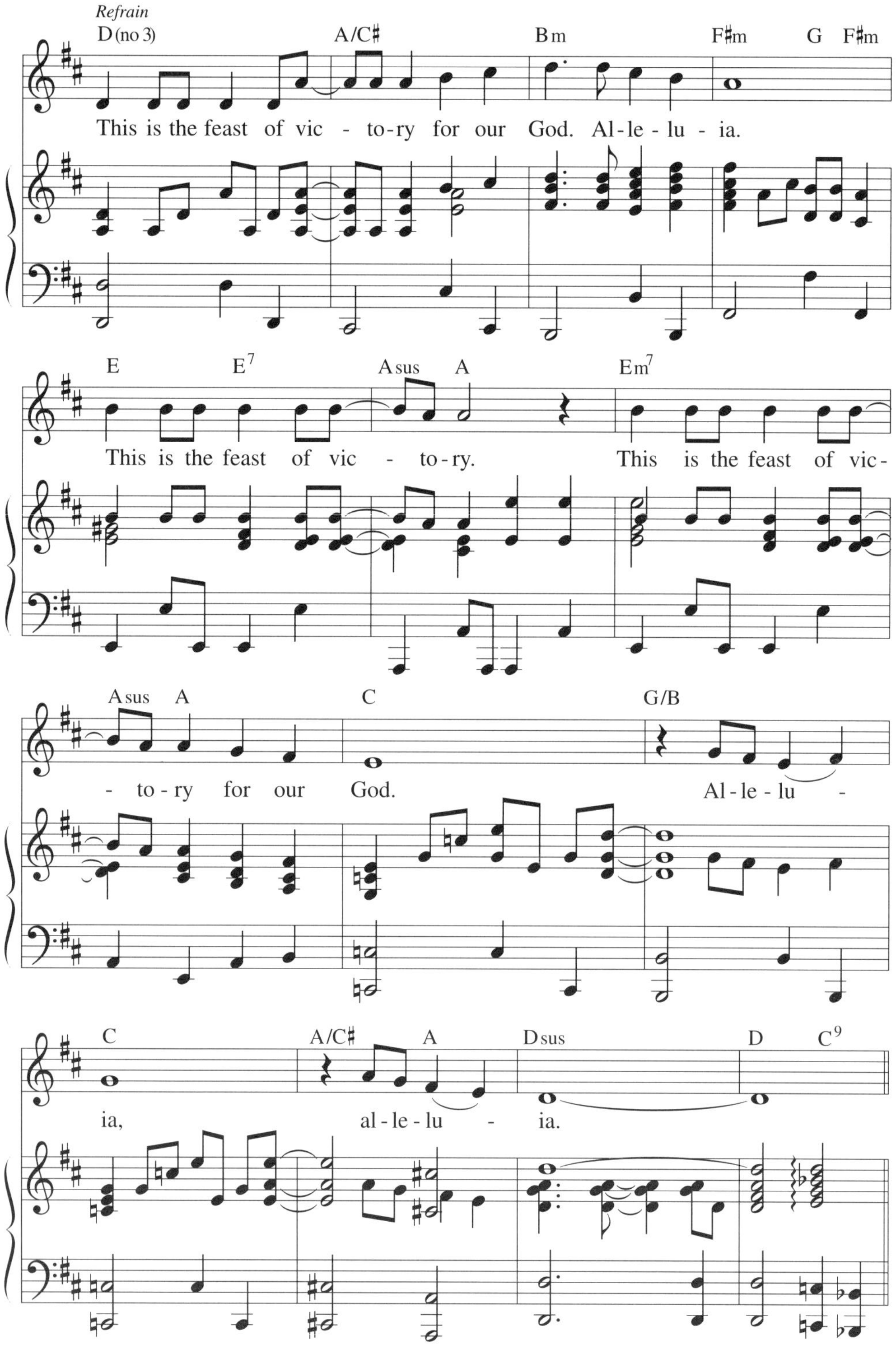

Refrain

This is the feast of vic-to-ry for our God. Al-le-lu-ia.

This is the feast of vic-to-ry. This is the feast of vic-

-to-ry for our God. Al-le-lu-

ia, al-le-lu-ia.

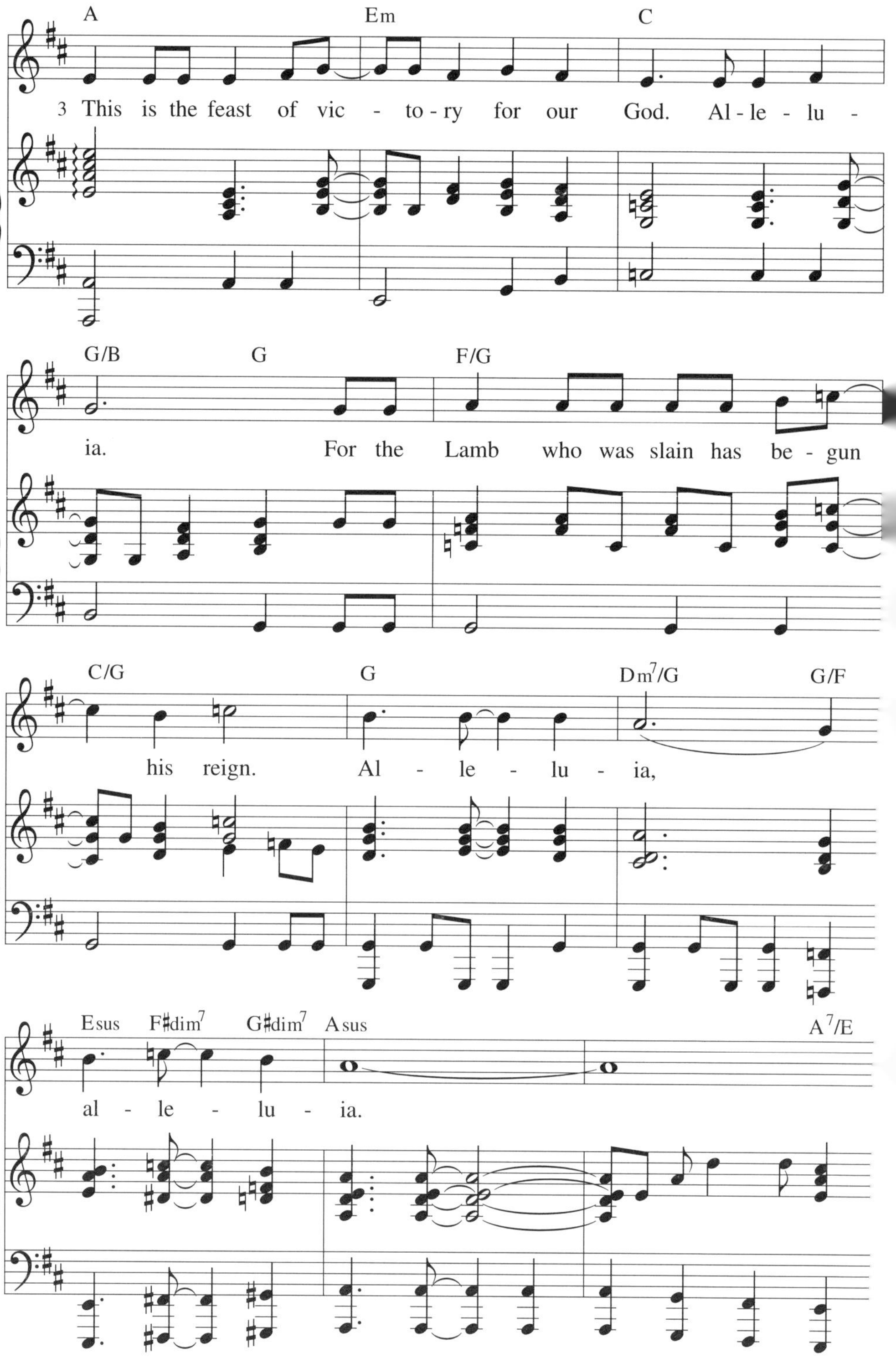

3 This is the feast of vic-to-ry for our God. Al-le-lu-

ia. For the Lamb who was slain has be-gun

his reign. Al-le-lu-ia,

al-le-lu-ia.

Text: John W. Arthur
Music: Jeremy Young
Text © 1978 *Lutheran Book of Worship*; music © 1999 Augsburg Fortress

143 Thy word

Text: Psalm 119:105
Music: Richard Webb
Music © 1998 Richard Webb, admin. Faith Inkubators

Thy word

Thy word is a lamp un-to my feet and a light un-to my path.

1 When I feel a - fraid, think I've lost my way,
2 I will not for - get your love for me, and yet my

still you're there right be - side me, and noth-ing will I fear as
heart for - ev - er is wan - der - ing. Je - sus, be my guide and

long as you are near. Please be near me to the end.
hold me to your side, and I will love you to the end.

...m 119:105, refrain; Michael W. Smith, stanzas
...my Grant
...usic © 1984 Meadowgreen Music, admin. EMI Christian Music Publishing; and Bug and Bear Music, admin. Word Music, Inc.

Waterlife

F² C Dm⁷sus | F C Dm⁷sus

1 Be-
2 A
3 My

F² C Dm⁷sus | F² C Dm⁷

fore I can re-mem-ber   the cov-e-nant was sealed   with
sim-ple sweet be-gin-ning,   a lov-ing place to start:
hope and ex-pec-ta-tion   for true com-mun-i-ty be-

F² C Dm⁷sus | F² C Dm⁷

Fa-ther, Son, and Spir-it,   in wa-ter was re-vealed. The
Christ be-gan the sing-ing   that swells with-in my heart. His
gins with res-ur-rec-tion,   his death and life in me. His

Gm F#aug Gm/F Bb/C

cleans-ing was for cer-tain,   with wa-ter and the Word;
love be-came my call-ing,   his life my min-is-try.
Spir-it fills the Bod-y: his church through wa-ter sees

F² C Dm⁷ | F² C Dm⁷sus

gen-tle words were spo-ken,   in heav-en they were heard.
name is my a-dop-tion   in-to his fam-i-ly.
prom-ise for to-mor-row,   his wa-ter-life in me.

Refrain

Dm⁷sus F/G Gm⁷ F/C Bb/C

They were sing-ing wa-ter-life,   be-gin-ning life,

wa-ter-life,   all   my life,   wa-ter-life,   Spir-

- it life,   wa - ter - life.

wa-ter-life,   wa-ter-life.

: Handt Hanson

sic: Handt Hanson, arr. Henry Wiens

and music © 1991 Prince of Peace Publishing, Changing Church, Inc.

We are an offering

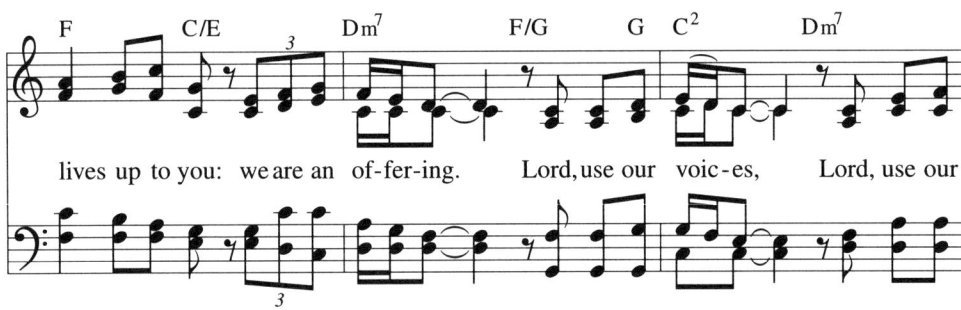

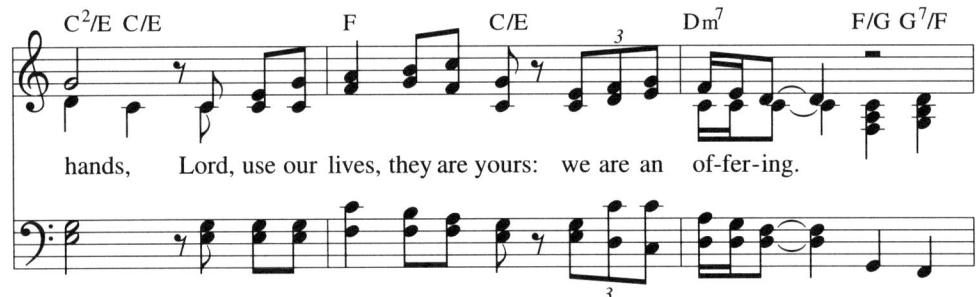

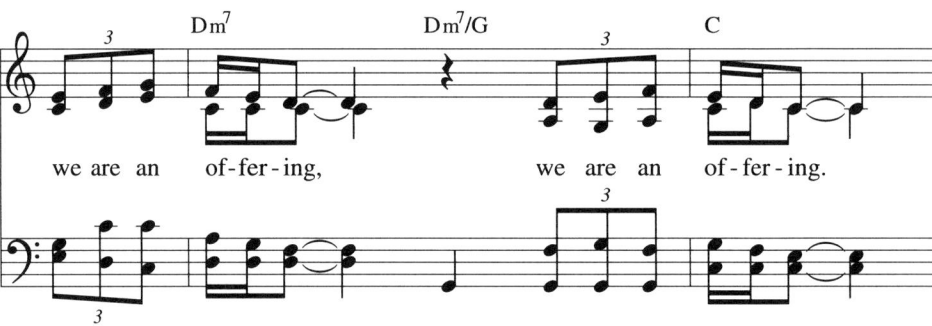

Text and music: Dwight Liles
Text and music © 1984 Bug and Bear Music, admin. Word Music, Inc.

We are called

G G/B C C/D D

1 Come! Live in the light!
2 Come! O - pen your heart!
3 Sing! Sing a new song!

Am7 G/B C C/D D

live in the free - dom of the cit - y of God.
ha - tred and blind - ness . . . will be . . . no more.
sis - ters and broth - ers . . . . u - nit - ed in love.

G G/B C D D/F#

Shine with the joy and the love of the Lord! We are
Show your . . . mer - cy to all those in fear! We are
Sing of that great day when all will be one! God will

Refrain
Am9 G/B C D D/F# C/G D/G G G/B

We are called to act with jus - tice, we are

Em Em7/D C G/B

called to be light for the king - dom, to
called to be hope for the hope - less so all
reign, and we'll walk with each oth - er as

C D Em Em7/D G/B C

called to love ten - der - ly; we are called to

serve one an - oth - er, to walk

hum - bly with God.

Text and music: David Haas
Text and music © 1988 GIA Publications

We are marching in the light of God

Siyahamba

We are march - ing in the light of God, we are march-ing in the
Si - ya - hamb' e - ku - kha - nyen' kwen-khos', si - ya - hamb' e - ku - kha-

light of God. We are march - ing in the light of God,
nyen' kwen-khos'. Si - ya - hamb' e - ku - kha - nyen' kwen-khos',

we are march-ing in the light of God.
si - ya - hamb' e - ku - kha - nyen' kwen - khos'.

we are march-ing in the light of, the light of God.
si - ya - hamb' e - ku - kha - nyen' kwen-, kha - nyen' kwen - khos'.

we are march-ing in the light of God.
si - ya - hamb' e - ku - kha - nyen' kwen - khos'.

We are march - ing   oo
Si - ya - ham - ba   oo

We are march - ing, march - ing, we are march-ing,   march - ing,
Si - ya - ham - ba, ham - ba, si - ya - ham - ba,   ham - ba,

we are march - ing in the light of God.
si - ya - hamb' e - ku - kha - nyen' kwen - khos'.

we are march-ing in the light of, the light of God.
si - ya - hamb' e - ku - kha - nyen' kwen-, kha - nyen' kwen - khos'.

we are march - ing in the light of God.
si - ya - hamb' e - ku - kha - nyen' kwen - khos'.

We are march - ing   oo
Si - ya - ham - ba   oo

We are march - ing, march - ing, we are march-ing,   march - ing,
Si - ya - ham - ba, ham - ba, si - ya - ham - ba,   ham - ba,

we are march - ing in the light of God.
si - ya - hamb' e - ku - kha - nyen' kwen - khos'.

Additional stanzas ad lib:
We are dancing…
We are praying…
We are singing…

Text: South African
Music: South African

You are Lord of cre-a-tion and Lord of my life, Lord of the land and the
sea. You were Lord of the heav-ens be-fore there was time, and
Lord of all lords you will be. We bow down and we
wor-ship you, Lord; we bow down and we wor-ship you, Lord; we bow
down and we wor-ship you, Lord; Lord of all lords you will be.

We bring the sac-ri-fice of praise in-to the house of the
Lord; we bring the sac-ri-fice of praise in-to the
house of the Lord. And we of-fer up to
you the sac-ri-fic-es of thanks-giv-ing; and we
of-fer up to you the sac-ri-fic-es of joy.

We re-joice in the grace of God poured up-on our lives;

lov-ing-kind-ness has come to us be-

cause of Je - sus Christ. We re-joice in the

grace of God, our hearts o - ver - flow.

What a joy to know the grace of God!

In bro-ken bread and the cup that we share, we re-

mem-ber you. In bro-ken bread and the

cup that we share, we re-mem-ber you.

We re-mem-ber you, Je - sus. We re-

mem-ber your love for us. We re-mem-ber th

Text and music: Rick Founds
Text and music © 1988 Maranatha! Music, admin. The Copyright Company

153   We see the Lord

Text: anonymous, based on Isaiah 6:1, 3
Music: anonymous; arr. Betty Pulkingham
Arr. © 1971 CELEBRATION, admin. The Copyright Company

1 We will glo - ri - fy the King of kings, we will glo - ri - fy the Lamb;
2 Lord Je - ho - vah reigns in maj - es - ty, we will bow be - fore his throne;
3 He is Lord of heav - en, Lord of earth, he is Lord of all who live;
4 Hal - le - lu - jah to the King of kings, hal - le - lu - jah to the Lamb;

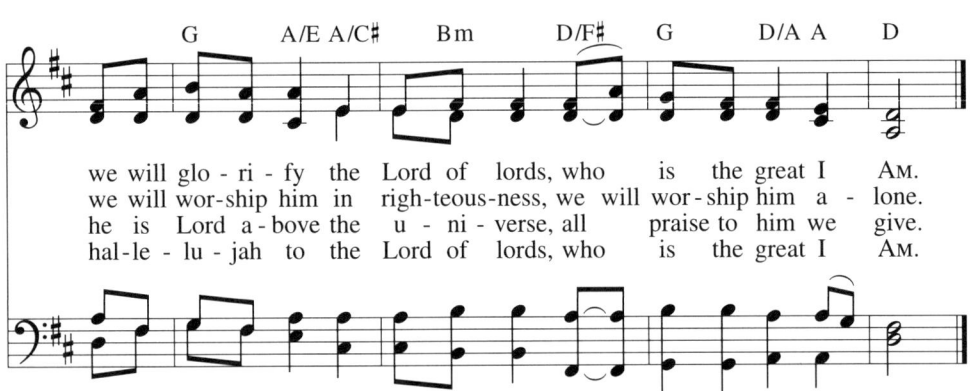

we will glo - ri - fy the Lord of lords, who is the great I AM.
we will wor - ship him in righ - teous - ness, we will wor - ship him a - lone.
he is Lord a - bove the u - ni - verse, all praise to him we give.
hal - le - lu - jah to the Lord of lords, who is the great I AM.

Text: Twila Paris
Music: Twila Paris; arr. David Allen
Text and music © 1982 Singspiration Music, a division of Brentwood-Benson Music Publishing

What a might - y Word God gives!

What a might - y Word God gives!

When he speaks, our faith is fed. Give us, Lord, our dai - ly bread.
God sent us the on - ly Son, who for us the vic - try's won.

What a might - y Word God gives!

Text: James Tallman
Music: anonymous
Text © 1996 James Tallman

What have we to offer?

1 What have we to of-fer? What have we to share?
2 What have we to of-fer? What have we to bring?
3 What have we to of-fer? What have we to give?

Coins from the cof-fer, hearts filled with care.
Love, ripe with laugh-ter; hope that we can sing;
Eyes that are wide o-pen; lies that we won't live;

God will not fal-ter; so let us dare
dreams of what we're af-ter; prom-is-es of when.
truth that must be spo-ken; jus-tice some-how.

lay it at the al-tar there.
Lay it at the al-tar then.
Lay it at the al-tar now.

4 What have we to of-fer? What have we to give?

Lives we will live.

Text and music: Ray Makeever
Text and music © 1982 Ray Makeever, admin. Augsburg Fortress

Wind of the Spir - it, move fresh as we wor - ship and

life is filled with mean-ing, and love is what we're breath-ing in the

wind of the Spir - it,

wind of the Spir - it.

fill us with hope ev - 'ry day.

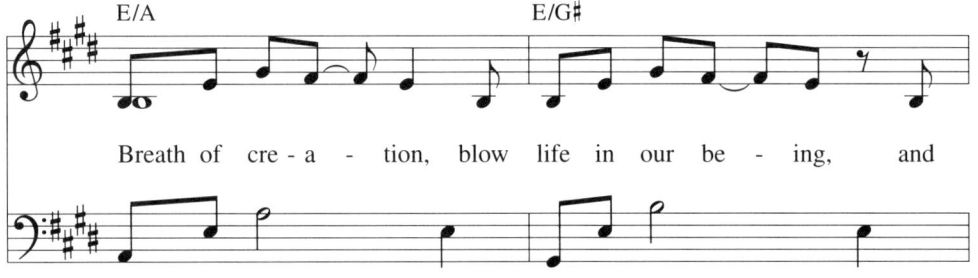

Breath of cre - a - tion, blow life in our be - ing, and

gift us with pur - pose, we pray; so our

Text: Handt Hanson and Paul Murakami
Music: Handt Hanson and Paul Murakami; arr. Henry Wiens

You are mine

A | D/A | A | E/G#

1 "I will come to you in the si - lence,
2 "I am hope for all who are hope - less,
3 "I am strength for all the des - pair - ing,
(4) am the Word that leads all to free - dom,
I

F#m⁷ | D | Esus | E

I will lift you from all your fear.
I am eyes for all who long to see.
heal - ing for the ones who dwell in shame.
am the peace the world can - not give.
(2) In the

A | D/A | C# | C#/E# | F#m

You will hear my voice, I claim you as my choice. Be
shad - ows of the night, I will be your light.
All the blind will see, the lame will all run free, and
I will call your name, em - brac - ing all your pain. Stand

Bm | A/C# | D | Esus | E | Esus | E

still and know I am here. *(To stanza 2)*
Come and rest in me. *(To refrain)*
all will know my name. *(To refrain)*
up, now walk and live! *(To refrain)*

Refrain
A | D/A | E/G# | F#m⁷ | D

Do not be a - fraid, I am with you. I have called you each by

Esus | E | A | D/A | E/G#

name. Come and fol - low me, I will bring you

home;   I   love you and you are   mine."

To stanzas | *Last time*

4 "I

Text and music: David Haas
Text and music © 1991 GIA Publications

159   You are my God

You are my God, I am your servant. You are my King, my Lord and Savior. You are my friend, my joy and comfort. You are my Lord, you are my God. Hear, hear the angels sing, all creation bring you the glory. And I will lift my heart in faith, lift my eyes to see you in holiness, in righteousness, in majesty; you are my God.

Text and music: Geoff Bullock and Gail Dunshea

Text and tune © 1992 Maranatha! Music, admin. Word Music
Arr. © 1997 Maranatha! Music, admin. Word Music

160   You are my hiding place

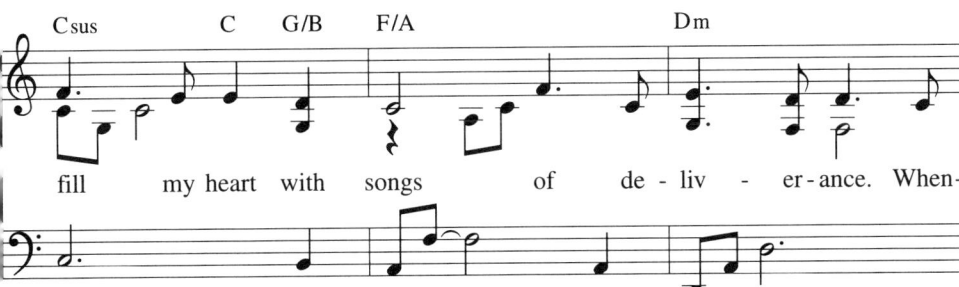

*may be sung in canon

Text and music: Michael Ledner
Text and music © 1981 Maranatha Praise, Inc., admin. The Copyright Company

You are the rock of my salvation
Rock of my salvation

You are the rock of my sal-va-tion,

you are the strength of my life. You are my hope and my in-

-spi-ra-tion; Lord, un-to you will I cry. I be-

lieve in you, be-lieve in you, for your faith-ful love to me.

You have been my help in time of need;

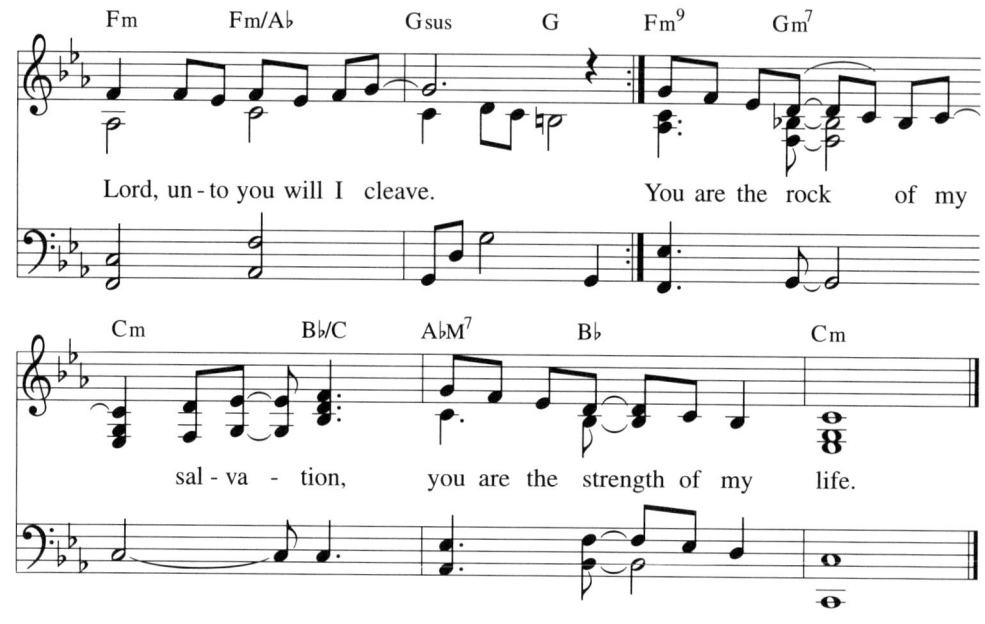

Lord, un-to you will I cleave. You are the rock of my

sal-va- tion, you are the strength of my life.

Text and music: Teresa Muller
Text and music © 1982 Maranatha! Music, admin. The Copyright Company

You, Lord

We stand here in awe be-fore you,

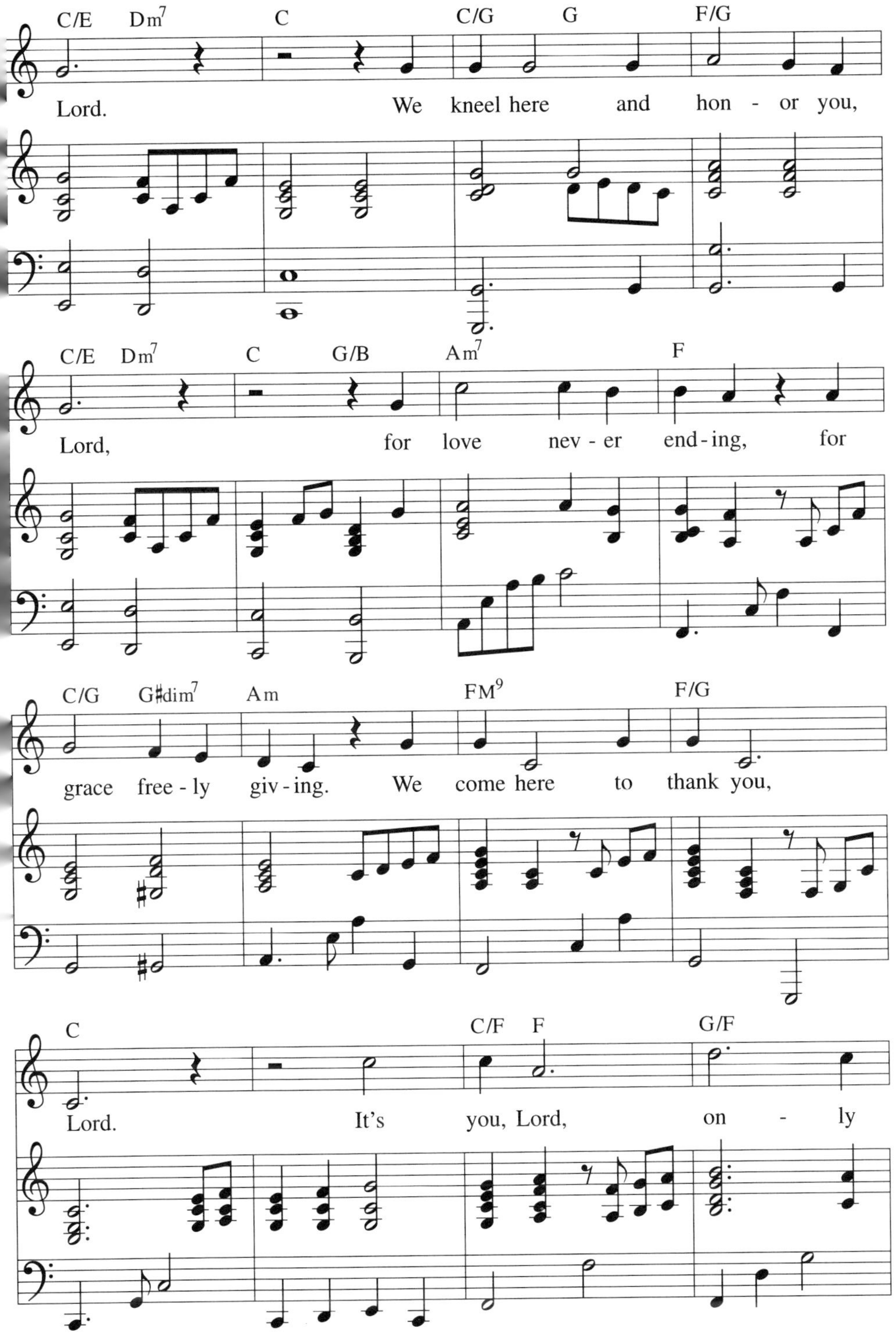
C/E Dm7 C C/G G F/G
Lord. We kneel here and hon - or you,
C/E Dm7 C G/B Am7 F
Lord, for love nev - er end - ing, for
C/G G♯dim7 Am FM9 F/G
grace free - ly giv - ing. We come here to thank you,
C C/F F G/F
Lord. It's you, Lord, on - ly

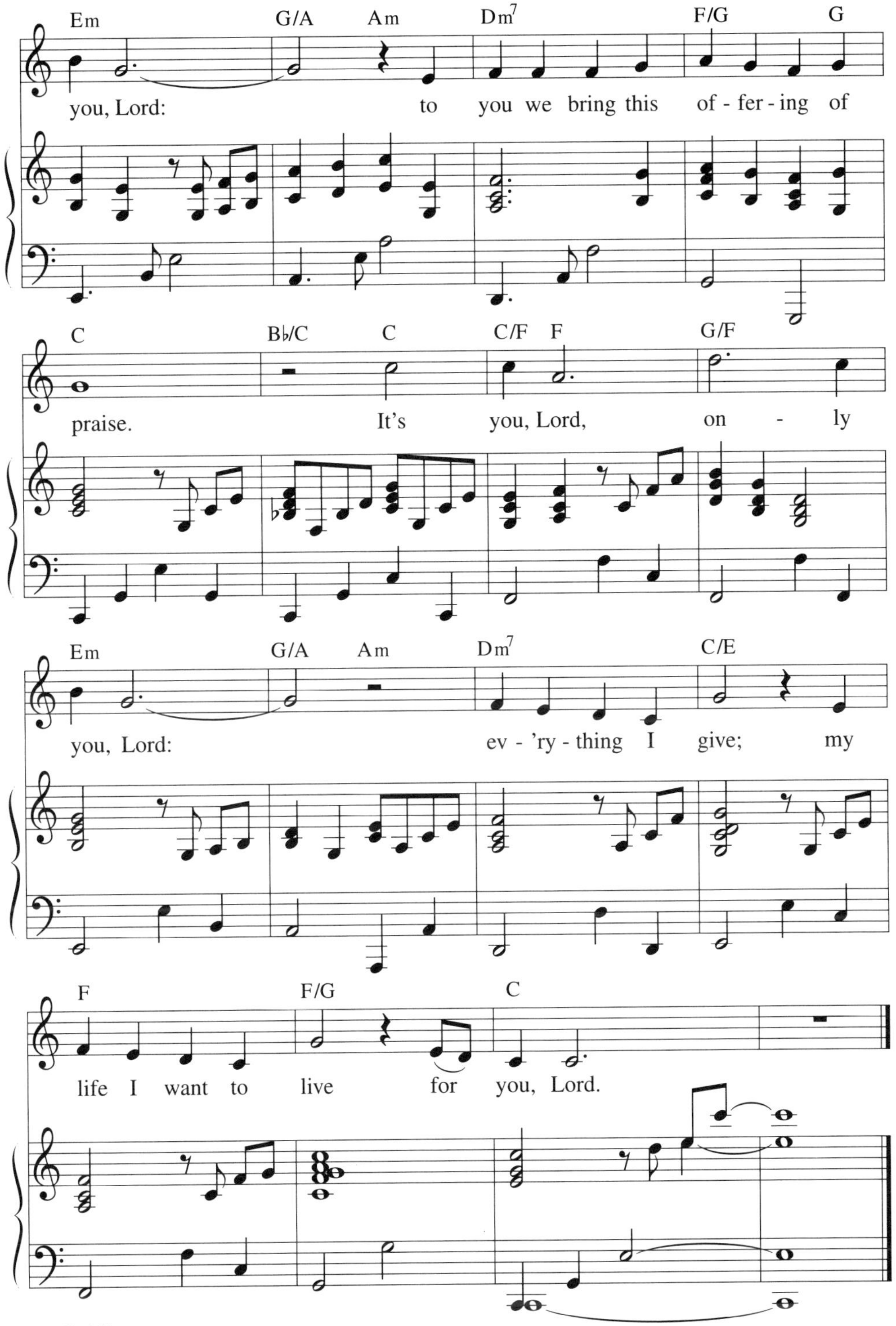
Em G/A Am Dm7 F/G G
you, Lord: to you we bring this of - fer - ing of
C B♭/C C C/F F G/F
praise. It's you, Lord, on - ly
Em G/A Am Dm7 C/E
you, Lord: ev - 'ry - thing I give; my
F F/G C
life I want to live for you, Lord.

Text: Handt Hanson
Music: Handt Hanson; arr. Henry Wiens

Using *Worship & Praise*

A vast body of worship songs in musical styles drawn from popular culture has emerged in the last several decades. "Contemporary" is a shorthand term often applied to these songs, although it hardly seems adequate to describe such a wide range of worship music styles, which includes folk, country, rock 'n' roll, praise and worship, alternative rock, guitar-based liturgical songs, older standards arranged in pop style, and more.

The sampling of these songs and musical styles in *Worship & Praise* is described in the preface as a collection of some of the most widely used and most broadly useful of this literature. What follows in this appendix is a guide to using the songs in *Worship & Praise*. The guide is intended especially for pastors, musicians, and other worship leaders as they prepare the worship of Christian assemblies.

This songbook has been developed in the context of two deep commitments: a commitment to word and sacrament as the central framework for worship, and a commitment to rich diversity in the ways that the people of God express themselves in worship and song. You will discover that this guide focuses upon holding these two commitments in a rich and complex harmony. How can the repertoire of contemporary song be used most effectively within the weekly gathering of Christians around word and sacrament?

The pattern for worship embraces many styles

Many of the songs in this collection originate from theological traditions in which gatherings for worship may not be focused on word and sacrament within the context of the church's ancient and ecumenical pattern. The words and melodies of these songs can find a home, however, in other gatherings that do regularly follow such a pattern. An enormous variety of musical styles can be incorporated within the liturgical pattern, building upon the foundational symbols and words of Christian worship.

What are the benefits of a consistent worship pattern that allows for rich variation?

1) By following a pattern of word and sacrament held in common by a majority of Christians and developed over the centuries, we are linked to the church around the world and throughout history.

2) We retell the Christian story over and over again, not only through the reading of scriptures, preaching, and singing, but through the recurring actions and words of the Christian assembly itself.

3) An established framework provides a base of familiarity for worshipers that enables them to be more receptive to new songs, seasonal variations, and challenging presentations of the word.

4) A practical consideration: because there is a structured pattern to worship, it is not necessary to begin anew each week. With the time saved, elements that make up the pattern can be enriched.

The pattern for Sunday

The foundational pattern for Christian worship begins with Sunday, the primary day on which Christians gather. On this day of Jesus' resurrection and his appearance to the disciples, the people of God gather to hear the word, to pray for those in need, to offer thanks to God for the gift of salvation, to receive the bread of life and the cup of blessing, and to be renewed for the daily witness of faith, hope, and love.

A common fourfold structure makes up this ecumenical pattern: *gathering, word, meal,* and *sending.* Each section of the structure allows for considerable variety. The following suggestions are offered to help worship planners use the resources of *Worship & Praise* within this pattern.

Gathering

Amid a culture rich with sound and activity, many worshiping communities gather in intentional and reflective silence. Other Christian assemblies embrace a more participatory gathering, which includes a time of singing using medleys or song sets, in any number of musical styles. In selecting appropriate music, it is helpful to observe how the words of the songs work together, in addition to musical relationships such as meter and key.

Songs of gathering invite the assembly into the worship of God, and encourage the people of God to express adoration and praise. The following combinations illustrate a few of the many possibilities for medleys. The topical and musical keys indexes in this volume can be useful tools in creating other combinations.

53	Great is the Lord
66	How majestic is your name
94	Majesty
150	We bring the sacrifice of praise
54	He has made me glad
80	King of kings
13	Awesome God
66	How majestic is your name

117	Praise the name of Jesus
77	Jesus, name above all names
140	There is a Redeemer

Even in a participatory gathering, silence is a powerful element as a context for prayer, meditation, and experiencing the presence of God. A time of silence may take place following a gathering medley, before proceeding to the confession and forgiveness, an opening song, or the prayer of the day.

After the people have assembled with singing, silence, and/or instrumental music, the elements of the gathering pattern for Sunday might include an entrance song, a biblical greeting ("The grace of our Lord Jesus Christ…"), a song of petition for God's mercy, a hymn of praise ("Glory to God" and "This is the Feast"), and the prayer of the day.

This pattern is easily enriched with contemporary song. For a **song of petition** or a **hymn of praise**, the following might be considered:

81	Kyrie eleison
83	Lamb of God (refrain)
44, 45	Glory to God
142	This is the feast

The hymn of praise is traditionally a song that glorifies God for the saving work of Christ. Songs that reflect this emphasis are not difficult to find. The following might be considered:

43	Glory and praise to our God
88	Lift up your heads
139	The trumpets sound, the angels sing
149	We bow down
154	We will glorify

The prayer of the day concludes the gathering section, often illustrating a theme of the day or season and helping to focus the congregation on hearing the word of God that follows.

Word

The proclamation of the word within the Sunday worship pattern has a responsive shape inherited from our ancestors in faith among the Hebrew people. God's word is proclaimed to us, and we respond in song. This natural rhythm still works today. The ecumenical order of this section includes a first reading (usually from the Hebrew scriptures), a psalm, a second reading (usually from the New Testament letters), a gospel acclamation, a reading from the gospels, a sermon, a hymn of the day, a creed, and the prayers.

Contemporary worship songs may be used for sung responses to the word. There are many settings of **psalms** and psalm verses included in this volume; see the scriptural index for a listing. For the **gospel acclamation**, a song that welcomes Christ who is present in the proclamation of the gospel, the following might be considered:

6	Alleluia
7	Alleluia. Lord, to whom shall we go?
118	Praise to you, O Christ, our Savior
155	What a mighty word God gives

Scripture songs, such as "Good soil" (52) and "For God so loved" (39), may also be incorporated into the rhythm of speaking and singing the word.

The **hymn of the day** is an important element in the Lutheran tradition of worship. This hymn or song usually follows the sermon and stands beside the reading of scripture and preaching as a proclamation or response to the word of God. Since many contemporary songs have not been created to fulfill this function, it may be difficult to find songs that engage in sustained reflection on biblical readings or seasons of the church year. New songs are being created to fill this gap. The following might be considered:

2	A story for all people
4	All is ready now
25	By grace have we been saved
32	Come to the mountain
115	Out in the wilderness
120	Rejoice in the mission
145	Waterlife

The hymn of the day is also a place to draw on the traditional hymnody of the church. The practice of blending newer musical forms with standard hymns reflects the universal nature of the church and its music. Many congregations have embraced different styles of music and types of musical leadership in the same worship context. It is not uncommon for a worship service to include both contemporary choruses led by a worship team and traditional hymns supported either by an organ or with arrangements for keyboards and instruments.

Meal

Following the word and prayers, the gathered community is invited to give thanks to God and to partake of the bread of life and cup of blessing. Elements of the eucharistic meal pattern include a greeting of peace, the gathering and presentation of gifts, a prayer of thanksgiving, the Lord's Prayer, the communion of the people, and a song and prayer after the communion. Songs from this collection can be used wherever singing is part of the pattern.

Music may accompany the gathering of money and other gifts, and is especially appropriate for the **presentation of the gifts** at the table. Songs that give thanks for God's gifts to us, and that refer to the dedication of our selves, our time, and our possessions to God are most helpful. The following might be considered:

34, 35	Create in me a clean heart
146	We are an offering
150	We bring the sacrifice of praise
156	What have we to offer?

In the context of the Lord's supper, texts that speak of preparing to receive the sacrament are also appropriate. The following might be considered:

10	As the grains of wheat
33	Come to the table
134	That we may be filled
139	The trumpets sound, the angels sing

Many contemporary settings of "Holy, holy, holy Lord" (Sanctus) and "Lamb of God" (Agnus Dei) are available for use during and following the **prayer of thanksgiving**. A few are sampled in this collection:

63, 64	Holy, holy, holy Lord
82, 83	Lamb of God

Singing is natural as people come to share the **communion**. Songs with easily remembered refrains are especially useful, allowing worshipers to sing without books or papers as they come to receive the bread and cup. The following might be considered:

9	As the deer
10	As the grains of wheat
18	Bind us together
23	Broken for me
30	Come and taste
58	Here is bread
76	Jesus, Lamb of God
78	Jesus, remember me
104	Now in this banquet
111	One bread, one body
121	Seed, scattered and sown
152	We remember you

After all have communed, a **song of thanksgiving** for God's gifts and a brief prayer may conclude the meal. If a song is not to be sung at the conclusion of the service, a song here could send worshipers from the table into the world. The following might be considered:

41	Give thanks
119	Praise to you, O God of mercy

Sending

Following a blessing, a **sending song** may be sung by all. The music leaders could reprise a song from earlier in the service. Songs that are simple and brief are usually most effective. The following might be considered:

46	Go in peace and serve the Lord
47	Go, make disciples
48	Go out with joy
49	Go ye therefore
138	The trees of the field
148	We are marching in the light of God

Words of dismissal such as "Go in peace. Serve the Lord" are perhaps best spoken after any sending song. After receiving God's blessing and these words of sending, the assembly is sent out to participate in God's mission to the world.

A pattern for morning and evening

The primary structure of Christian worship is the weekly pattern of gathering around word and sacrament. Another pattern has evolved over time for worship gatherings at the hinges of the day: morning and evening. The structures of morning and evening prayer are ancient, flowing orders that lend themselves to a variety of musical styles. What are the elements of this pattern for daily prayer at morning and evening? How can songs in this collection be incorporated?

Opening

Opening sentences, spoken or sung between leader (lay or ordained) and people, may begin the service. For example, "Now the day has drawn to a close" (105) may be sung in alternation between leader and congregation at the opening of evening prayer, or it may be sung by all as an evening song.

Another sung element at the opening of evening prayer may be a hymn of light, such as "Joyous light of glory" (79). A spoken or sung prayer of thanksgiving for the day and for the gift of light may follow.

Psalms

Psalms are central to the ecumenical pattern for daily prayer. Psalm 95:1-7a is often associated with morning prayer; contemporary settings based on this psalm include "Come, let us worship and bow down" (31) and "Oh, come, let us sing" (107). Psalm 141:1-4, 8 is especially fitting at evening; see "Let my prayer be a fragrant offering" (86). The scripture references index of this collection suggests contemporary settings of other psalms. Consider also more traditional methods of singing or chanting the psalms, or speaking them, possibly with an instrumental accompaniment. A period of silence after each psalm offers time for the meditative slowing that is a welcome aspect of daily prayer in a fast-paced world. A brief psalm-based prayer may conclude the silence.

Song or hymn

The rhythm of daily prayer provides a space for another song or hymn as a "keynote" for the service. Set next to biblical songs, this song is often a setting of words from the rich treasury created by the church's poets and songwriters, and is chosen to relate to the time of day, the season, or the readings that follow. The following might be considered:

22	Bring forth the kingdom
43	Glory and praise to our God
50	God be with you
51	God has done marvelous things
75	In the morning
84	Lead me, guide me
98	Morning has broken
126	Sing out, earth and skies
140	There is a Redeemer

Readings

One or two biblical readings follow the song or hymn. Following the readings, a time of silence can help worshipers reflect on the word of God. After the silence, a song that reflects the spirit of the reading might be sung.

Song from the gospels

In the ecumenical pattern for daily prayer, a reading from the gospels is not always included, but one of the songs (canticles) from the biblical gospels is typically sung. The song of Zechariah (Luke 1:67-79) is associated with morning prayer; see "Blessed be the Lord God of Israel" (20). The song of Mary (Luke 1:46-55) is associated with evening prayer; see the paraphrase of Mary's Magnificat, "Canticle of the turning" (26).

Prayer

The services conclude with prayers, the Lord's Prayer, and a blessing. Singing the prayers, or at least including a sung refrain between petitions, is a possibility. The following might be considered:

92	Lord, listen to your children praying
108	O Lord, hear our prayer

The gift of silence

Worship includes both sound and silence. Stillness, however, may be countercultural in a society in which "dead air" is to be avoided at all costs. Worshipers need the opportunity to collect their thoughts, to meditate on God's word, and to pray in their own words. Silence might be built into the service order at appropriate places. Sometimes instrumentalists can help the worshipers move naturally into silence, by gradually bringing down the intensity and volume at the end of a song. Brief verbal or printed instructions can help people use silence constructively; comfort and skill with silence is something that worship leaders can encourage and model for others.

The song of the people

People who love contemporary worship songs often also appreciate singing older familiar hymns. Because those hymns have been around for so long, they cover many subjects and ideas in addition to those found in contemporary song. Consider bringing popular musical styles to some of these older favorites — the results may surprise you!

In some contemporary songs, musical style may be more prominent than the words of the song. But since music is a servant to the word of God, the actual texts that worshipers sing deserve careful attention. Regardless of their function, all texts which are sung and prayed need to have integrity. No single song will cover the whole story of creation, salvation, and sanctification. Song texts, however, can be selected and placed so that each says something suitable for that point in worship, while also building into a rich summation with all the texts sung in worship.

The song of God's people gathered for worship is at the heart of all music-making in worship. What words will best express their faith on this day and in this place? What melodies will they sing with confidence? What style of leadership will encourage people to sing rather than listen? What volume and depth of sound will support and enable the congregation's song rather than overpower it?

For all who lead God's people in prayer and song, the resources of *Worship & Praise* are offered as models and patterns for encouraging God's people in song as they celebrate the gifts of word and sacrament.

Guitar chords

A♭   A♭m   A♭⁷   A♭m⁷   A♭M⁷   A♭m⁷⁽♭⁵⁾   A♭dim⁷

A♭sus   A♭⁷sus   A♭²   A♭⁶   A♭m⁶   A   Am

A⁷   Am⁷   AM⁷   Am⁷⁽♭⁵⁾   Adim⁷   Asus   A⁷sus

A²   A⁶   Am⁶   B♭   B♭m   B♭⁷   B♭m⁷

B♭m⁷⁽♭⁵⁾   B♭dim⁷   B♭sus   B♭⁷sus   B♭²   B♭⁶   B♭m⁶

B   Bm   B⁷   Bm⁷   BM⁷   Bm⁷⁽♭⁵⁾   Bdim⁷

Bsus   B⁷sus   B²   B⁶   Bm⁶   C   Cm

C⁷   Cm⁷   CM⁷   Cm⁷⁽♭⁵⁾   Cdim⁷   Csus   C⁷sus

C²   C⁶   Cm⁶   C♯/D♭   C♯m/D♭m   C♯⁷/D♭⁷   C♯m⁷/D♭m⁷

C♯M⁷/D♭M⁷   C♯m⁷⁽♭⁵⁾/D♭m⁷⁽♭⁵⁾   C♯dim⁷/D♭dim⁷   C♯sus/D♭sus   C♯⁷sus/D♭⁷sus   C♯²/D♭²   C♯⁶/D♭⁶

C♯m⁶/D♭m⁶   D   Dm   D⁷   Dm⁷   DM⁷   Dm⁷⁽♭⁵⁾

Ddim⁷   Dsus   D⁷sus   D²   D⁶   Dm⁶   E♭

E♭m   E♭⁷   E♭m⁷   E♭M⁷   E♭m⁷⁽♭⁵⁾   E♭dim⁷   E♭sus

E♭⁷sus   E   Em   E⁷   Em⁷   EM⁷   Em⁷⁽♭⁵⁾

Guitar chords

$Edim^7$ $Esus$ E^7sus E^2 E^6 Em^6 F

Fm F^7 Fm^7 FM^7 $Fm^{7(\flat5)}$ $Fdim^7$ $Fsus$

F^7sus F^2 F^6 Fm^6 $F\sharp$ $F\sharp m$ $F\sharp^7$

$F\sharp m^7$ $F\sharp M^7$ $F\sharp m^{7(\flat5)}$ $F\sharp dim^7$ $F\sharp sus$ $F\sharp^7sus$ $F\sharp^2$

$F\sharp^6$ $F\sharp m^6$ G Gm (3fr.) G^7 Gm^7 GM^7

$Gm^{7(\flat5)}$ $Gdim^7$ $Gsus$ G^7sus G^2 G^6 Gm^6

Drum kit patterns

8 Beat a

Waltz a
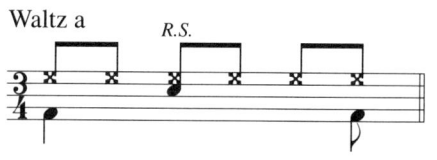

8 Beat b

Waltz b
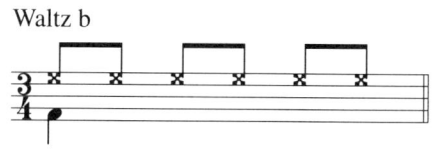

8 Beat c

Gospel

8 Beat d

Swing
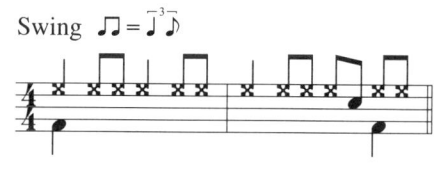

4 Beat

Rock ballad

Acknowledgments

Consultants and contributors are gratefully acknowledged: Jay Beech, Marshall Bowen, Robin Cain, Dori Erwin Collins, Robert Buckley Farlee, Mark Glaeser, Rob Glover, Heidi Hagstrom, Handt Hanson, Ben Houge, David Householder, David Jahn, Phil Kadidlo, Dean Krippaehne, Terri McLean, Ralph C. Sappington, John Ylvisaker, Jeremy Young

Additional reviewers are gratefully acknowledged: Katie Adelman, Arletta Anderson, Kevin Anderson, Carole Lea Arenson, Donald M. Brandt, Linda Bronstein, Lorraine Brugh, Bill Chouinard, Richard Colligan, William Eaton, Rusty Edwards, Steven B. Eulberg, Donna J. Hackler, Dave Janzer, Jeff Kjellberg, Dale Olson, Larry Olson, Karen Reynolds, Marty Schaefer, Kris Simon, Cathy Skogen-Soldner, Phil Spencer, James Tallman, David Tryggestad, Kathy Donlan Tunseth, Scott Tunseth, Erik Whitehill, Tim Wright, Michael Zehnder

ELCA publishing house and churchwide staff: Norma Aamodt-Nelson, Ruth Allin, Suzanne Burke, Katherine Carter, D. Foy Christopherson, Ann Delgehausen, Ryan French, Lynn Joyce Hunter, Lynette Johnson, Aaron Koelman, Rebecca Lowe, David Meyer, Paul Nelson, Kristine Oberg, Linda Parriott, Rachel Riensche, Douglas Schmitz, Ted Schroeder, Martin A. Seltz, Frank Stoldt, Eric Vollen, Karen Ward, Scott Weidler, Richard Webb, Mark Weiler, Eileen Zahn

Cover art and design: Greg Lewis Studios

Music engraving and preparation: Thomas Schaller, Mensura Music Preparation; Becky Brantner-Christiansen, J. David Moore

Material from the following sources is acknowledged: *Lutheran Book of Worship*, © 1978 Lutheran Church in America, The American Lutheran Church, The Evangelical Lutheran Church of Canada, and The Lutheran Church—Missouri Synod: texts of "Alleluia. Lord, to whom shall we go?" (#2) and "This is the feast of victory" (#142).

Praying Together, © 1988 English Language Liturgical Consultation: texts of "Glory to God in the highest" (#43), "Holy, holy, holy Lord" (#63, 64), and "Lamb of God" (#82).

Copyright acknowledgment: The publisher gratefully acknowledges all copyright holders who have granted permission to reproduce copyrighted materials in this book. Every effort has been made to determine the owner(s) and/or administrator(s) of each copyright and to secure needed permission. The publisher will, upon written notice, make necessary corrections in subsequent printings.

Permission information: Permission to reproduce copyrighted words or music contained in this book must be obtained from the copyright holder(s) of that material. A list of the major copyright holders represented in this book follows, with information current as of the year of publication of *Worship & Praise*. Some of the songs may be covered under one or more major licensing agencies, but because this status may change from time to time, it is best to verify this information with the copyright holder or licensing agency at the time of use. For contact information of copyright holders not listed here or for further copyright information, please contact Augsburg Fortress.

Copyright holders and administrators

A.P. WATT, LTD.
20 John Street
London WC1N 2DR UK
011-44-71-405-6774
011-44-71-831 2154 FAX

AUGSBURG FORTRESS
PO Box 1209
Minneapolis, MN 55440-1209
(800) 426-0115
(612) 330-3252 FAX

BEECH, JAY
c/o Baytone Music
1330 8th Ave. N., Suite 102
Moorhead, MN 56560
(218) 291-1386

BMG MUSIC PUBLISHING
One Music Circle North
Nashville, TN 37203-4310
(615) 780-5420

BRENTWOOD-BENSON MUSIC PUBLISHING
365 Great Circle Road
Nashville, TN 37228
(615) 742-6800
(615) 742-6950 FAX

C.A. MUSIC
c/o Music Services
Franklin, TN 37069
(615) 794-9015
(615) 794-0793 FAX

CHANGING CHURCH, INC.
200 East Nicollet Blvd
Burnsville, MN 55337-4521
(612) 435-8107

THE COPYRIGHT CO.
40 Music Square East
Nashville, TN 37203
(615) 244-5588
(615) 244-5591 FAX

DAKOTA ROAD MUSIC
PO Box 90344
Sioux Falls, SD 57109
(605) 362-9554

DAVID HIGHAM ASSOCIATES, LTD.
5-8 Lower John Street
Golden Square
London W1R 4HA UK
011-44-71-437-7888
011-44-71-437-1072 FAX

EKKLESIA MUSIC
PO Box 22967
Denver, CO 80222
(303) 757-4853

EMI CHRISTIAN MUSIC PUBLISHING
101 Winners Circle
Brentwood, TN 37024-5085
(615) 371-4400
(615) 371-6897 FAX

GAITHER MUSIC MANAGEMENT
PO Box 737
1703 S. Park Avenue
Alexandria, IN 46001
(765) 724-8233
(765) 724-8290 FAX

GIA PUBLICATIONS, INC.
7404 South Mason Avenue
Chicago, IL 60638
(800) 442-1358
(708) 496-3828 FAX

HOPE PUBLISHING CO.
380 South Main Place
Carol Stream, IL 60188
(800) 323-1049
(630) 665-2552 FAX

INTEGRITY MUSIC, INC.
1000 Cody Road
Mobile, AL 36695
(334) 633-9000
(334) 633-5202 FAX

KEVIN MAYHEW PUBLISHERS
Buxhall, Stowmarket
Suffolk IP14 3DJ UK
011-44-973-7978
011-44-973-7834 FAX

THE LORENZ CORP.
Box 802
Dayton, OH 45401-0802
(800) 444-1144
(513) 223-2042 FAX

MANNA MUSIC, INC.
35255 Brooten Road
PO Box 218
Pacific City, OR 97135
(503) 965-6112
(503) 965-6880 FAX

MUSIC SERVICES
209 Chapelwood Dr.
Franklin, TN 37069
(615) 794-9015
(615) 794-0793 FAX

NEW DAWN MUSIC
PO Box 18030
Portland, OR 97213-0248
(800) 548-8749
(503) 282-3486 FAX

OCP PUBLICATIONS
PO Box 18030
Portland, OR 97213-0248
(800) 548-8749
(503) 282-3486 FAX

PRINCE OF PEACE PUBLISHING
See Changing Church, Inc.

ROCKSMITH MUSIC
c/o Trust Music Management, Inc.
PO Box 22274
Carmel, CA 93922
(831) 626-1030
(831) 626-1026 FAX

SELAH PUBLISHING CO.
58 Pearl Street
Kingston, NY 12401-0902
(914) 338-2816
(914) 338-2991 FAX

SOVEREIGN MUSIC UK
PO Box 356
Leighton Buzzard
Bedfordshire LU 7 8 WP UK
011-44-52-538-5578
011-44-52-537-2743 FAX

YLVISAKER, JOHN
New Generation Publishers, Inc.
Box 321
Waverly, IA 50677-0321
(319) 352-0765

UNICHAPPELL MUSIC, INC.
c/o Hal Leonard Corp.
7777 West Bluemound Road
PO Box 13819
Milwaukee, WI 53213-0819
(414) 774-3630
(414) 774-3259 FAX

WALTON MUSIC CORP.
170 NE 33rd Street
Fort Lauderdale, FL 33334
(305) 563-1844

WORD MUSIC, INC.
c/o Acuff-Rose Music Publishing, Inc.
65 Music Square West
Nashville, TN 37203
(615) 321-5000
(615) 327-0560 FAX

Topics and themes

14	Baptized and set free	113	Open our eyes, Lord	
19	Bless his holy name	116	Praise, praise, praise the Lord	
20	Blessed be the Lord God of Israel	123	Shine, Jesus, shine	
21	Blessing, honor, and glory	124	Shout to the Lord	
29	Come and see	125	Sing a new song	
30	Come and taste	126	Sing out, earth and skies	
31	Come, let us worship and bow down	130	Spirit song	
32	Come to the mountain	131	Stand in the congregation	
33	Come to the table	132	Step by step	
36	Emmanuel	136	The King of glory	
37	Father, I adore you	139	The trumpets sound, the angels sing	
40	From where the sun rises	141	This is the day	
41	Give thanks	142	This is the feast of victory	
42	Glorify thy name	143, 144	Thy word	
43	Glory and praise to our God	146	We are an offering	
44, 45	Glory to God	148	We are marching in the light of God	
51	God has done marvelous things	149	We bow down	
53	Great is the Lord	150	We bring the sacrifice of praise	
54	He has made me glad	151	We rejoice in the grace of God	
55	He is exalted	153	We see the Lord	
59	Holy ground	154	We will glorify	
60	Holy, holy	157	Wind of the Spirit	
66	How majestic is your name	159	You are my God	
67	I love you, Lord	162	You, Lord	
68	I was glad	**Good Friday**		
70	I will call upon the Lord	11	At the foot of the cross	
71	I will celebrate	39	For God so loved	
72	I will delight	78	Jesus, remember me	
73	I will sing, I will sing	140	There is a Redeemer	
74	I will sing of the mercies of the Lord	**Grace**		
75	In the morning	25	By grace we have been saved	
77	Jesus, name above all names	38	For by grace	
80	King of kings	58	Here is bread	
81	Kyrie eleison	65	How can I be free from sin?	
85	Let justice roll like a river	68	I was glad	
87	Let there be praise	69	I was there to hear your borning cry	
88	Lift up your heads	73	I will sing, I will sing	
90	Lord, I lift your name on high	86	Let my prayer be a fragrant offering	
94	Majesty	90	Lord, I lift your name on high	
98	Morning has broken	100	Name above all names	
99	Mourning into dancing	112	Only by grace	
100	Name above all names	140	There is a Redeemer	
103	Now God our Father	145	Waterlife	
107	Oh, come, let us sing	151	We rejoice in the grace of God	
112	Only by grace	162	You, Lord	

Healing

2	A story for all people
14	Baptized and set free
24	Broken in love
45	Glory to God
58	Here is bread
93	Lord, my strength

Holy Baptism

14	Baptized and set free
18	Bind us together
47	Go, make disciples
49	Go ye therefore
56	He who began a good work in you
69	I was there to hear your borning cry
110	On eagle's wings
127	Song over the waters
137	The summons
145	Waterlife
162	You, Lord

Holy Communion

1	A song of unity
6	Alleluia
8	Amazing love
23	Broken for me
24	Broken in love
33	Come to the table
34, 35	Create in me a clean heart
58	Here is bread
65	How can I be free from sin?
76	Jesus, Lamb of God
78	Jesus, remember me
82, 83	Lamb of God
104	Now in this banquet
106	Now we remain
111	One bread, one body
121	Seed, scattered and sown
133	That Christ be known
134	That we may be filled
139	The trumpets sound, the angels sing
152	We remember you

Holy Cross Day

11	At the foot of the cross
25	By grace we have been saved
65	How can I be free from sin?
140	There is a Redeemer

Holy Trinity

37	Father, I adore you
42	Glorify thy name
59	Holy ground
60	Holy, holy
62	Holy, holy, holy
63, 64	Holy, holy, holy Lord
87	Let there be praise
130	Spirit song
140	There is a Redeemer

Hope

9	As the deer
17	Beauty for brokenness
46	Go in peace and serve the Lord
56	He who began a good work in you
70	I will call upon the Lord
75	In the morning
97	May you run and not be weary
100	Name above all names
102	No longer strangers
104	Now in this banquet
105	Now the day has drawn to a close
106	Now we remain
114	Our confidence is in the Lord
128	Soon and very soon
136	The King of glory
158	You are mine
161	You are the rock of my salvation

Joy

55	He is exalted
59	Holy ground
80	King of kings
87	Let there be praise
88	Lift up your heads
99	Mourning into dancing
107	Oh, come, let us sing
131	Stand in the congregation
138	The trees of the field
139	The trumpets sound, the angels sing
141	This is the day

Justice

17	Beauty for brokenness
22	Bring forth the kingdom
81	Kyrie eleison
85	Let justice roll like a river
95	Make me a channel of your peace

96	Make me a servant
104	Now in this banquet
126	Sing out, earth and skies
127	Song over the waters
147	We are called
156	What have we to offer?
158	You are mine

Kingdom of God

17	Beauty for brokenness
22	Bring forth the kingdom
78	Jesus, remember me
122	Seek ye first

Lent

9	As the deer
11	At the foot of the cross
17	Beauty for brokenness
22	Bring forth the kingdom
25	By grace we have been saved
30	Come and taste
34, 35	Create in me a clean heart
39	For God so loved
65	How can I be free from sin?
72	I will delight
81	Kyrie eleison
84	Lead me, guide me
92	Lord, listen to your children praying
95	Make me a channel of your peace
104	Now in this banquet
108	O Lord, hear our prayer
109	O Lord, my heart is not proud
110	On eagle's wings
113	Open our eyes, Lord
115	Out in the wilderness
118	Praise to you, O Christ, our Savior
120	Rejoice in the mission
127	Song over the waters
133	That Christ be known
134	That we may be filled
136	The King of glory
137	The summons
140	There is a Redeemer
152	We remember you

Light

3	All hail King Jesus
79	Joyous light of glory
104	Now in this banquet

123	Shine, Jesus, shine
127	Song over the waters
143, 144	Thy word
147	We are called
148	We are marching in the light of God

Love

1	A song of unity
2	A story for all people
8	Amazing love
13	Awesome God
18	Bind us together
23	Broken for me
24	Broken in love
25	By grace we have been saved
28	Change my heart, O God
30	Come and taste
39	For God so loved
42	Glorify thy name
52	Good soil
53	Great is the Lord
67	I love you, Lord
87	Let there be praise
95	Make me a channel of your peace
97	May you run and not be weary
104	Now in this banquet
113	Open our eyes, Lord
122	Seek ye first
123	Shine, Jesus, shine
124	Shout to the Lord
125	Sing a new song
126	Sing out, earth and skies
130	Spirit song
134	That we may be filled
137	The summons
139	The trumpets sound, the angels sing
140	There is a Redeemer
143, 144	Thy word
147	We are called
152	We remember you
156	What have we to offer?
157	Wind of the Spirit
158	You are mine
162	You, Lord

Marriage

18	Bind us together
50	God be with you
69	I was there to hear your borning cry
87	Let there be praise

Mary, mother of our Lord

| 2 | A story for all people |
| 26 | Canticle of the turning |

Maundy Thursday

1	A song of unity
23	Broken for me
24	Broken in love
96	Make me a servant
104	Now in this banquet
133	That Christ be known
134	That we may be filled
152	We remember you

Mercy

8	Amazing love
22	Bring forth the kingdom
39	For God so loved
45	Glory to God
53	Great is the Lord
78	Jesus, remember me
82, 83	Lamb of God
85	Let justice roll like a river
118	Praise to you, O Christ, our Savior

Ministry

22	Bring forth the kingdom
95	Make me a channel of your peace
96	Make me a servant
120	Rejoice in the mission
146	We are an offering
147	We are called

Morning

50	God be with you
75	In the morning
98	Morning has broken
107	Oh, come, let us sing

Name of Jesus

3	All hail King Jesus
12	At the name of Jesus
21	Blessing, honor, and glory
36	Emmanuel
66	How majestic is your name
77	Jesus, name above all names

94	Majesty
100	Name above all names
117	Praise the name of Jesus

Offertory

1	A song of unity
4	All is ready now
5	All that we have
10	As the grains of wheat
24	Broken in love
34, 35	Create in me a clean heart
41	Give thanks
87	Let there be praise
96	Make me a servant
104	Now in this banquet
106	Now we remain
111	One bread, one body
121	Seed, scattered and sown
146	We are an offering
149	We bow down
150	We bring the sacrifice of praise
156	What have we to offer?
162	You, Lord

Palm Sunday

29	Come and see
88	Lift up your heads
136	The King of glory

Peace

48	Go out with joy
50	God be with you
52	Good soil
81	Kyrie eleison
85	Let justice roll like a river
91	Lord, listen to your children
95	Make me a channel of your peace
102	No longer strangers
109	O Lord, my heart is not proud
127	Song over the waters
158	You are mine

Pentecost, the Holy Spirit

9	As the deer
22	Bring forth the kingdom
42	Glorify thy name
47	Go, make disciples
49	Go ye therefore
59	Holy ground
60	Holy, holy

Service

1	A song of unity
32	Come to the mountain
47	Go, make disciples
96	Make me a servant
146	We are an offering
156	What have we to offer?
159	You are my God
160	You are my hiding place

Sorrow, suffering

8	Amazing love
11	At the foot of the cross
17	Beauty for brokenness
23	Broken for me
27	Cares chorus
65	How can I be free from sin?
160	You are my hiding place

Thanksgiving

1	A song of unity
41	Give thanks
43	Glory and praise to our God
44, 45	Glory to God
54	He has made me glad
72	I will delight
73	I will sing, I will sing
87	Let there be praise
112	Only by grace
119	Praise to you, O God of mercy
134	That we may be filled
138	The trees of the field
146	We are an offering
150	We bring the sacrifice of praise
151	We rejoice in the grace of God
156	What have we to offer?

Transfiguration

3	All hail King Jesus
13	Awesome God
21	Blessing, honor, and glory
29	Come and see
32	Come to the mountain
53	Great is the Lord
55	He is exalted
59	Holy ground
66	How majestic is your name
77	Jesus, name above all names
80	King of kings
94	Majesty
123	Shine, Jesus, shine
148	We are marching in the light of God
153	We see the Lord

Travelers

9	As the deer
16	Be my home
50	God be with you
84	Lead me, guide me
110	On eagle's wings
132	Step by step
148	We are marching in the light of God

Trust

5	All that we have
9	As the deer
20	Blessed be the Lord God of Israel
28	Change my heart, O God
38	For by grace
43	Glory and praise to our God
53	Great is the Lord
56	He who began a good work in you
58	Here is bread
69	I was there to hear your borning cry
70	I will call upon the Lord
74	I will sing of the mercies of the Lord
79	Joyous light of glory
84	Lead me, guide me
89	Lord, be glorified
91	Lord, listen to your children
93	Lord, my strength
96	Make me a servant
99	Mourning into dancing
104	Now in this banquet
105	Now the day has drawn to a close
108	O Lord, hear our prayer
110	On eagle's wings
114	Our confidence is in the Lord
115	Out in the wilderness
124	Shout to the Lord
131	Stand in the congregation
132	Step by step
145	Waterlife
158	You are mine
160	You are my hiding place

Unity

1	A song of unity
2	A story for all people
10	As the grains of wheat
14	Baptized and set free
18	Bind us together
23	Broken for me
33	Come to the table
40	From where the sun rises
58	Here is bread
68	I was glad
102	No longer strangers
111	One bread, one body
119	Praise to you, O God of mercy
121	Seed, scattered and sown
125	Sing a new song
127	Song over the waters
130	Spirit song
133	That Christ be known
134	That we may be filled
135	The church song
137	The summons
140	There is a Redeemer
145	Waterlife
147	We are called
152	We remember you
156	What have we to offer?
157	Wind of the Spirit
158	You are mine

Victory

12	At the name of Jesus
13	Awesome God
15	Be bold, be strong
45	Glory to God
55	He is exalted
59	Holy ground
71	I will celebrate
80	King of kings
88	Lift up your heads
94	Majesty
102	No longer strangers
124	Shout to the Lord
131	Stand in the congregation
136	The King of glory
139	The trumpets sound, the angels sing
142	This is the feast of victory
155	What a mighty word God gives

Vision

16	Be my home
22	Bring forth the kingdom
120	Rejoice in the mission
138	The trees of the field
140	There is a Redeemer
148	We are marching in the light of God
151	We rejoice in the grace of God

Witness

22	Bring forth the kingdom
43	Glory and praise to our God
46	Go in peace and serve the Lord
47	Go, make disciples
48	Go out with joy
49	Go ye therefore
52	Good soil
115	Out in the wilderness
118	Praise to you, O Christ, our Savior
120	Rejoice in the mission
123	Shine, Jesus, shine
133	That Christ be known
135	The church song
136	The King of glory
139	The trumpets sound, the angels sing
146	We are an offering
147	We are called
148	We are marching in the light of God
151	We rejoice in the grace of God
156	What have we to offer?
162	You, Lord

Word of God

22	Bring forth the kingdom
32	Come to the mountain
48	Go out with joy
52	Good soil
72	I will delight
98	Morning has broken
118	Praise to you, O Christ, our Savior
119	Praise to you, O God of mercy
121	Seed, scattered and sown
122	Seek ye first
129	Spirit of the living God
143, 144	Thy word
155	What a mighty word God gives

Scripture references

<table>
<tr><td colspan="3">Genesis</td></tr>
<tr><td>1:1-2</td><td>157</td><td>Wind of the Spirit</td></tr>
<tr><td>1:2</td><td>127</td><td>Song over the waters</td></tr>
<tr><td>1:5</td><td>98</td><td>Morning has broken</td></tr>
<tr><td>2:7</td><td>157</td><td>Wind of the Spirit</td></tr>
<tr><td colspan="3">Exodus</td></tr>
<tr><td>3:5</td><td>59</td><td>Holy ground</td></tr>
<tr><td>3:14</td><td>154</td><td>We will glorify</td></tr>
<tr><td>15:1</td><td>71</td><td>I will celebrate</td></tr>
<tr><td>15:2</td><td>93</td><td>Lord, my strength</td></tr>
<tr><td>15:11</td><td>13</td><td>Awesome God</td></tr>
<tr><td colspan="3">Deuteronomy</td></tr>
<tr><td>10:17</td><td>13</td><td>Awesome God</td></tr>
<tr><td>32:11</td><td>1</td><td>A song of unity</td></tr>
<tr><td colspan="3">Joshua</td></tr>
<tr><td>1:5, 9</td><td>15</td><td>Be bold, be strong</td></tr>
<tr><td colspan="3">Samuel</td></tr>
<tr><td>2:2</td><td>161</td><td>You are the rock of my salvation</td></tr>
<tr><td>3:10</td><td>137</td><td>The summons</td></tr>
<tr><td colspan="3">Samuel</td></tr>
<tr><td>22:2-3</td><td>114</td><td>Our confidence is in the Lord</td></tr>
<tr><td>22:47</td><td>70</td><td>I will call upon the Lord</td></tr>
<tr><td colspan="3">Chronicles</td></tr>
<tr><td>16:23</td><td>126</td><td>Sing out, earth and skies</td></tr>
<tr><td>29:11</td><td>55</td><td>He is exalted</td></tr>
<tr><td>29:11</td><td>94</td><td>Majesty</td></tr>
<tr><td>29:13</td><td>66</td><td>How majestic is your name</td></tr>
<tr><td>29:14</td><td>156</td><td>What have we to offer?</td></tr>
<tr><td colspan="3">Nehemiah</td></tr>
<tr><td>1:5</td><td>13</td><td>Awesome God</td></tr>
<tr><td colspan="3">Esther</td></tr>
<tr><td>9:22</td><td>99</td><td>Mourning into dancing</td></tr>
<tr><td colspan="3">Psalms</td></tr>
<tr><td>1:2-3</td><td>72</td><td>I will delight</td></tr>
<tr><td>4:1</td><td>108</td><td>O Lord, hear our prayer</td></tr>
<tr><td>5:1-3</td><td>91</td><td>Lord, listen to your children</td></tr>
<tr><td>5:1-3</td><td>92</td><td>Lord, listen to your children praying</td></tr>
<tr><td>8</td><td>29</td><td>Come and see</td></tr>
<tr><td>8:1, 9</td><td>66</td><td>How majestic is your name</td></tr>
<tr><td>16:2</td><td>159</td><td>You are my God</td></tr>
<tr><td>18:1</td><td>67</td><td>I love you, Lord</td></tr>
<tr><td>18:3, 46</td><td>70</td><td>I will call upon the Lord</td></tr>
<tr><td>22:22</td><td>131</td><td>Stand in the congregation</td></tr>
<tr><td>23:4</td><td>15</td><td>Be bold, be strong</td></tr>
<tr><td>24:7-10</td><td>88</td><td>Lift up your heads</td></tr>
<tr><td>24:7-10</td><td>136</td><td>The King of glory</td></tr>
<tr><td>25:1-2, 5</td><td>70</td><td>I will call upon the Lord</td></tr>
<tr><td>28:7</td><td>9</td><td>As the deer</td></tr>
<tr><td>28:7</td><td>93</td><td>Lord, my strength</td></tr>
<tr><td>30:5</td><td>75</td><td>In the morning</td></tr>
<tr><td>30:5, 11</td><td>99</td><td>Mourning into dancing</td></tr>
<tr><td>32:7</td><td>160</td><td>You are my hiding place</td></tr>
<tr><td>33</td><td>53</td><td>Great is the Lord</td></tr>
<tr><td>33</td><td>55</td><td>He is exalted</td></tr>
<tr><td>34</td><td>17</td><td>Beauty for brokenness</td></tr>
<tr><td>34:3</td><td>66</td><td>How majestic is your name</td></tr>
<tr><td>34:8</td><td>30</td><td>Come and taste</td></tr>
<tr><td>34:8</td><td>139</td><td>The trumpets sound, the angels sing</td></tr>
<tr><td>42:1</td><td>9</td><td>As the deer</td></tr>
<tr><td>46:1</td><td>16</td><td>Be my home</td></tr>
<tr><td>46:10</td><td>158</td><td>You are mine</td></tr>
<tr><td>47:5</td><td>88</td><td>Lift up your heads</td></tr>
<tr><td>48</td><td>146</td><td>We are an offering</td></tr>
<tr><td>50:1-6</td><td>17</td><td>Beauty for brokenness</td></tr>
<tr><td>51:10</td><td>28</td><td>Change my heart, O God</td></tr>
<tr><td>51:10-12</td><td>34</td><td>Create in me a clean heart</td></tr>
<tr><td>51:10-12</td><td>35</td><td>Create in me a clean heart</td></tr>
<tr><td>55:1</td><td>108</td><td>O Lord, hear our prayer</td></tr>
<tr><td>55:22</td><td>27</td><td>Cares chorus</td></tr>
<tr><td>59:9</td><td>114</td><td>Our confidence is in the Lord</td></tr>
<tr><td>61:1</td><td>108</td><td>O Lord, hear our prayer</td></tr>
<tr><td>61:2</td><td>84</td><td>Lead me, guide me</td></tr>
<tr><td>62:2</td><td>114</td><td>Our confidence is in the Lord</td></tr>
<tr><td>62:2</td><td>161</td><td>You are the rock of my salvation</td></tr>
<tr><td>62:6</td><td>107</td><td>Oh, come, let us sing</td></tr>
<tr><td>63:4</td><td>60</td><td>Holy, holy</td></tr>
<tr><td>63:5-8</td><td>105</td><td>Now the day has drawn to a close</td></tr>
<tr><td>65</td><td>43</td><td>Glory and praise to our God</td></tr>
<tr><td>65:2</td><td>108</td><td>O Lord, hear our prayer</td></tr>
<tr><td>66</td><td>43</td><td>Glory and praise to our God</td></tr>
<tr><td>66:1-4</td><td>126</td><td>Sing out, earth and skies</td></tr>
<tr><td>68:35</td><td>13</td><td>Awesome God</td></tr>
<tr><td>71:1-3</td><td>161</td><td>You are the rock of my salvation</td></tr>
<tr><td>71:3</td><td>114</td><td>Our confidence is in the Lord</td></tr>
<tr><td>86:12</td><td>42</td><td>Glorify thy name</td></tr>
<tr><td>89:1</td><td>74</td><td>I will sing of the mercies of the Lord</td></tr>
<tr><td>91</td><td>110</td><td>On eagle's wings</td></tr>
<tr><td>91</td><td>160</td><td>You are my hiding place</td></tr>
<tr><td>91:2</td><td>117</td><td>Praise the name of Jesus</td></tr>
<tr><td>93</td><td>21</td><td>Blessing, honor, and glory</td></tr>
<tr><td>93</td><td>94</td><td>Majesty</td></tr>
<tr><td>95:1</td><td>73</td><td>I will sing, I will sing</td></tr>
<tr><td>95:1-7</td><td>107</td><td>Oh, come, let us sing</td></tr>
<tr><td>95:6</td><td>149</td><td>We bow down</td></tr>
<tr><td>95:6-7</td><td>31</td><td>Come, let us worship and bow down</td></tr>
<tr><td>96</td><td>73</td><td>I will sing, I will sing</td></tr>
<tr><td>96</td><td>125</td><td>Sing a new song</td></tr>
<tr><td>97</td><td>126</td><td>Sing out, earth and skies</td></tr>
<tr><td>98</td><td>73</td><td>I will sing, I will sing</td></tr>
<tr><td>98</td><td>125</td><td>Sing a new song</td></tr>
<tr><td>98:1</td><td>51</td><td>God has done marvelous things</td></tr>
<tr><td>98:1</td><td>71</td><td>I will celebrate</td></tr>
<tr><td>99:5</td><td>60</td><td>Holy, holy</td></tr>
<tr><td>100</td><td>87</td><td>Let there be praise</td></tr>
<tr><td>100</td><td>150</td><td>We bring the sacrifice of praise</td></tr>
<tr><td>100:4</td><td>54</td><td>He has made me glad</td></tr>
<tr><td>100:5</td><td>5</td><td>All that we have</td></tr>
<tr><td>103:1</td><td>19</td><td>Bless his holy name</td></tr>
<tr><td>104</td><td>154</td><td>We will glorify</td></tr>
<tr><td>104:1</td><td>94</td><td>Majesty</td></tr>
<tr><td>104:3-4</td><td>127</td><td>Song over the waters</td></tr>
<tr><td>113:3</td><td>40</td><td>From where the sun rises</td></tr>
<tr><td>116:17</td><td>150</td><td>We bring the sacrifice of praise</td></tr>
<tr><td>118:24</td><td>54</td><td>He has made me glad</td></tr>
<tr><td>118:24</td><td>141</td><td>This is the day</td></tr>
<tr><td>118:26</td><td>64</td><td>Holy, holy, holy Lord</td></tr>
<tr><td>119:105</td><td>105</td><td>Now the day has drawn to a close</td></tr>
<tr><td>119:105</td><td>143</td><td>Thy word</td></tr>
<tr><td>119:105</td><td>144</td><td>Thy word</td></tr>
<tr><td>119:105</td><td>155</td><td>What a mighty word God gives</td></tr>
<tr><td>119:114</td><td>160</td><td>You are my hiding place</td></tr>
<tr><td>119:26</td><td>63</td><td>Holy, holy, holy Lord</td></tr>
<tr><td>119:90</td><td>5</td><td>All that we have</td></tr>
<tr><td>121</td><td>105</td><td>Now the day has drawn to a close</td></tr>
<tr><td>121</td><td>160</td><td>You are my hiding place</td></tr>
<tr><td>121:1-2</td><td>159</td><td>You are my God</td></tr>
<tr><td>122:1</td><td>68</td><td>I was glad</td></tr>
<tr><td>126:3</td><td>41</td><td>Give thanks</td></tr>
<tr><td>126:5</td><td>73</td><td>I will sing, I will sing</td></tr>
<tr><td>131</td><td>109</td><td>O Lord, my heart is not proud</td></tr>
<tr><td>139</td><td>69</td><td>I was there to hear your borning cry</td></tr>
<tr><td>141</td><td>86</td><td>Let my prayer be a fragrant offering</td></tr>
<tr><td>141:2</td><td>146</td><td>We are an offering</td></tr>
<tr><td>143:1</td><td>108</td><td>O Lord, hear our prayer</td></tr>
<tr><td>145</td><td>60</td><td>Holy, holy</td></tr>
<tr><td>145:13-16</td><td>155</td><td>What a mighty word God gives</td></tr>
<tr><td>145:3</td><td>53</td><td>Great is the Lord</td></tr>
<tr><td>146:10</td><td>13</td><td>Awesome God</td></tr>
<tr><td>146:2</td><td>90</td><td>Lord, I lift your name on high</td></tr>
<tr><td>147:1-6</td><td>17</td><td>Beauty for brokenness</td></tr>
<tr><td>147:1-8</td><td>126</td><td>Sing out, earth and skies</td></tr>
<tr><td>148</td><td>51</td><td>God has done marvelous things</td></tr>
<tr><td>148</td><td>124</td><td>Shout to the Lord</td></tr>
<tr><td>148</td><td>150</td><td>We bring the sacrifice of praise</td></tr>
<tr><td>148:13</td><td>87</td><td>Let there be praise</td></tr>
<tr><td colspan="3">Isaiah</td></tr>
<tr><td>4:6</td><td>16</td><td>Be my home</td></tr>
<tr><td>6:1-3</td><td>153</td><td>We see the Lord</td></tr>
<tr><td>6:3</td><td>29</td><td>Come and see</td></tr>
<tr><td>6:3</td><td>61</td><td>Holy, holy, holy</td></tr>
<tr><td>6:3</td><td>62</td><td>Holy, holy, holy</td></tr>
<tr><td>6:3</td><td>63</td><td>Holy, holy, holy Lord</td></tr>
<tr><td>6:3</td><td>64</td><td>Holy holy, holy Lord</td></tr>
<tr><td>7:14</td><td>36</td><td>Emmanuel</td></tr>
<tr><td>9:2</td><td>147</td><td>We are called</td></tr>
<tr><td>9:6</td><td>80</td><td>King of kings</td></tr>
<tr><td>12:2</td><td>93</td><td>Lord, my strength</td></tr>
<tr><td>24:14</td><td>53</td><td>Great is the Lord</td></tr>
<tr><td>25:6-10</td><td>139</td><td>The trumpets sound, the angels sing</td></tr>
<tr><td>26:4</td><td>161</td><td>You are the rock of my salvation</td></tr>
<tr><td>28</td><td>17</td><td>Beauty for brokenness</td></tr>
<tr><td>40:11</td><td>130</td><td>Spirit song</td></tr>
<tr><td>40:31</td><td>97</td><td>May you run and not be weary</td></tr>
<tr><td>41:10</td><td>15</td><td>Be bold, be strong</td></tr>
<tr><td>42:1</td><td>96</td><td>Make me a servant</td></tr>
</table>

17:24	13	Awesome God

Romans

3:21-26	25	By grace we have been saved
3:21-26	112	Only by grace
3:24	151	We rejoice in the grace of God
5	95	Make me a channel of your peace
5	151	We rejoice in the grace of God
5:1	25	By grace we have been saved
6:4	102	No longer strangers
6:9	21	Blessing, honor, and glory
6:18	14	Baptized and set free
8	95	Make me a channel of your peace
8:2	14	Baptized and set free
8:26	129	Spirit of the living God
8:26	134	That we may be filled
9:21	28	Change my heart, O God
9:21	103	Now God our Father
10:15	25	By grace we have been saved
12:1	146	We are an offering
12:1	156	What have we to offer?
14:7-9	106	Now we remain
15:6	42	Glorify thy name

1 Corinthians

1:18	11	At the foot of the cross
1:30	140	There is a Redeemer
2:2	65	How can I be free from sin?
2:12	129	Spirit of the living God
6:20	89	Lord, be glorified
10:4	161	You are the rock of my salvation
10:16	111	One bread, one body
10:16	152	We remember you
10:16-17	10	As the grains of wheat
10:16-17	58	Here is bread
10:16-17	121	Seed, scattered and sown
10:16-17	133	That Christ be known
10:31	89	Lord, be glorified
11:23-25	23	Broken for me
11:23-25	24	Broken in love
11:23-26	134	That we may be filled
11:24-26	152	We remember you
11:26	33	Come to the table
11:26	58	Here is bread
12	111	One bread, one body
12:4-11	133	That Christ be known
15:10	151	We rejoice in the grace of God
15:51-52	32	Come to the mountain
15:54-57	142	This is the feast of victory

2 Corinthians

3:12-18	123	Shine, Jesus, shine
12:10	41	Give thanks

Galatians

3:28	18	Bind us together
3:28	111	One bread, one body
5:16-25	129	Spirit of the living God
6:14	11	At the foot of the cross

Ephesians

1	136	The King of glory
1:9	133	That Christ be known
1:17-18	113	Open our eyes, Lord
2:1-8	102	No longer strangers
2:1-8	112	Only by grace
2:4-8	65	How can I be free from sin?
2:8	25	By grace we have been saved
2:8	38	For by grace
2:19	102	No longer strangers
3:12	114	Our confidence is in the Lord
3:14-20	2	A story for all people
3:17	130	Spirit song
4:1	137	The summons
4:4	102	No longer strangers
4:4-5	14	Baptized and set free
4:11-16	18	Bind us together
5:1-2	146	We are an offering
5:1-2	162	You, Lord
5:8	104	Now in this banquet
5:8	148	We are marching in the light of God
5:18	129	Spirit of the living God
5:18-20	119	Praise to you, O God of mercy
5:26	145	Waterlife
6:10	15	Be bold, be strong

Philippians

1:6	56	He who began a good work in you
1:20	89	Lord, be glorified
2:5	127	Song over the waters
2:8	11	At the foot of the cross
2:9	77	Jesus, name above all names
2:9-11	55	He is exalted
2:9-11	100	Name above all names
2:10-11	12	At the name of Jesus
2:10-11	73	I will sing, I will sing
4:7	95	Make me a channel of your peace
4:18	162	You, Lord

Colossians

1:18	135	The church song
2:13	65	How can I be free from sin?
3:12-17	119	Praise to you, O God of mercy
3:14	18	Bind us together
3:15-17	41	Give thanks

1 Thessalonians

4:16-17	139	The trumpets sound, the angels sing

2 Thessalonians

2:15	131	Stand in the congregation

1 Timothy

1:14	151	We rejoice in the grace of God
3:15	135	The church song

2 Timothy

2:1	160	You are my hiding place
2:11	106	Now we remain

Hebrews

1:1	20	Blessed be the Lord God of Israel
1:3	79	Joyous light of glory
8:1	94	Majesty
12:1	97	May you run and not be weary
13:15	87	Let there be praise
13:15	150	We bring the sacrifice of praise
13:16	146	We are an offering

1 Peter

1:18-21	140	There is a Redeemer
2:9-10	135	The church song
2:21	132	Step by step
3:12	92	Lord, listen to your children praying
4:11	89	Lord, be glorified

1 John

1:1	106	Now we remain
4:19	67	I love you, Lord
5:4	142	This is the feast of victory
5:14	114	Our confidence is in the Lord

Revelation

1:18	102	No longer strangers
4:8	60	Holy, holy
4:8	61	Holy, holy, holy
4:8	62	Holy, holy, holy
4:8	63	Holy, holy, holy Lord
4:8	64	Holy, holy, holy Lord
4:11	29	Come and see
5:12	6	Alleluia
5:12	64	Holy, holy, holy Lord
5:12	76	Jesus, Lamb of God
5:12-13	21	Blessing, honor, and glory
5:12-13	154	We will glorify
5:12-14	142	This is the feast of victory
7:9-12	55	He is exalted
7:10	44	Glory to God
7:10	45	Glory to God
19:1	6	Alleluia
19:6-7	55	He is exalted
19:16	3	All hail King Jesus
19:16	80	King of kings
19:16	94	Majesty
21:4	26	Canticle of the turning
21:4	99	Mourning into dancing
21:4	128	Soon and very soon
21:6	14	Baptized and set free
21:22-26	148	We are marching in the light of God
22:3, 5	4	All is ready now
22:16	3	All hail King Jesus
22:20	128	Soon and very soon

Authors, composers, and sources

Musical keys

Titles and first lines

Alternate titles and first lines that differ from
song titles are listed in italics.

ISBN 0-8066-3851-6